*CASE STUDIES in*

# ORGANIZATIONAL BEHAVIOUR AND HUMAN RESOURCE MANAGEMENT

SECOND EDITION

Edited by Dan Gowler,
Karen Legge and Chris Clegg

P·C·P
Paul Chapman
Publishing Ltd

82004

Paul Chapman Publishing Ltd
144 Liverpool Road
London
N1 1LA

Typeset by Setrite Typesetters Ltd, Hong Kong
Printed and bound by Athenaeum Press, Gateshead, Tyne & Wear.

C D E F G H 9 8 7 6 5

British Library Cataloguing in Publication Data
Case Studies in Organizational Behaviour and
Human Resource Management 2nd edition
   I. Gowler, Dan
   658.00722

   ISBN 1−85396−177−9

# Contents

| | | |
|---|---|---|
| *Dedication* | | vii |
| *Preface* | | ix |
| *Notes on the Contributors* | | x |
| *Introduction* | | 1 |

**PART I FLEXIBILITY, QUALITY AND HRM IN MANUFACTURING** — 19

Case 1   Digital Equipment, Scotland: The VLSI Story — 21
*David Buchanan and James McCalman*

Case 2   Japanization in the UK: Experiences from the Car Industry — 30
*Nick Oliver and Barry Wilkinson*

Case 3   The Implementation of High-Performance Work-Teams — 42
*Sharon K. Parker and Paul R. Jackson*

Case 4   Valleyco: Total Quality on the Shopfloor — 56
*Rick Delbridge and Mike Noon*

Case 5   A Greenfield Site: Cableco — 67
*Helen Newell*

**PART II THE FLEXIBLE FIRM, MANPOWER PLANNING AND BARGAINING** — 73

Case 6   The Permanent Search for Temporary Staff — 75
*Dorothy Wong*

Case 7   Finding New Employees for High Reliability Operations — 82
*Gary Brown*

Case 8   The Open Door? Women and Equal Opportunity at Com/Co (North) — 92
*Janette Webb*

Case 9   Multi-Plant Industrial Relations: Fast Foods — 106
*Nicholas Kinnie*

**PART III   DEVELOPING CULTURES OF QUALITY IN THE
              SERVICE SECTOR**                                            115
Case 10   Culture and Commitment: British Airways                        117
          *Heather Hopfl*
Case 11   Culture Change and Quality Improvement in British Rail         126
          *David E. Guest, Riccardo Peccei and Amanda Fulcher*
Case 12   Close to the Customer: Employee Relations in Food Retailing    134
          *Mick Marchington*
Case 13   Evaluating Teleworking in an Educational Establishment         144
          *Jean F. Hartley and Mike Fitter*

**PART IV   TOWARDS AN ENTERPRISE CULTURE?**                             157
Case 14   The Case of Aborted New-Company Formation:
          Organizational Failure or Emergent Potentiality?               159
          *Gemma M. Cox*
Case 15   Decision-Making and Accounting: Resource Allocation in
          the National Health Service                                    166
          *Janine Nahapiet*
Case 16   Southglam: Managing Organizational Change in a District
          Health Authority                                               177
          *Michael Reed and Peter Anthony*
Case 17   The 'Perfect Professional'                                     190
          *Susan Walsh*
Case 18   The Introduction of a Performance Appraisal System             197
          *Barbara Townley*
Case 19   Ownership and Management:
          The Case of Fulham Football Club                               207
          *Nick Woodward*

**PART V   STRATEGY, STRUCTURE AND MANAGEMENT
             DEVELOPMENT IN A COMPETITIVE ENVIRONMENT**                  215
Case 20   Falkner Wilks: Managing Growth in a Professional Firm          217
          *Tim Morris and Helen Lydka*
Case 21   The Growing Pains of Harvey (Engineers) Ltd                    227
          *Fiona E. Mills*
Case 22   Muddle in the Middle: Restructuring in Autospares              238
          *Sue Dopson*
Case 23   Management Development: A Tale of Two Companies                246
          *John Storey*
Case 24   Assessment for Development: Product Development –
          Ford Motor Co. Ltd                                            256
          *Russell J. Drakeley, Ivan T. Robertson and Mike G. Gregg*

*Subject Index*                                                          267

# *Dedication*

During the final stages of editing this book, Dan Gowler died suddenly. The respect, affection and love felt for Dan were testified by the attendance of hundreds of his friends at his funeral and subsequent memorial service. This is not the place for a full obituary, in any case already written by people better qualified than myself, but perhaps for a brief personal comment.

I have known Dan since 1975 when, along with Karen, we joined the Social and Applied Psychology Unit in Sheffield. Since then he has been a friend, confidant and mentor, as I know he has for many, many others. His learning, his ideas, his warm encouragement, his commitment to his students, his friends and his subject, all of these he was so ready to give and share. So too will we remember his sharp and learned wit and his ready debunking of the pompous and the powerful.

Above all, however, I think of his wonderful enthusiasm, so warmly and richly conveyed to all who had the good fortune to work with, or be taught by, him. The *University Dictionary* defines enthusiasm as an ecstasy of the mind as if from divine or spiritual influence; as ardent zeal; as an elevation of fancy.

Just so. This book is dedicated to Dan Gowler.

Chris Clegg
*July 1992*

# Preface

This book of original case studies is a sequel to two earlier volumes we have edited. The first, *Case Studies in Organizational Behaviour*, was published in 1984, and the second, *Case Studies in Information Technology, People and Organizations*, in 1991.

All three books demonstrate a strong commitment, both on our part and by the individual authors of each case, to the case study method as research practice, as teaching aid and, more generally, as a means of investigating, analysing, understanding and coping with complex problems in the real world.

Luckily for us as editors, there appears no shortage of first-class British (and other) social scientists prepared to face the challenge of describing their research in ways that are socially relevant and useful, theoretically sophisticated and challenging, and that, at the same time, provide a good, interesting read. We are delighted with this − long may it continue! Social science of this kind, explicitly addressing practical, theoretical and pedagogic concerns, represents an exciting set of challenges and we hope some of this spirit is conveyed in this book and its accompanying *Teacher's Manual*. Overall we believe the standard of cases in this book is higher than ever. We hope you find them stimulating, educational and enjoyable.

Dan Gowler
Karen Legge and
Chris Clegg,
*1992*

# Notes on the Contributors

*Professor Peter Anthony* is a Lecturer at Swansea Institute of Higher Education.

*Gary Brown* is a Doctoral student at Templeton College, Oxford.

*David Buchanan* is Professor of Human Resource Management at the Human Resource and Change Management Research Unit, Loughborough University Business School.

*Ms Gemma M Cox* is a Lecturer in Organizational Behaviour at the Glasgow Business School.

*Rick Delbridge* is Research Associate at the Cardiff Business School, University of Wales.

*Ms Sue Dopson* is a Research Fellow in Organizational Behaviour at Templeton College, Oxford.

*Dr Russell J Drakeley* is a Director of Craig, Gregg and Russell Limited.

*Mike Fitter* is a Senior Research Fellow at MRC/ESRC Social and Applied Psychology Unit, University of Sheffield.

*Ms Amanda Fulcher* is a Research Assistant in the Department of Occupational Psychology, Birkbeck College, University of London.

*Dr Mike G Gregg* is a Director of Craig, Gregg and Russell Limited.

*David E Guest* is a Professor in the Department of Occupational Psychology, Birkbeck College, University of London.

*Dr Jean F Hartley* is Senior Lecturer in the Department of Occupational Psychology, Birkbeck College, University of London.

*Dr Heather Hopfl* is Research Director at the Bolton Business School, Bolton Institute of Higher Education.

*Dr Paul R Jackson* is a Senior Researcher at the MRC/ESRC Social and Applied Psychology Unit, University of Sheffield.

*Dr Nicholas Kinnie* is a Lecturer at the School of Management, University of Bath.

*Ms Helen Lydka* is a Lecturer in Human Resource Management at the Henley Management College.

*Dr James McCalman* is Director of the MBA programme and a Senior Lecturer in the Department of Management Studies and Human Resource Management, University of Glasgow Business School.

*Dr Mick Marchington* is Senior Lecturer in Human Resource Management at Manchester School of Management, UMIST.

*Ms Fiona E Mills* is TQM Coordinator, Corporate Management Services, British Nuclear Fuels plc.

*Dr Tim Morris* is a Lecturer at the London Business School.

*Ms Janine Nahapiet* is a Fellow in Strategic Management at Templeton College, Oxford.

*Dr Helen Newell* is a Lecturer at the School of Industrial and Business Studies, University of Warwick.

*Dr Mike Noon* is a Lecturer in Organizational Behaviour at the Cardiff Business School, University of Wales.

*Dr Nick Oliver* is a Lecturer at the Judge Institute of Management Studies, University of Cambridge.

*Ms Sharon K Parker* is a Doctoral Student at the MRC/ESRC Social and Applied Psychology Unit, University of Sheffield.

*Riccardo Peccei* is a Research Fellow in the Department of Industrial Relations, London School of Economics.

*Dr Michael Reed* is a Senior Lecturer in the Department of Behaviour in Organizations, the Management School, University of Lancaster.

*Ivan T Robertson* is Professor of Occupational Psychology at the Manchester School of Management, UMIST.

*Dr John Storey* is Director of the Human Resource and Change Management Unit at the Loughborough University Business School.

*Professor Barbara Townley* is Associate Professor in the Department of Organizational Analysis, University of Alberta, Canada.

*Dr Susan Walsh* is a Lecturer in the Department of Psychology at the University of Sheffield, and a clinical psychologist in the National Health Service.

*Dr Janette Webb* is Lecturer in Organization Studies in the Department of Business Studies, University of Edinburgh.

*Barry Wilkinson* is Professor of Human Resource Management at the Cardiff Business School, University of Wales.

*Ms Dorothy Wong* is a Doctoral Student at University College, Oxford.

*Nick Woodward* is a Fellow in Organizational Behaviour at Templeton College, Oxford.

# Introduction

It is now almost ten years since our first book of *Case Studies in Organizational Behaviour* (1984) appeared. Ironically both books have experienced cyclical lag. Whereas many of the cases in our first book reflected research undertaken during the economic recession of the early 1980s, but were read and used in the period of recovery that followed, so now, to some extent, the situation is reversed. Many of the cases here are based on research undertaken in the late 1980s and very early 1990s, when the heady days of economic boom were only beginning to downturn and enthusiasms for greenfield sites, human resource management (HRM) initiatives, enterprise culture and so on were riding high. The 'new realism' that underlies many of these cases refers to the marginalization of traditional industrial relations' concerns rather than that resulting from the sharp shock of renewed economic recession. Nevertheless, the problematic nature of competitive environments and the HRM initiatives designed to achieve competitive advantage, even before the full onslaught of recession, represent major themes in these cases.

Although there are similarities between the 1984 and 1993 publications, inevitably there are major differences. As in the earlier book, all the cases are research based and most have kept to the same structure of *context, problem/ issue, specific questions, essential* and *additional reading*. Similarly, the *Teacher's Manual* provides notes on the appropriate *theoretical background* to each case, a description of *what actually happened* where organizations actively tried to resolve their problems; a set of *answers* to the questions set and a bibliography of *further reading*. We describe a typical case and teacher's manual entry in the next section of this Introduction. Our discussion in the 1984 book of the strengths and weaknesses of the case study method still stands but, in the interests of space, will not be repeated here.

The differences between the two books are major. In the first place the industrial sectors from which the cases are drawn reflect changes in the British economic structure. First, whereas in the 1984 book a quarter of the cases (26 per cent) were derived from the service sector, now over half the cases (57 per cent) are from that sector. Perhaps surprisingly, almost two thirds (62 per cent) of the present book's service sector cases come from the public sector — but this reflects the massive changes in developing market and customer (as opposed to non-market and client) oriented and, in some cases, pseudo-privatized, services. In the private service sector, the retail and distribution industries feature more prominently in this book and a new addition is a case from the leisure industry. What is absent, though, are cases from the financial services sector and the recently privatized public sector utilities. The reason for this is that we dealt with these sectors — and the major impact of information technology (IT) on their structures, processes and culture — in a recent companion book of case studies, entitled *Case Studies in Information Technology, People and Organizations* (Legge, Clegg and Kemp, 1991). Second, the choice of manufacturing industry cases in the present book, as compared to the 1984 publication, is more heavily biased towards industry where change in productivity has been most evident (i.e. engineering, particularly car components and assembly, and electronics).

Perhaps more significant, however, is the difference in substantive approach. The 1984 book was divided into three parts: organizational behaviour (cases placed in order from micro-level issues — for example, job design and stress — to the macro — for example, organization development and organizational structure and design), personnel management, and industrial relations. The latter two parts, in particular, have a mildly geriatric feel after a further decade of the enterprise culture. The personnel management part, although placing issues in organizational and environmental context (and hence showing an awareness of broader concerns) scarcely mentioned the concepts of strategy, culture or competitive advantage although, to the more sophisticated reader, these ideas are implicit. The industrial relations part evokes waves of nostalgia in anyone sceptical of the merits of individualism and free-market forces with its cases on collective bargaining, industrial disputes, strike organization and even a 'lock-out'! Compliance rather than commitment was the spirit evoked in those cases, in spite of the inclusion of three on new technology, participation and trade-union democracy (a hint of 'new realism' emerging in the early 1980s!).

In contrast this book reflects the moods of the late 1980s and early 1990s. The majority of the cases are not single issue focused (whether on absenteeism, power, job design or redundancy, for example) as in the earlier book. Rather they all, to a greater or lesser extent, reflect the interface between organizational behaviour HRM and strategy issues. This is evident in the titles of the parts into which we have organized the book:

- Flexibility, quality and HRM in manufacturing.
- The flexible firm, manpower planning and bargaining.
- Developing cultures of quality in the service sector.
- Towards an enterprise culture?
- Strategy, structure and management development in a competitive environment.

We say more about these issues and themes later in this Introduction.

## A Typical Case and *Teacher's Manual* Entry

All the case studies in this book are based on the first-hand experiences of their authors trying to make 'theoretical sense' of practical problems and changes in the real world as means of understanding and action.

A typical case study is organized into three sections. First, the authors describe the situation in which they have worked, in as much detail as space permits. The aim here is to allow the reader to develop insights into, and a feel for, the problems and difficulties faced by the particular organization and the people working in it. Second, the authors set the readers some tasks or questions for deliberation. These usually focus on asking for some theoretical understanding of what is happening and some theory-derived prescriptions for change. Such questions usually involve some form of group working and plenary discussion. In addition, since our experiences have convinced us that users of such case studies enjoy role-play exercises, nine of the cases in this book explicitly include extended role-play activities. And, third, each case provides a list of essential and supplementary reading to help students make sense of what is happening.

The case book has an accompanying *Teacher's Manual*, again with material organized on a case-by-case basis. The manual entry for each case is written by the authors of the case. A typical entry in the manual is organized into four sections. There is a summary of the appropriate theoretical background, identifying key issues and themes for the case. Second, there is a brief account, where this is known, of what actually happened next in the case, perhaps when the organization or its members took action to make changes. Third, the authors give their 'answers' to the questions they set in the case itself. And, fourth, there is a list of further reading, which may be helpful to the tutor. Where role-play exercises have been included in the case, the manual entry provides further material to help the tutor set up the necessary roles. It must be stressed here that the notes for the tutors are in no way intended as a set of 'correct prescriptions' or definitive answers. We hope and trust that tutors and users of the manual will develop their own solutions.

## The Book's Structure and How to Use It

The 24 cases in the book are organized into five main parts. As mentioned earlier, these are

- flexibility, quality and HRM in manufacturing;
- the flexible firm, manpower planning and bargaining;
- developing cultures of quality in the service sector;
- towards an enterprise culture?; and
- strategy, structure and management development in a competitive environment.

Table I.1 provides a description of the different parts and the cases within them. For example, looking at Part I, there are five cases all of which are

Table I.1

| Case | Sector | Major theme(s) | Key concepts and ideas | Role play included |
|---|---|---|---|---|
| *Part I Flexibility, Quality and HRM in Manufacturing* | | | | |
| Case 1: *Digital Equipment, Scotland* (Buchanan and McCalman) | Computer assembly | Work organization | Flexible production systems; self-managing teams; role of supervision; management structure; functional boundaries; socio-technical systems; training and development; multi-skilling | No |
| Case 2: *Ford and Nissan* (Oliver and Wilkinson) | Car manufacture | Japanese manufacturing methods | Work organization; TQM; JIT production; personnel practices; control strategies; role of trade unions; flexibility; power and conflict; culture; organizational change | No |
| Case 3: *Norahs & Luap* (Parker and Jackson) | Electronics company | High-performance work-teams | Work organization; functional relationships; role of specialists; skilling; quality; training; recruitment and selection; appraisal and reward systems; evaluation of change; culture | Yes |
| Case 4: *Valleyco* (Delbridge and Noon) | Parts manufacture for car industry | Total quality | TQM; JIT manufacturing; work organization; training; management commitment; socio-technical systems; responsible autonomy; payment systems | Yes |
| Case 5: *Cableco* (Newell) | Manufacture of electrical cables | Greenfield site | Flexibility; team-working; single status; selection and recruitment; payment systems; skills; training; single union deals; involvement and communication; internal labour market | No |

*Part II The Flexible Firm, Manpower Planning and Bargaining*

| Case | Sector | Topic | Themes | |
|---|---|---|---|---|
| Case 6: *Home Cosy* (Wong) | Retail distribution | Staff recruitment and retention | Flexible firm; numerical and functional flexibility; core and peripheral staff; competitive advantage; job content; skills; payment systems; human resources vs. personnel management | No |
| Case 7: *Air traffic controllers* (Brown) | Civil aviation | Recruitment and training | Recruitment and selection; training; learning; labour market; manpower planning; flexible firm; occupational communities; reliability in hazardous operations | No |
| Case 8: *ComCo* (Webb) | Manufacturer of computing and telecommunication systems | Equal opportunities | Equal opportunities; affirmative action; personal and career development; performance appraisal, training and remuneration; individualistic ethos; sexual division of labour; corporate culture; recruitment, selection and promotion; role of personnel function | Yes |
| Case 9: *Fast Foods* (Kinnie) | Food production | Multi-plant industrial relations | Collective bargaining; decision-making; centralization/decentralization; control and autonomy; role of shop stewards; pay and costs | Yes |

*Part III Developing Cultures of Quality in the Service Sector*

| Case | Sector | Topic | Themes | |
|---|---|---|---|---|
| Case 10: *British Airways* (Hopfl) | Private transport | Culture and commitment | Cultural change; organizational values; individual commitment; service quality; training and education; profits; personal costs; management of meaning; rites and rituals; leadership; redundancy | No |

**Table I.1** *Continued*

| Case | Sector | Major theme(s) | Key concepts and ideas | Role play included |
|---|---|---|---|---|
| *Case 11: British Rail* (Guest, Peccei and Fulcher) | Public transport | Culture change and quality improvement | Cultural change; quality of service; centralization/decentralization; training; top-down change; structural and attitudinal change; evaluation | No |
| *Case 12: Hiclas* (Marchington) | Food retailing | Employee relations and human resource management | Communications and involvement; pay, job evaluation and grading; selection and induction; labour turnover; training; customer service; role of trade unions; flexible firm; control commitment; responsible autonomy | No |
| *Case 13: University of Minterne* (Hartley and Fitter) | Higher education | Teleworking and computer conferencing | Impact of technical change for service providers and customers; formative and summative evaluation; stakeholders; training and support; work organization; effectiveness; flexibility; culture; power | Yes |
| *Part IV Towards an Enterprise Culture?* | | | | |
| *Case 14: Applied Expertise Centre* (Cox) | Government research laboratory | Formation of new private company | New company formation; organizational emergence; permanent failure; professionals and expert knowledge; privatization; financial resources; changing cultures | No |
| *Case 15: Regional health authority* (Nahapiet) | National Health Service | Decision-making and resource allocation | Decision-making; ambiguity; resource allocation; accounting; managing change; conflict; uncertainty; politics; rationality | Yes |

| | | | | |
|---|---|---|---|---|
| *Case 16: Southglam* (Reed and Anthony) | National Health Service | Managing organizational change | Politics of structural and cultural change; stakeholders; organizational restructuring; decision-making; resistance to change; ideology; finances; control and performance | Yes |
| *Case 17: Professional clinicians* (Walsh) | National Health Service | Coping with change | Support and self-care; professionalism; strain and burn-out; gender; appraisal; performance; organizational values and climate; responses to organizational and cultural change | No |
| *Case 18: University lecturers* (Townley) | Higher education | Performance appraisal | Performance appraisal of professionals; collegiate vs. managerial assumptions; control; professional autonomy; public vs. private sector management; knowledge and power; role of trade unions | Yes |
| *Case 19: Fulham Football Club* (Woodward) | Professional football | Ownership and management | Ownership; management; mergers; stakeholders; power and mobilization of bias; culture clash; community vs. business interests; NIMBY; business ethics; decision-making; business strategy | Yes |

*Part V   Strategy, Structure and Management Development in a Competitive Environment*

| | | | | |
|---|---|---|---|---|
| *Case 20: Falkner Wilks* (Morris and Lydka) | Small firm of professional surveyors | Managing growth | Management of a professional firm; organization and management of firm; organization strategy; hybrid organizations; financial controls; autonomy; morale; professional and career expectations | Yes |

Table I.1  *Continued*

| Case | Sector | Major theme(s) | Key concepts and ideas | Role play included |
|------|--------|----------------|------------------------|--------------------|
| Case 21: *Harvey (Engineers) Ltd* (Mills) | Civil engineering | Organizational growth and retrenchment | Organizational life-cycle and transitions; organizational growth and change; strategies for change; organization structure; permanent failure; management development; cultural change | No |
| Case 22: *Autospares* (Dopson) | Motorspares dealers | Restructuring middle management | Organization structure; decentralization; downsizing; delayering; organization strategy; changing roles; payment systems; entrepreneurship; career paths; managing change | No |
| Case 23: *Smiths and Watanabe* (Storey) | Electrical engineering | Management training and development | Strategic approach to management development; training; competencies; functional chimneys; human resource practices in Japan; organization structure | No |
| Case 24: *Ford* (Drakeley, Robertson and Gregg) | Car manufacture | Assessment for career development | Personnel selection and assessment; career development; psychometric testing; individual differences; competencies; fast-tracking | No |

concerned with various aspects of flexibility, quality and HRM in manufacturing environments. Column 1 in the table names the organization in which the case is set, and also gives the name(s) of the author(s) of the case. Column 2 shows the business sector within which the organization operates. For example, in Part III, Cases 10 and 11 are both based in the transport sector. Column 3 describes the major theme on which the case concentrates. For example, in Part I, Japanese manufacturing methods form the focus of Case 2.

Column 4 lists the key concepts and ideas incorporated within each case. This information is crucially important for tutors making choices about which case(s) to use. For example, culture and cultural change are of central importance in Cases 2, 3, 8, 10, 11, 13, 14, 16, 17, 19 and 21. Such issues may also, of course, be of relevance in other cases. Finally, column 5 shows whether or not the case includes explicit role-play material. This may be useful for tutors in selecting cases. This book has a subject indexes, which give further detail of overlapping issues and ideas.

As editors we have tried to ensure the cases cover a wide range of topics, ideas and themes. In our earlier book of case studies, each case was focused on a particular topic, such as job design or stress. This book is different: here the cases are focused around substantive themes with several issues arising.

Clearly we do not expect readers to work sequentially through a case book of this kind. Rather we hope this Introduction and, in particular Table I.1, allow teachers to select and develop case material that supplements their other teaching activities.

## Users of this Book

This book is aimed at a wide range of users, including students and teachers of business studies, organizational behaviour and theory, HRM, personnel management, industrial relations, organizational and occupational psychology, and industrial sociology. They may be studying at universities, business schools or colleges of higher and further education on a range of full-time, part-time, distance-learning, day-release or post-experience courses, towards higher national diplomas, undergraduate or postgraduate degrees, or professional qualifications. Certainly, many individuals and organizations are grappling with many of the issues and themes addressed here; we hope these case studies help.

## Issues and Themes

The cases here reflect several changes, experienced in the 1980s and early 1990s in both the UK and USA, in both product and labour markets, changes mediated by technological development and a swing to right-wing political ideologies. Several buzz words signify these changes: intensification of international competition, the Japanese Janus (threat/icon), cultures of excellence, IT, knowledge-working, high value-added, the enterprise culture. The phrase that encapsulates them all is 'the search for competitive advantage'. This is the

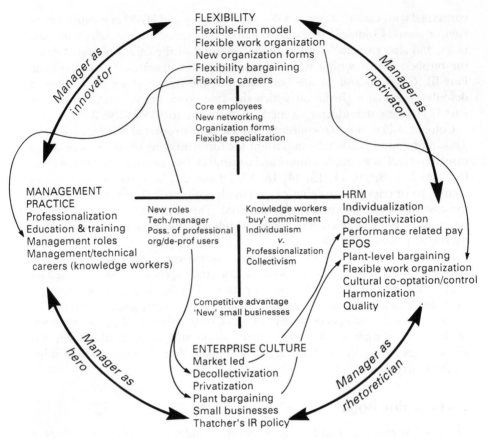

FLEXIBILITY
Flexible-firm model
Flexible work organization
New organization forms
Flexibility bargaining
Flexible careers

Core employees
New networking
Organization forms
Flexible specialization

*Manager as innovator*

*Manager as motivator*

MANAGEMENT
PRACTICE
Professionalization
Education & training
Management roles
Management/technical
  careers (knowledge workers)

New roles
Tech./manager
Poss. of professional
org/de-prof users

Knowledge workers
'buy' commitment
Individualism
v.
Professionalization
Collectivism

HRM
Individualization
Decollectivization
Performance related pay
EPOS
Plant-level bargaining
Flexible work organization
Cultural co-optation/control
Harmonization
Quality

Competitive advantage
'New' small businesses

*Manager as hero*

*Manager as rhetoretician*

ENTERPRISE CULTURE
Market led
Decollectivization
Privatization
Plant bargaining
Small businesses
Thatcher's IR policy

**Figure I.1**

theme that integrates this book, interweaving or, at the very least, providing a background to all the cases. Some major themes that cut across the cases are summarized in Figure I.1 and in the discussion that follows.

## Market Changes

The 1980s and early 1990s have been marked by the increased globalization of markets, and intensification of competition (Sisson, 1989; 1990–1). The rise of the Pacific economies, first Japan, then South Korea, Taiwan, Singapore and so on – combining modern technology with (initially) relatively cheap labour – has posed a massive challenge to European and US economies. From a US point of view, the European Economic Community (EC) poses another; from a UK point of view, the UK competitive position is challenged within the EC by the greater effectiveness of German, French and, arguably, Italian economies. The shift from 'command' to 'market' economies in Eastern Europe not only further enlarges the international economy but, given relative labour costs, also represents another competitive threat (or marketing opportunity, given pent-up consumer demand).

The globalization of markets facilitated by an IT-induced speeding up of worldwide communication has gone hand in hand with the emergence of multinational companies, operating on a worldwide basis. This has resulted in an international division of labour, where regions specialize according to their source of competitive advantage (cheap, low-skilled labour providing low-cost assembly; well-educated, high-skilled knowledge workers providing high value-added goods and services; commodity producers − Nolan and O'Donnell, 1991). Not only is production located where it is most cost effective but also multiple-sourcing of products and services is used to encourage internal competition to enhance effectiveness (see Cases 1, 2 and 4). Furthermore, production is organized for effective access to chosen markets − hence, from a UK point of view, the patterns of inward investment to gain access to EC markets (e.g. Japanese investment in 'screwdriver' factories) and the outward investment into Continental Europe and the USA, the latter assisted by Conservative government policies of financial deregulation (see Case 2).

Deregulation has combined with instabilities in the global political order instanced by a reduction of trade barriers, a breakdown of international trade treaties (such as GATT) and volatile exchange rates; major politico-economic shocks to commodity prices, such as oil; recessions of 1973−4, 1979−81 and 1989−92 ending the long post-war Keynesian period of stability and growth; and the US/Japanese trade imbalance culminating in the Stock Market crash of 1987. All these have increased the volatility of trading.

Focusing on the UK, this intensification of international competition has forced many companies to become more strategically aware (see Cases 1, 5, 20, 23 and 24). Should they pursue a policy of 'asset management' or 'value-added' (Capelli and McKersie, 1987)? This has encouraged analysis of their sources of competitive advantage. If we take manufacturing industry in the UK, such an analysis confronts management with a series of dilemmas surrounding investment policy and working practices. Manufacturing in the UK is rooted in such mature industries as general engineering, steel and glass production, shipbuilding and textiles, where competition is price sensitive. If a firm chooses a 'value-added' strategy, two main courses of action are open: to increase efficiency and/or to go up-market with higher-quality, high design-input products that are less price sensitive. Both strategies, logically, require investment in human and technical capacity, often involving new selection and training strategies (see Cases 1, 3, 4, 5, 8, 23 and 24), greenfield sites (see Case 5) and new working practices (see Cases 1, 2, 3, 4 and 5), if long-term repositioning is to be achieved. Here both the 'hard' and 'soft' HRM models implicit in most of the cases have a palatable message. The 'hard' model looks to the integration of human resource policies with business strategy. Will cost effectiveness best be achieved by relocating production to low-cost areas and/or with market access advantages (see, for example, the strategies of GKN, IMI and Pilkington, and Case 9)? Or, if higher-quality, greater customer responsiveness is required, what about those 'soft' HRM policies that speak of generating greater employee flexibility and commitment, necessary if integrated manufacturing systems require multi-skilling, total quality management (TQM), just in time (JIT) and so forth (see Cases 3, 4, 5, and 8)?

The HRM models speak equally to those organizations, often originally based in manufacturing, that have preferred to adopt an 'asset management' policy of closures, divestment and diversification in pursuit of profitable investment. For many, a long-term investment policy in British manufacturing industry has been judged an ineffective use of assets given the extent of the investment gap (in the UK) in new plant, infrastructure, education and training as compared to Continental European and Pacific competitors (see Keep, 1989). Such views received reinforcement in both the early 1980s and, presently, in the early 1990s, when government monetarist policies involving the lethal combination of high interest and exchange rates have made investment very expensive and profitability very uncertain. Diversification away from manufacturing (e.g. BAT), closure of unprofitable plant (e.g. BTR) and overseas investment (e.g. Hanson) have seemed a better route to profitability. In such circumstances the 'hard' model of HRM preaches an important message: tailor the management of its labour resource to the business strategy of each constituent business unit – take a contingent rather than absolutist approach to what HRM should involve for each business (see Cases 21 and 22).

These product market changes are mirrored in labour market changes in the UK and USA (Sisson, 1990–1, pp. 2–3). The long-term shift in employment from manufacturing to the service sector, exacerbated by the 1979–81 recession (for a discussion, see MacInnes, 1987; Legge, 1988), and the greater technical sophistication of much surviving manufacturing, has resulted in a decline in manual jobs relative to non-manual jobs. This has had several knock-on effects. First, the workforce has become increasingly polarized between those undertaking jobs requiring the skills of 'knowledge-workers' (see Cases 7, 14, and 20) and consequently high levels of education and training, and those performing routinized, low-skill service jobs (checkout, shelf-filling, fast-food catering – see Cases 6, 7, 12, 14, and 20). Second, the workforce is becoming feminized, as it has become the norm for women to work with only a minimal break for child-rearing and as service sector jobs are available. Third, due to demographic trends, the workforce will become increasingly 'middle aged' in the 1990s. Again the unitaristic message of the HRM models find a less hostile environment than in the days when the 'worker' was seen as predominantly male and manual working in unionized manufacturing industry. Today, arguably, managers can see the advantages of co-opting rather than confronting 'core' knowledge workers, aiming for commitment via cultural management and marginalization of unions, rather than compliance through collective bargaining (see Case 10). Further, growth in employment has occurred in a sector (private service) and among a category of employees (women working part time) that traditionally are not highly unionized (see Case 6).

## The Japanese Janus and Models of Excellence

Janus, the Roman god of doorways, gates and openings, looks in opposite directions, with a friendly and a hostile face. At the risk of stereotyping, this image is not inappropriate to the UK's and USA's reaction to Japan. On the one hand, Japan's hostile face is recognized as an erstwhile wartime enemy, that is now turning the tables on an over-generous victor, using 'unfair' tactics in economic combat. On the other hand, though, is admiration and envy: after the destruction by Allied bombing and nuclear attack, how could the Japanese have become the second most powerful world economy, in the space of forty years? What lessons can we learn from the benign face of economic success? Two cases (Cases 2 and 23) look comparatively at UK and Japanese management practice.

The 'lessons' learnt in the early 1980s stemmed from influential publications — Ouchi's (1981) *Theory Z*, and Peters and Waterman's (1982) *In Search of Excellence* — that claimed a similarity between company 'excellence' (defined largely in terms of financial criteria) and the adoption of management practices reminiscent of those of Japan. In the eyes of these influential texts this boiled down to combining the 'hard' — tight controls on results — with the 'soft' — facilitating autonomy in definitions of priorities, decisions and actions (Wood, 1989, p. 383). The argument was that American management practice had traditionally placed too much emphasis on a centrally imposed rationality, expressed through excessive emphasis on the measurable, and involving the manipulation of complex structures to achieve compliance and results. The Japanese, on the other hand, prioritized the creation of a shared vision, a culture of collective commitment to achieving organizational goals, often expressed in philosophical ('quality', being the 'best') rather than in quantitative terms. The Americans had neglected this 'transformational' leadership, in favour of a shorter-term 'harder' transactional style. But the comforting message was that all was not lost. Where US companies had adopted management practices that resembled those of the Japanese ('Theory Z'; Peters and Waterman's 'eight attributes'), they had achieved financial success. The lesson was clear: cultural management that secured the commitment of employees as valued assets — hallmarks of the 'soft' HRM model — should be the order of the day. Supported by the six 'pillars' of Japanese employment practice (lifetime employment, company welfare, quality consciousness, enterprise unions, consensus management and seniority-based reward systems) — all suitably adapted to local context, of course (in particular in relation to pay) — this would facilitate the adoption of other Japanese practices (Kanban/JIT; Kaizen/continuous improvement) that call for flexible utilization of resourceful humans (see Cases 2, 4, 5, and 23).

It should be noted that the underpinnings of this equation of Japanese management, including HRM practices, with success in US companies is shaky to say the least. First, the research design and empirical basis of Peters and Waterman's research is highly suspect, raising doubts as to the genuine excellence (even financial!) of the companies identified, and the reliability of the eight attributes (for an excellent critique, see Guest, 1992). Second, the typification of Japanese management practice rests on stereotypes that neglect such important qualifications as Japan's dualistic industrial structure and the extent to which traditional HRM policies have never been universally applied and, indeed, are in the process of erosion in the light of demographic change, internationalization and technological development (for a short summary, see Thompson and McHugh, 1990, pp. 202–6; for longer accounts, see Clark, 1979; Godet, 1987; Okubayashi, 1988; Whittaker, 1990). Nevertheless, the imagery of the Japanese Janus and the rhetoric associated with models of excellence resonates with the messages contained in the 'soft' HRM model.

## The Enterprise Culture

If market changes, the Japanese Janus and models of excellence pointed both to an intensification of competition and strategies for meeting it, at a macro-level, government ideology and resultant policies, in the UK and USA, provided just the right growing medium (or should we say, compost) for the ideas contained in HRM models to flourish.

In both the UK and USA in the 1980s, under Mrs Thatcher and President Reagan, national government swung to the right. Although their respective economic policies differed (compare, for example, the monetarism – later relaxed – of the early days of the first Thatcher government with the runaway budget deficits of the Reagan years), at the level of ideology both administrations preached the virtues of a 'rugged entrepreneurial individualism' (Guest, 1990, p. 31), of the central value of 'enterprise' to national economic well-being. Enterprise, though, as Keat (1991) and Fairclough (1991) point out, has a dual meaning. It can convey the meaning of a noun – the 'commercial enterprise' – as well as that of a verb – to be 'enterprising', by taking risks, showing initiative, self-reliance and so on. In the UK, in the 1980s, government has attempted to equate these meanings in the politico-economic environment it has sought to create.

The desirability of the model of the 'commercial enterprise' – that is, the privately owned firm operating in a free market economy – has found expression in policies aimed at extending the domain of the 'free market' and intensifying competition therein. The cases in Parts III and IV, in particular, are illustrative of this trend. Such policies include a rejection of Keynesian demand management economic policies, aimed at the maintenance of full employment – 'the business of government is not the government of business', as Nigel Lawson declared – in favour of monetarist supply management, aimed at squeezing inflation out of the economy, through the control of the money supply (M3, PSBR). Levels of employment then find their own 'natural' level through the operation of the forces of supply and demand in the market-place. Firms' survival and growth depend on their 'leanness' and 'fitness' in dealing with the rigours of the market-place, no longer feather-bedded by artificially protective fiscal measures. Over the decade there has been an end of exchange controls, a deregulation of financial services and the removal of non-market restrictions governing the conduct of some professions. For organizations erstwhile protected by public funding and ideologies at odds with the market-place (public good/need), there have been institutional reforms designed to introduce market principles and commercially modelled forms of organization (see Cases 16, 17, and 18). Hence, in the UK, the 1980s have seen the privatization of State-owned industries and public utilities and the introduction of quasi-markets in the organization of public services (e.g. the 'opting-out' of schools, 'trust' status and 'fund management' in the NHS, competitive tendering in local authorities – see Cases 10 and 16). Expressive of these changes has been the introduction of the concept of 'consumer' into situations where the terminology of professional dominance (cf. 'student', 'patient', 'client') previously prevailed. Whether in the service or manufacturing, public or private sectors, 'meeting the demands of the "sovereign consumer" [has become] the new and institutional imperative' (Keat, 1991, p. 3 – see Cases 3, 4, 5, 10, 11, 12, 13, and 14).

Used as a verb, 'enterprising' has connotations of initiative, energy, independence, boldness, self-reliance and a willingness to take risks and to accept responsibility for one's actions. In this sense an enterprise culture is one in which the acquisition and exercise of these qualities is valued and encouraged. When combined with knowledge-working, as a 'modern professional', the symbol of the enterprise culture became the much maligned 'yuppy'. While there may be no 'yuppies' in this set of cases, nevertheless several (e.g. Cases 7, 14, 17 and 20) reflect the tensions arising from the confrontation of traditional professional values and expectations with a climate of entrepreneurialism and the increased importance of the 'bottom line'. Furthermore, in the UK, such encouragement of enterprise has taken the form of attempts to neutralize and reverse the influence of institutions that are supposedly inimical to the spirit of enterprise: the trades unions and the Welfare State.

The trade unions have been considered doubly inhibiting. On the one hand they are seen by protagonists of the enterprise culture as fettering the free will of 'captive' individuals through imposing the shackles of collective bargaining and by impeding the free working of market forces by such institutions as the closed shop, restrictive practices and legal immunities. On the other hand, they are regarded as protective of employees' collective interests in a way that encourages the diminution of individual responsibility and aspiration, creating a culture of dependency. It is noticeable how few of our cases, compared to the 1984 volume, deal explicitly with trade-union issues (for an exception, see Case 9).

Such a view has not only resulted in a rejection of conventional incomes policies, and a general shift from direct to indirect taxation, but also an approach to employment legislation designed to weaken trade-union power and strengthen the employer's hand *vis-à-vis* employees in the fight against inflation. Thus, the two parliamentary orders of July 1979 served to restrict employment protection, particularly in relation to unfair dismissal. The Employment Acts 1980 and 1982 largely dismantled the 'minimum conditions' props to collective bargaining – the latter being completely side-stepped by legislation imposing a pay settlement in the case of the teachers' pay dispute, 1987. The Employment Acts 1980 and 1982, and the Trade Union Act 1984, chopped back union immunities in relation to industrial action, with restrictive clauses in particular on picketing, secondary action, action to extend recognition and negotiation, the definition of trade disputes, dismissal of strikers and strike ballots. Similarly, the 1982 and 1984 Acts, by imposing liability on unions in tort, undermined union strength and security. The same effect was aimed for in the 1980 and 1982 Acts, by the attack on the closed shop (or as the government saw it, freeing a 'conscript army' of unionists). Finally, and in the same spirit, the 1984 Act sought to 'democratize' internal trade-union affairs by compelling ballots in trade-union elections and over the continuance of the political levy (for further details, see, for example, Wedderburn, 1986, pp. 69–83).

Gone was the image of trade-union leaders walking the corridors of power, and enjoying 'beer and sandwiches at No 10'. Consistently, the government refused to discuss economic issues with the Trades Union Congress. Instead, in the public sector, it lent ideological and financial support to managements' attempts to reassert control, at the risk of prolonged strike action (the 1984 dispute at the Department of Health and Social Security in Newcastle; the coal miners' strike, 1984–5). Individuals' membership of unions, in special cases, was considered as incompatible with their status as employees (the Government Communications Headquarters dispute); some 'militant' unions, notably the National Union of Mineworkers, were presented as led by demagogues threatening democracy. As Wedderburn (*ibid.* pp. 85–6) succinctly put it:

> Those who opposed the new policies increasingly ran the risk of being seen not as critics with whom to debate and compromise (the supreme pluralist virtue) but as a domestic enemy within, which must be defeated. In such circumstances the old tradition of compromise was squeezed out: [quoting a government spokesman].
> The mining dispute cannot be *settled*. It can only be won.

And this is to ignore the legislation of the late 1980s! (See the annual reviews in *British Journal of Industrial Relations*, 1985–91).

Hence, in the context of events of the 1980s and early 1990s – two major recessions and the resulting decimation of manufacturing in the early 1980s, and of the 'High Street' and property markets in the 1990s; continuing high levels of unemployment throughout most of the period and a changing structure of surviving employment; and a consequent decline in trade-union membership and finances – there has emerged a new realism in trade-union–management relations (reflective of and reinforced by a fourth Conservative party election in 1992), less ideologically opposed to the values of 'excellence' and the 'enterprise culture' than in the 1970s and early 1980s.

Turning to the Welfare State, UK governments of the 1980s have considered that receiving, as of right, a wide range of welfare and unemployment benefits, pensions, housing, even aspects of education and health, have also contributed to attitudes of dependency and passivity. Hence, to quote Keat (1991, p. 5),

> Along with increasingly stringent criteria for the receipt of benefits by right, in which the principle of need is modified by a strongly voluntaristic conception of desert, a key strategy is to encourage the commodification of previously state-supplied goods, replacing them by consumer purchasable products – e.g., private pensions, health insurance, home ownership, and so on. Individuals become non-dependent and 'responsible' by taking financial responsibility for these matters, as consumers; and the sphere of consumption thus becomes an important training ground for the enterprising self.

Indeed, public sector service organizations have sometimes been stigmatized as equally passive and dependent, in need of the disciplines of the market-place and enhanced cost and service accountability (see Cases 11, 13, 15, 16 and 18). The two meanings of the enterprise culture come together in the view that the management of commercial enterprises is the field of activity in which enterprising qualities are best put to use and developed. As enterprising qualities are seen as virtues, this justifies and validates the workings of a free market economy (see Case 19). At the same time, in order to maximize the benefits of a 'free enterprise' economic system, firms and their participants must be seen to act in ways that express enterprising qualities, at whatever personal or organizational cost (Keat, 1991, pp. 3–4 – see Cases 17 and 18).

Now clearly major criticisms can be raised about many of the assumptions that lie behind this vision of enterprise culture and the politico-economic policies that have been adopted in its pursuit (see, for example, Keat, 1991, pp. 7–9). But as a political rhetoric presenting a particular gloss to the intensification of competition discussed earlier, its message is consonant with assumptions embodied in both the 'hard' and 'soft' models of HRM. The individualistic values (and anti-union bias) that pervade the rhetoric of the enterprise culture are consistent with the individualistic and unitarist values of stereotypical normative HRM models. Its emphasis on the primacy of the market and the need to create enterprising individuals and firms to compete successfully in the market-place finds echoes in the hard model's emphasis on external integration – of the match between strategy and environment, and of HRM policy, procedures and practices with business strategy. The image of enterprising individuals as keen to take responsibility, goal oriented and concerned to monitor their progress towards goal achievement, motivated to acquire the skills and resources necessary to pursue these goals effectively (see Cases 23 and 24), seeing the world as one of opportunity rather than constraint (Keat, 1991, pp. 5–6), is consistent with the values of commitment and flexibility embodied in the 'soft' model. One could argue too that the rhetoric about the sovereignty of the consumer is consistent with the ideas about quality, also central to the 'soft' model. Finally, the ideas about competitive advantage that pervade HRM and the models of excellence are part of the rhetoric of a free market economy, the bed-rock of the enterprise culture.

Since the research, teaching and practice of organizational behaviour reflect and in some measure help formulate the concerns of our times, it should come as no surprise that the themes that underlie and pervade these cases are quite different from those of our earlier books of case studies.

Our modern times have their own rhetoric, a lexicon incorporating the words and phrases of the early 1990s: accountability, commitment, competition, competitive advantage, consumer, culture, enterprise, entrepreneurship, excellence, flexibility, free markets, human resources, individualism, Japanization, performance, quality (even total quality), value-added. Unwittingly, perhaps through what they include and exclude, collections of cases like these may provide their own social history of our times.

# References

Capelli, P. and McKersie, R. B. (1987) Management strategy and the redesign of work rules, *Journal of Management Studies*, Vol. 24, no. 5, pp. 441–62.

Clark, R. (1979) *The Japanese Company*, Yale University Press, New Haven, Conn.

Clegg, C., Kemp, N. J. and Legge, K. (eds.) (1984) *Case studies in Organizational Behaviour*, Paul Chapman, London.

Fairclough, N. (1991) What might we mean by 'enterprise culture'?, in R. Keat and N. Abercrombie (eds.) *Enterprise Culture*, Routledge, London.

Godet, M. (1987) Ten unfashionable and controversial findings on Japan, *Futures*, August, pp. 371–84.

Guest, D. (1990) Human resource management and the American Dream, *Journal of Management Studies*, Vol. 27, no. 4, pp. 376–97.

Guest, D. (1992) Right enough to be dangerously wrong: an analysis of the *In Search of Excellence* phenomenon, in G. Salaman *et al.* (eds.) *Human Resource Strategies*, Sage, London.

Keat, R. (1991) Introduction, Starship Britain or universal enterprise? in R. Keat and N. Abercrombie (eds.) *Enterprise Culture*, Routledge, London.

Keep, E. (1989) A training scandal?, in K. Sisson (ed.) *Personnel Management in Britain*, Blackwell, Oxford.

Legge, K. (1988) *Personnel Management in Recession and Recovery: A Comparative Analysis of What the Surveys Say (Personnel Review Monograph*, Vol. 17, no. 2, pp. 1–72).

Legge, K., Clegg, C. and Kemp, N. J. (eds.) (1991) *Case Studies in Information Technology, People and Organizations*, NCC/Blackwell, Manchester and Oxford.

MacInnes, J. (1987) *Thatcherism at Work*, Open University Press, Milton Keynes.

Nolan, P. and O'Donnell, K. (1991) Restructuring and the politics of renewal: the limits of flexible specialization, in A. Pollert (ed.) *Farewell to Flexibility*, Blackwell, Oxford.

Okubayashi, K. (1986) Recent problems of Japanese personnel/management, *Labour and Society*, Vol. 11, no. 1.

Ouchi, W. (1981) *Theory Z: How American Business Can Meet the Japanese Challenge*, Addison-Wesley, Reading, Mass.

Peters, T. J. and Waterman, R. H. (1982) *In Search of Excellence: Lessons from America's Best Run Companies*, Harper & Row, New York, NY.

Sisson, K. (1989) Personnel management in perspective, in K. Sisson (ed.) *Personnel Management in Britain*, Blackwell, Oxford.

Sisson, K. (1990–1) Introducing the *Human Resource Management Journal, Human Resource Management Journal*, Vol. 1, no. 1, pp. 1–11.

Thompson, P. and McHugh, D. (1990) *Work Organizations: A Critical Introduction*, Macmillan, London.

Wedderburn, K. W. (1986) *The Worker and the Law* (3rd edn), Penguin Books, Harmondsworth.

Whittaker, D. H. (1990) The end of Japanese style employment?, *Work, Employment and Society*, Vol. 4, no. 3, pp. 321–47.

Wood, S. (1989) New wave management?, *Work, Employment and Society*, Vol. 3, no. 2, pp. 379–402.

# PART I

Flexibility, Quality
and HRM
in Manufacturing

# CASE 1

## Digital Equipment, Scotland: The VLSI Story

### David Buchanan and James McCalman

## The Company

It is January 1989. You are employed as a consultant to the seven-member Assembly Staff Group — the management team — of the Very Large Scale Integration (VLSI) assembly business at Digital Equipment Corporation's plant near Ayr in Scotland. You have been asked to advise the management team, who are undecided about organizational changes that have been proposed.

Digital Equipment Corporation's VLSI facility at Ayr assembles and tests semiconductors for Digital's own range of business computers. Digital is one of the largest computer manufacturing companies in the world. The VLSI business at Ayr has one of the largest semiconductor cleanroom facilities in Europe. The operation began in 1983 as a small-scale test facility, but as the assembly operations were added, total employment in VLSI — assembly and test combined — grew to around 470. The plant is non-unionized, and the assembly operation works a 24-hour, three-shift system turning finished silicon wafers into packaged integrated circuits, worth around £300 each.

## What about the Workers?

VLSI Assembly in 1989 employs around 230 people (around 75 operators and four supervisors on each shift), and occupies 25,000 square feet, including 10,000 square feet of cleanroom. When you speak to operators on the shopfloor, as management invited you to do, there is no reluctance or hesitation in offering views. The following comments are representative of their feelings:

> Working conditions here are fine. Training and scope for individual development are not too good though, and the jobs you get can depend on whether your face fits with the supervisor. There is no shortage of good-quality people wanting to come and work here, and those who come here do tend to stay for a long time.

> The people I work with are great and the company has a strong local reputation as an extremely good employer. There's a lot of hierarchical

decision-making that's not explained to us. We would like more trust and more communication from management. Communication is not as good as it should be.

Work is organized in the manner traditional for semiconductor plants, with operators employed at individual stations in the assembly process, trained to work single machines or processes, and with limited knowledge of the production process as a whole. The individual jobs are repetitive, but there does not seem to be much complaint about that. One group of shopfloor employees tells you that 'Abilities are not being used — that's a general opinion. Managers and supervisors are assuring us this will improve, but it's not getting through. There's too much management input'.

One of the supervisors tells you that

The main problem as far as management is concerned is making sure that our people are adequately trained for the job to which they have been allocated, and that we provide appropriate retraining to cope with change, which is always happening in this operation by the way — new product specifications, new equipment ...

The company norm is one first-line supervisor to sixteen employees. The supervisors pass on information and management directives, allocate tasks and solve routine production problems. Process adjustments, maintenance and improvements are the responsibility of engineering technicians. Some of the direct employees have previously worked for other semiconductor plants in Scotland, but many have no relevant previous experience, including some ex-miners. The workforce is mixed, but there are no 'male' or 'female' tasks. One of the shopfloor operators tells you that

We are dependent on traditional management. Communications are poor. There is very little feedback to the ground level. We are not told how well, or how badly, we have done. The information may be there if you want to go and find it out, but it is not communicated to the floor.

One manager has suggested that the production operators could do a lot of their own regular and preventive maintenance if they were given the right training. For this to happen, the engineering technicians would have to be prepared to run 'technical operator' training courses for the shopfloor and effectively work themselves out of this job.

## The Production Process

What does the work actually involve? The semiconductor manufacturing process has four main stages.

### Design

The chips are designed in America. This is a complex and sophisticated process carried out by professional staff generating chip layouts on computerized design systems.

## Fabrication

Chips are etched onto a wafer of silicon, typically 4−6 inches in diameter. Each wafer contains from 150 to 2,000 chips, depending on circuit size and complexity. Each circuit is tested electrically before shipment to assembly (from either Hudson in America or from South Queensferry in Scotland).

## Assembly

This is done at Ayr and involves three basic stages. First, individual chips are cut from the silicon wafer and are mounted into ceramic packages or onto metal leadframes. Second, the connections are made between the chips and the pins which will form the electrical connection to the module or printed circuit board. Third, the ceramic packages have lids attached, and the leadframes are encapsulated in plastic, to protect the chips from the external environment. The end result forms the central processing unit of a computer.

## Test

Also at Ayr, extensive testing is carried out on each device to ensure only good chips proceed to module manufacturing.

There are thus a number of interrelated assembly stages which affect final product quality and process yields, and which demand constant attention to detail. The first step in the operation concerns the receipt and sorting of wafers from the fabrication plants at Hudson and South Queensferry near Edinburgh. The wafers are washed, given a 'gross visual inspection', and loaded into manufacturing containers. These are then moved into the cleanroom. Each die is then visually inspected to identify physical defects. The wafers are prepared for further handling by mounting them onto a film frame. Next, the individual circuits or die are sawn from the wafer. The saw used to separate individual wafers is four thousandths of an inch thick. The die are then attached to their packages using either a silver loaded glass paste or by forming a gold-alloy mix type of solder, depending on the product type. The positioning of the die relative to the package is critical.

Using automatic wire bonders, the contact pads on the die are attached to corresponding posts on the package. Products vary from 40 to 250 wires − or more. The more wires or contacts, the more complex the assembly task, and the wire count is always increasing. This operation is followed by another optical inspection (checking the process for physical defects) before the die is sealed. The product is then hermetically sealed using either a ceramic or metal lid. The lids are placed manually. Gas content and conditions inside the sealed product are also critical to quality. The sealed products are then thermally stressed, and tests are made for leakages in the package sealing. The lead frames are tin plated, again using an automated process.

The products are then taken from the cleanroom for the final operations.

The product type, lot number, date of manufacture and origin are manually branded onto the package. Some product is loaded into an anti-static carrier, while others require trimming in a hydraulic press. Following final inspection of all aspects of the package quality, the product is loaded into shipping tubes and transferred to the separately run VLSI Test Group.

The assembly operation is conducted in a sophisticated cleanroom designed to protect products before they are sealed from contamination from air, static discharge, people, liquids, equipment, chemicals and other particles, and items normally present in a manufacturing environment. The cleanroom floor, wall and ceiling materials are smooth and non-shedding, and air is ducted into the cleanroom through microfilters to scrub it clean of airborne contamination, particularly dust. The cleanroom pressure is higher than in the rest of the factory, to improve cleanliness standards, and entry and exit is effected through double airlocked doors.

The manufacturing process is laid out in sequence of production operation. Figure 1.1 shows a simple schematic diagram of the cleanroom layout with the product moving clockwise through the various stages of the assembly operation.

## The Management Position

Management views are divided about possible changes to management practices and working methods. Figure 1.2 shows the current organization structure.

Typical management responses to the comments you've collected from the shopfloor are

> That's a typical set of shopfloor gripes you've collected and, as you've also heard, we've got a satisfied workforce on the whole. We get the odd complaint about conditions, but there's nothing unusual about that, in this business or any other. Sure we can improve our communications, and maybe we could do with more supervisory training. We've got a complex organization structure because we've got a technically complex business that needs a lot of specialists to keep up with all the product developments and other changes.

> We can improve on what we've got. We don't need to change any of that, and besides it's both effective and successful. It ain't broke, so why fix it?

You hear that last comment repeated several times in your conversations with management. The Ayr plant, and the VLSI business in particular, has a consistent history of success. The plant opened in 1976 with 25 people, as a pilot final assembly and test operation sourcing the British and European markets. This involved order consolidation for small- and medium-range computer systems, add-ons, assembling components and testing systems made in and imported from America. The plant grew to over 365,000 square feet in 1989, and is now a complex site with multiple businesses employing over 1,400 people manufacturing the range of Digital's small-business products, from workstations to MicroVAX and VAXstation products, as well as the VLSI assembly and test businesses.

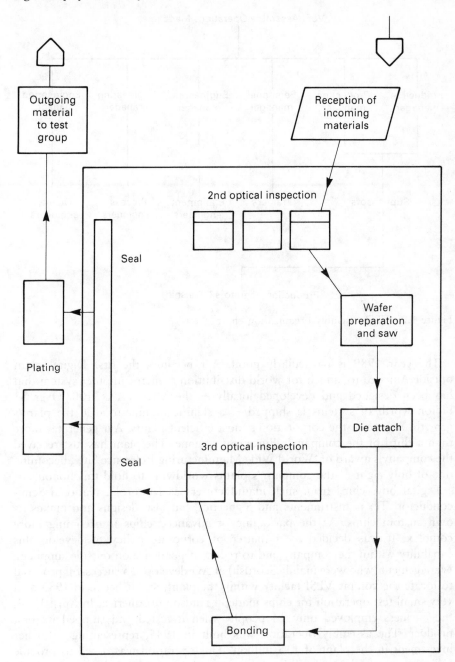

**Figure 1.1** Schematic diagram of cleanroom layout

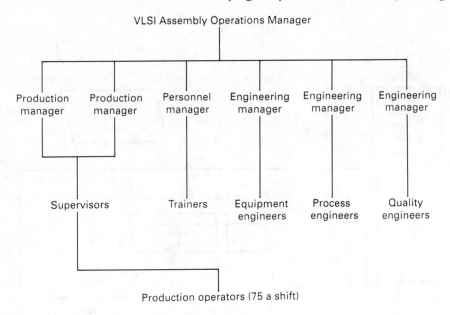

**Figure 1.2**   VLSI assembly organization chart

The year 1989 is particularly good. Ayr becomes the first Digital plant outside America to launch for world distribution a microcomputer system that has been designed and developed locally — the MicroVAX 3100. Over $1 billion worth of systems is shipped — a significant milestone in the plant's growth. As one of the corporation's most efficient plants, Ayr generates more than a third of the company's European revenue. The plant has just received the company's award of 'World Wide Manufacturing Reference Site', becoming one of only eight of the company's plants worldwide to hold this honour.

Digital buys chips from such manufacturers as Motorola, National Semi-conductor, Texas Instruments and Signectics, but also designs and makes its own custom chips. As the packaging of advanced chips is becoming more complex, it was decided as a matter of corporate policy to develop this capability within the company and to reduce dependence on outside suppliers. Management (who were mainly Scottish) at Ayr developed a successful proposal to locate the volume VLSI facility within the plant, and it began in 1983 as a very small test operation for chips made in Hudson in America. In April 1984, the business employed only 14 people when it tested and shipped its first product. The assembly operation was built in 1985, representing a further investment in the plant of £15 million. This operation was asked to provide full assembly and test facilities for up to 80 per cent of the corporation's worldwide custom semiconductor needs. A new advanced semiconductor wafer facility was then built at South Queensferry, near Edinburgh in Scotland, with a further investment of £150 million.

From the end of 1985 until 1989, the growth in VLSI production volumes was dramatic. The number of units assembled and tested per week in 1985 was 2,000. Assembly volumes rose to around 35,000 a week in 1989, covering devices in five main package families, with 40 different product types, in lot or batch sizes of 50 to 100. However, the devices are becoming increasingly sophisticated, by increasing the number of contacts required, and by the introduction of new packaging options, making constant new demands on engineering and assembly skills, and on investment in appropriate new test equipment.

In this type of manufacturing operation, the need to improve productivity is less important than the need to be able to handle increasing product complexity, the need to reduce the wastage rate (or to increase the 'yield' of chips that make it successfully through the manufacturing process), the need to reduce manufacturing cycle times to meet customer requirements, and the flexibility to handle small batches of specialized and varied product quickly.

Some managers feel that their uninterrupted record of achievement is due to the organization structure on which VLSI assembly is based. To change that now, they argue, will put the future success of the business at risk. The management voices dissenting from this view, on the other hand, point to the following issues:

> I accept that we've seen a steady increase in production volumes achieved with a conventional organization structure and no significant organizational problems. But we've gone up the ramp and it's started to level off. We've got an ideal opportunity here to stand back and look at the organization and see how it can be improved.

> Because of our traditional management approach, most of the assemblers in the cleanroom are unskilled. We've got people pushing buttons who aren't involved in decision-making. They haven't a clue what's going on half the time beyond their piece.

> I'm not sure how else we could have developed the type of operation we're running today from scratch. But now we've done that, maybe there's a better way forward. We've got some kind of window here, now that the business has started − relatively − to stabilize. We're glad of this breather now that build requirements have levelled off, and they even reduced for a brief period a few months back. We can use this opportunity to concentrate on training and skills development for our people.

> We've got a tradition here in our small computers business of multi-skilled self-managing teamwork. Maybe we should be looking at this for VLSI too − maybe have cells without direct supervision, and try to speed up decision-making and improve flexibility in assembly operations. This method has never been tried in the semiconductor business.

The organization hierarchy also has its critics, as these managers explain:

> We've built up a significant hierarchy around the business to co-ordinate and control it. There's a lot of engineering support and other specialists and decision-makers who seem to be needed around the assembly group, and this is consistent with conventional semiconductor manufacturing. But it is slow to respond to fast change; it's difficult to manage in a fluid environment.

Yeah, and another thing – the invisible barriers between our functional groups. With functional groups, there is a lot of stress and conflict. Whoever you work with, you are at loggerheads with on some issues, and I take a step back from it and think, why? If quality and engineering are in conflict, why is that?

You overhear the following debate about these issues in a management meeting:

*Manager A:*   I think that what we have to do here is to stand back and redraw the hierarchy and the lines of management responsibility and reporting. We just need to clarify our functional boundaries to avoid conflict.

*Manager B:*   That won't address the real problems we're facing. Why don't we set up a small management team with collective responsibility for the business, have no direct functional boundaries inside that group?

*Manager A:*   Sounds great, idealistic, and it'll never work in practice. What will you do with the managers you make redundant with your new team structure? Look, our hierarchy creates some problems, but these are quite normal and we understand them, and this is the structure that built the business. The effective strategy now is to pay more attention to communications – and that's risky in a changing environment.

*Manager B:*   Those managers have skills that can be used in other ways to develop the business. You're talking about strengthening the functional barriers, I'm concerned about removing them. It's not just a communications problem.

The debate you overhear is inconclusive.

## Case Study Tasks

Is there a problem? You are a consultant to the Assembly Staff Group for the VLSI assembly business. What organizational changes will you recommend, if any? As the old engineering proverb says, if it ain't broke, why fix it? Some managers in the VLSI business clearly feel this way about the existing organization structure and working practices. The key business goals include high standards of product quality and reliability, customer satisfaction, and the ability to respond effectively to rapid change. What recommendations will you make to help ensure that these business goals are achieved effectively in the 1990s?

1. What changes – if any – would you recommend with respect to the organization of work in the assembly operation, and why?
2. What changes – if any – would you recommend with respect to the supervisory function, and why?
3. What recommendations – if any – would you make concerning the management structure, and why?

4. What are the training and development implications of your recommendations?
5. What evidence do you have concerning this organization's readiness at this time to accept change?
6. How do you think your decisions would differ if the Ayr plant was unionized?

## Essential Reading

Buchanan, D. A. and McCalman, J. (1989) *High Performance Work Systems: The Digital Experience*, Routledge, London.
Hoerr, J. (1989) The payoff from teamwork, *Business Week*, 10 July, pp. 56–62.

## Additional Reading

Dumaine, B. (1990) Who needs a boss?, *Fortune*, no. 10, 7 May, pp. 40–7.
Lawler, E. E. (1986) *High Involvement Management: Participative Strategies for Improving Organizational Performance*, Jossey-Bass, San Francisco, Calif.
Mohrman, S. A., Ledford, G. E. and Lawler, E. E. (1986) Quality of worklife and employee involvement, in C. L. Cooper and I. Robertson (eds.) *International Review of Industrial and Organizational Psychology*, Wiley, New York, NY, pp. 189–216.
Peters, T. (1987) *Thriving on Chaos: Handbook for a Management Revolution*, Macmillan, London.
Wickens, P. (1987) *The Road to Nissan: Flexibility, Quality, Teamwork*, Macmillan, Basingstoke.

# CASE 2

# Japanization in the UK:
# Experiences from the Car Industry

## Nick Oliver and Barry Wilkinson

## Introduction

During the 1980s there was a surge of interest in Japanese manufacturing methods on the part of Western manufacturers. By the late 1980s the term 'Japanization' had been coined to describe (somewhat contentiously) a particular configuration of management practices spanning manufacturing methods, supplier relations and human resource policies typically found among the major Japanese manufacturing companies. These management practices have found their purest expression in the automotive industry, a sector in which Western companies felt the full impact of Japanese competition in the 1980s and 1990s.

In the early 1990s a major international consulting group asked a UK business school to prepare some briefing materials on the transfer of Japanese manufacturing methods to the West, with particular reference to the vehicle industry. The Consulting Group was planning to develop its consulting profile in this area and, as an initial step, was in search of basic 'awareness-raising' material. This document contains notes from various sources collated in response to this request.

## Notes from a Seminar Given by an Auto-Industry Expert

During the 1970s and 1980s the Japanese car producers assumed an increasingly important role in the international vehicle industry. By the end of the 1980s Japan controlled approximately 30 per cent of world output of cars; the impact of this growth has not been limited to market share. A major study published in 1990 into the performance of car producers by Womack, Jones and Roos demonstrated enormous differentials in both productivity and quality between Japanese and Western producers. On average it takes 16.8 hours to assemble a medium-sized car in Japan compared to 36.7 hours in Europe. The defect rate (for faults attributable to the assembly operation) in Japanese vehicles is 60 per 100 vehicles compared to 105 per 100 for European vehicles. 'Adapt or die' is the message many Western producers are taking from these figures. This message is all the more pressing as Japanese car producers establish factories in the West.

## Japanese Manufacturing Techniques: Notes from Various Sources

The irony about many of the manufacturing practices now being hailed as 'Japanese' is that many are in fact of Western origin, picked up and developed by Japanese industry in the 1950s. The key elements of the 'package' include the following.

### Total Quality Control

This involves a strong 'customer' orientation, extending inside the organization in the form of the internal customer; responsibility for quality at the point of production, rather than in the hands of a specialist quality-control department; an emphasis on 'getting it right first time'; and an ethos of continuous improvement, often manifested by such shopfloor problem-solving groups as quality circles.

### Just-in-Time (JIT) Production

The principle of JIT is that all the stations in a production process, from suppliers through to final assembly, should produce products and components in exactly the right quantity 'just in time' for them to be used in the next process. Materials thus pass through the system very quickly. Stock is minimized, which has the effect of making any problems in the production process very apparent. JIT principles extend to bought-out components. In Japan, many of Toyota's suppliers make several deliveries of the same components each day, often delivering to the exact point on the production line where the components will be used.

### Work Organization

Supporting conditions necessary for JIT and total quality to work successfully include forms of shopfloor organization that focus responsibility and accountability; flexibility of labour; and a workforce willing and able to participate in continuous improvement activities.

### Personnel Practices

In Japan the major Japanese corporations typically display paternalistic practices towards their employees, including life-time employment (at least for some sectors of the workforce), selective recruitment, seniority-based payment and promotion systems and consensual decision-making. Unions are based around the enterprise, not crafts or occupations. Managerial job rotation around the functions is the norm in order to foster a company-wide, rather than a sectional, perspective.

'Japanization' is sometimes used as a short-hand term to describe two processes: the emulation of Japanese practice by Western organizations and the impact of Japanese direct investment in host countries. The legitimacy of the term has been a hotly debated issue in the late 1980s and early 1990s.

## Nissan Motor Manufacturing (UK) – Notes from Various Sources

### Background

In 1990 Nissan was the world's fourth largest motor manufacturer and produced over 2.5 million vehicles. The company began manufacturing operations at its Sunderland plant in North-East England in 1986. The plant initially produced Bluebird models, which were superseded by the Primera model range in 1990. In this year the plant produced 76,000 vehicles, with a forecast of 120,000 for 1991, and a capacity rising to 220,000 when the plant starts producing Micra models alongside the Primera (*The Financial Times*, 22 March 1991).

### Inside the Sunderland Factory

Peter Wickens, Nissan's UK's Personnel Director, has stated that Nissan has introduced a Japanese tripod of working practices, namely 'teamwork, quality and flexibility'. Nissan offers everyone on the production line the same terms and conditions of employment. There is a common canteen and car park. All staff are paid monthly within a salary range, but the position of an individual within that range is determined by individual performance, as graded annually by the supervisor. There is no system of 'clocking on' at Nissan. On the shopfloor there are four basic occupations: manufacturing staff, technicians, team leaders and supervisors. The grade of senior supervisor was added when two-shift working was introduced.

### Shopfloor Organization

Staff work in production teams that typically comprise a supervisor and 20 manufacturing staff. Two of these staff are team leaders. Peter Wickens comments that supervisors are central figures and have 'Responsibility for everything that happens in their area ... a return to the old-style foreman before the specialists took away and diminished many of his tasks'. Supervisors act as mini-managers of their areas. They and the team leaders are taught every function of their team in considerable detail. At the beginning of 1989 Nissan employed 1,100 people in its manufacturing operations, including 70 supervisors and 120 team leaders. In contrast to traditional practice in the motor industry, Nissan's supervisors are not necessarily those who have worked their way up from the assembly line, because of the need for supervisors to possess managerial skills. Consequently, supervisors are often recruited externally.

At the beginning of each shift there are daily work-area meetings. These often focus on quality issues, but such matters as production schedules, the distribution of work, training and social events are also considered. Nissan encourage 'Kaizen' (continuous improvement) teams. Kaizen activity seeks to 'involve every individual in finding better ways of doing his or her job. It means continually seeking to find small improvements in quality, productivity, ease of working or simply making a better working environment'. Nissan claim that as a result of Kaizen, 90 per cent of all changes in the body shop have come from the employees working in that area. Up to 50 Kaizen teams may be operating in the manufacturing area at any one time.

At the end of the assembly process there is a vehicle evaluation system (VES). This provides information on defects expressed as numerical values. Industry analysts Garrahan and Stewart (1991) describe how the system enables faults to be traced back to particular workteams and hence to individual operators who may be awarded daily or weekly scores for their quality performance. Nissan has deliberately kept the area for the repair of finished vehicles small to force vehicles to be rectified in the area where the fault originally arose.

## Suppliers

Due in part to grant aid received, Nissan is under pressure to source components locally ('local' means from Europe). Many components are single sourced; where possible these are supplied on a JIT basis. Nissan has taken a share-holding in some of its suppliers, a number of which have located in close physical proximity to the Sunderland plant. Prior to entering into a contract with a supplier, Nissan looks in detail at the supplier's cost structure, quality-control procedures, materials stocks and purchasing policies. Industrial relations, work practices and strike record are also examined.

## Recruitment and Selection

At start-up Nissan recruited 470 people, 85 per cent from the locality. Approximately 11,500 applications were received for these jobs. These were narrowed down to 1,900, largely on the basis of answers to a questionnaire included with the application form. This number was further reduced (to 1,100) by the use of aptitude, numerical, verbal fluency and mechanical comprehension tests. There then followed a series of practical exercises. Nissan's Personnel Director commented that 'At all times we were looking for their attitude and approach to problems, and this was further reinforced by a general discussion involving candidates and supervisors'. By 1989 Nissan employed approximately 2,000 people. The average age of the workforce is in the mid-20s.

Nissan spends at least six hours in selecting, testing and interviewing each new member of the manufacturing staff. All applicants undergo the same procedure as described above for the original applicants. Practical tests and a general discussion take place before interviews conducted by the supervisors. The *supervisor* makes the final selection decision on whether to employ someone in his team.

New employees are given a one-day induction course, followed by on-the-job instruction. A minimum of one month or 1,500 job cycles under the supervision of their team leader is usual. Supervisors typically attend courses on leadership, problem-solving, organization, communication and quality. (The use of temporary workers in peak periods on the production line at Nissan marks a break with usual British practice.)

## Unions

Nissan has a single union agreement with the AEU, which was signed prior to production at the plant commencing. Commentators split in their opinions on this arrangement. The view of critical social-science commentators, such as Crowther and Garrahan (1988, p. 56), is that 'By offering the carrot of exclusive recruitment rights to a single union, but stipulating in advance which union, Nissan split them through competition and ensured agreement on its own terms'. It is estimated that only about 30 per cent of the workforce are members of the union.

There is a 'Company Council'. Representatives of all groups of employees sit on this body, which has three main functions: a consultative forum; ultimate authority in the in-house grievance procedure; and an arena in which pay and conditions are negotiated. The Chair and Secretary of the Council are Nissan managers, and workforce representatives are elected from the various sections of the plant. The representatives are not necessarily union members, and the company has a veto over who can stand.

## Work Experience

The experience of work in factories run according to Japanese principles is a debated topic. Nissan has attracted controversy in this area. On its application forms Nissan states that

All applicants should carefully consider the following points:

- The pace of work will be dictated by a moving production line and will be very demanding.
- Work assignments will be carefully defined and will be repetitive.
- You may be moved on to a new operation or transferred into a different department at very short notice.

Within a year of the plant commencing production shopfloor complaints about working conditions appeared in the national press. These complaints included allegations that the lines moved so fast that people had to work unpaid before shifts began and during breaks to meet targets; overtime being imposed; and pay being stopped when people were off sick because supervisors did not believe them (*The Daily Telegraph*, 6 May 1987). Nissan disputed these allegations.

A recent study of the work experience of Nissan workers by Garrahan and Stewart (1991) reported that many employees did find the work pace gruelling, but that there were some positive feelings; these were largely inspired by the 'togetherness' of team working. Garrahan and Stewart conclude that many workers at Nissan are engaging in a rational choice by accepting tough industrial work in exchange for employment in 'a good family firm'.

# Ford UK – Notes from Various Sources

## Background

The Ford Motor Company began manufacturing cars in the UK in 1911. It currently has two plants which assemble cars (Dagenham in Essex and Halewood on Merseyside) and a plant that produces light commercial vehicles in Southampton. Ford has a number of other UK plants that manufacture vehicle components. Ford of Britain employs approximately 48,000 people in total. The company has a further four assembly plants on the Continent.

## Inside the Factories

The management systems of the Ford Motor Company have historically been seen as the epitome of scientific management principles. At the macro-organizational level, the functional groupings of the company are very strong, with the route to advancement being to enter a particular function (finance, production, marketing, personnel and so on) and to stay within that function and be promoted within it. (Such systems typically create functional 'chimneys' where the understanding of one function by another is limited, with relations often being un-cooperative and sometimes antagonistic.)

## On the Shopfloor

Historically very little responsibility or discretion has been given to the shopfloor, engendering an 'I'm not paid to think' mentality. Jobs are rigidly defined and, at the start of the 1980s, there were 500 job titles on the factory floor. Specialization and a division of labour around functions has encouraged a fragmentation of responsibilities. For example, the role of the production supervisor has been to keep production volumes up, preventing line stops at all costs. Production supervisors largely come from the ranks of (unskilled) production workers. Skilled maintenance workers, whose input is essential to keep the lines running and to deal with breakdowns, come under a specialist section. Responsibility for quality has historically lain with a specialist quality-control department, which inspects the vehicles and sends those with defects to a rework area to be rectified. Some plants have a dedicated 'rework line', purely to rectify defects in the finished vehicles. The personnel department deals with the vast majority of employee relations matters, such as recruitment, selection, disciplinary and grievance issues.

## Unions

Labour relations at Ford have been restless. The multiplicity of job grades have their corollary in the presence of a number of unions representing the interests of different groups of Ford workers. In 1988 there were five main manual unions at Ford UK (including the TGWU, the AEU and the EETPU), a handful of smaller manual unions and two unions for white-collar workers. In addition to management/worker divides, there are tensions between skilled and unskilled groups, between different craft groups and between white- and blue-collar groups.

From 1945 (the year in which unions were first recognized at Ford UK) until the 1960s, management/union negotiations were handled by national union officials. Shop stewards were largely excluded from this forum. Labour unrest during the late 1960s and early 1970s led to arrangements that incorporated shop stewards into the bargaining procedure. According to industry analysts Starkey and McKinlay (1989), these arrangements were based on the assumption that negotiating agreements with unions was the best method of improving productivity by ensuring harmonious employee relations.

At a national level, Ford's unions and Ford management agreed common terms and conditions across the company's UK sites in a document known as the *Blue Book*. This national agreement did *not* prevent management/union conflict at plant level.

## After Japan

Since the late 1970s Ford worldwide has engaged in a number of initiatives to improve its performance in all areas of its operations. For Ford Europe, one of the key events was a trip to Japan by its President in the late 1970s who, according to Starkey and McKinlay (1989) returned 'in a state of shock' at what he had seen. Prior to this, within Ford it had been assumed that the Japanese challenge lay in cheap labour and a protected domestic market, rather than in the way they managed their operations. The most concrete manifestation of this realignment was a productivity campaign dubbed 'After Japan'. An important perception that lay behind this campaign was that the management style found in Japanese factories was consensual, and drew on the skills and creative abilities of the workforce in working towards company goals.

In 1979 Ford began to introduce quality circles, with three objectives in mind: the improvement of productivity; fostering greater motivation among shopfloor workers; and providing a direct communication channel between management and the shopfloor. Ford invested substantial sums of money in the programme, including training circle leaders and members in techniques of problem-solving and analysis. Plant managers were responsible for circle activities in their plants.

## Impact of 'After Japan'

Some early successes are documented (for example, a 2.5-per-cent saving in scrap at the Bridgend engine plant), but the campaign soon ran into union resistance and within two years the unions had withdrawn their support from the programme. According to an analysis by Guthrie (1987), the programme was branded a 'resounding failure' in terms of its aims of improving work attitudes and generating cost savings.

Ford management took the view that the programme failed largely because of union bloody-mindedness. Unions were concerned that circles were intended to by-pass the shop-steward system, by encouraging workers to communicate directly with management rather than via the trade-union structure. Middle and lower management were also concerned about the introduction of quality circles. Guthrie (*ibid*. p. 30) reports that many supervisors 'Were sceptical of a new "vogue" management technique, or even felt threatened by their lack of control over quality circles and vulnerable to criticism of the quality and legitimacy of their decisions'. These sentiments sometimes found expression in an unwillingness to implement circle proposals, aggravating shopfloor cynicism. Although training was provided to shopfloor workers, in some plants the largely immigrant and poorly educated workforces were not well suited to group discussions with the English supervisors and found problem-solving techniques difficult to grasp. In addition, the average age of the Ford workforce was over 40, making changes in attitudes less likely.

## More Initiatives

During the mid-1980s, Ford UK announced its intentions of implementing other elements of the Japanese-style management package. JIT and total-quality ideas were introduced, both in Ford's own factories and among its suppliers. By the mid-1980s, Ford was the acknowledged leader in introducing quality systems into its suppliers. (Up to 70 per cent of a modern vehicle comprises bought-in components, so the quality of the finished vehicle is crucially determined by the quality of bought-in parts.)

During the 1980s, Ford Europe developed an integrated production system, involving minimum stock (following JIT principles) and single or dual sourcing of parts (within Ford Europe, many major components are built by the company in one country and then fitted to cars assembled in another). This regime offers greater economies of scale at the component manufacturing plants and reduced costs of stock holding.

Inside its UK plants, Ford has been trying to push through reforms based on the Japanese model of manufacturing. In 1985 agreement was reached to increase flexibility in working practices. This agreement reduced the number of job classifications on the shopfloor from 550 to 52, permitting some flexibility across skilled grades and giving production workers responsibility for simple maintenance and housing-keeping activities. This move was not welcomed by all Ford workers. One assembly-line worker commented:

Flexibility means that every 102 seconds a car comes by, and not only do you have to screw something into the car, but in between you have to tidy up, check your tools, repair things and check you've got enough parts. You do not have a single job any more. If there is no work on the line they move you to where there is work. You are working the whole time.

(*The Financial Times*, 8 February 1988)

In 1988 Ford sought further reforms in working practices, to extend flexibility further and to introduce team working into its plants. A central component of the team-working concept as proposed by Ford is 'area working'. This scheme is similar to the structure used by Nissan. The aim is to have 'area foremen' responsible, as the title suggests, for a discrete area of the factory and the majority of the functions within it (such as quality control, production and maintenance). This represents a refocusing of the tasks that historically had been taken away from the supervisor and vested in the hands of specialist departments. Under the area foremen are group leaders, recruited from the shopfloor, who will lead work teams of between 8 and 10 workers. The group leaders have responsibility for routine supervisory activities covering work allocation, technical problem-solving and quality. The UK plans are modelled on practices at Ford's Valencia engine plant, where the central maintenance shop has been virtually disbanded and area foremen given responsibility for maintenance (*The Financial Times*, 11 February 1988). Other changes sought by Ford were for each UK plant to adopt a quality statement, the establishment of 'quality discussion groups' (another phrase for quality circles), harmonization of pay and conditions between white- and blue-collar workers and the establishment of a single bargaining forum for all workers.

## The 1988 National Strike

Negotiations over these changes were tied up with the 1988 pay deal, and culminated in February 1988 in an all-out strike of Ford UK's manual workers, largely around the issue of changes in working practices.

The emulation of Japanese methods in terms of low stocks and single sourcing at European level meant that the effects of this stoppage quickly rippled through the whole system. The day after the strike began, Ford announced that 2,000 workers were to be laid off at Genk; within a few days this had risen to 9,700 and production of Escort and Orion models at Saarlouis was cut (*Guardian*, 10 February 1988). Two weeks into the strike Ford made concessions acceptable to the workforce and the strike was over. The company marginally improved its pay offer, cut the period of the pay offer to two years (originally a three-year deal had been sought) and conceded to a 'non-imposition clause', which meant that all reforms would be introduced only by local agreement (*The Financial Times*, 20 February 1988).

Some months prior to the strike, in October 1987, Ford had announced plans to construct a £40 million electronics component plant at Dundee in Scotland. The company signed a single-union agreement with the AEU, an agreement that included provision for team working, flexibility and rates of pay in line with the Scottish electronics industry rather than other Ford plants. The deal thus fell outside the *Blue Book* union–management agreement on wages and conditions. It appears that Ford were using the opportunity of a greenfield site to try to break the mould of its UK employee relations and working practices.

The announcement of the deal immediately gave rise to an inter-union dispute on three issues: that Dundee would fall outside the *Blue Book*, which should hold at all plants; that wages and conditions at Dundee would be less than at equivalent Ford plants elsewhere; and that it should be workers who chose what union was going to represent them, not management. It was reported that the Ford unions' national negotiating committee threatened to black components coming out of Dundee (an allegation subsequently denied by union officials). In March 1988, just weeks after the end of the national strike, Ford announced it was withdrawing from the project, and in August 1988 it was reported that the factory was to be built in Spain (*Guardian*, 6 August 1988).

In the early 1990s this pattern continued. Attempts to push through changes in work practices and organization continue, as do instances of industrial unrest. In 1990 the Halewood plant on Merseyside was shut down for seven weeks because of a stoppage by skilled workers over Ford's failure to sort out problems with the pay structure, a stoppage that coincided with the build up to the launch of the new Escort. Ford claim 39,500 vehicles were lost as a consequence of the dispute and, in early 1991, set a deadline to improve efficiency at the plant. One element of this included the implementation of outstanding agreements on the reduction of demarcation, job progression on merit, more flexible shifts and 'bell-to-bell' working (*Guardian*, 20 May 1991). This dispute affected other Ford plants, including the Bridgend engine plant and, in early 1990, Ford cancelled a £225 million investment there and redirected the investment to Cologne, claiming that the unreliability of supplies from its British plants was an important factor in its decision (*The Financial Times*, 10 April 1990).

## Performance Data

Despite these attempts at reform, the performance of Ford's UK plants lags behind those of its other European plants, as the data in Table 2.1 demonstrate. In 1991 the European car market slumped, with the UK – Ford's major market – being particularly badly hit. Ford suffered more than most manufacturers and, in mid-1991, was forced to cut the prices of many of its models by 10 per cent.

In 1991, some European manufacturers successfully lobbied the EEC to restrict imports from Japan to the 1989–90 levels until 1999 (*Japan Times*, 31 July 1991). The hope is that the European car industry can survive and catch up in competitiveness before protectionist measures are lifted.

Table 2.1  Productivity at Ford's European plants

| Plant | Vehicles per employee | Hours per car | |
|---|---|---|---|
| Saarlouis | 42 | — | |
| Valencia | 38 | 33 | (Fiesta) |
| Genk | 34 | 40 | (Sierra)[†] |
| Halewood | 29 | 59 | (Escort) |
| Southampton | 23 | 79 | (Transit) |
| Dagenham | 22 | 57 | (Fiesta) |
| | | 67 | (Sierra)[*†] |

*Notes*
[*] Sierra production ceased on this site in 1990; [†] Ford estimate that Nissan UK only requires 26 hours to manufacture a Sierra-size vehicle.

Performance with respect to vehicle quality largely mirrors that of productivity. Dagenham-produced Fiestas average 62.2 warranty repairs per 100 vehicles after a month of service compared to 28.6 for Fiestas from Ford's Valencia plant.

(*Source: The Financial Times*, 26 June 1990.)

## Questions for Discussion

1. What are the key elements of work organization at shopfloor level at Nissan and Ford? What are their similarities? What are their differences?
2. On the basis of these cases, what appear to be the supporting conditions necessary for Japanese manufacturing practices, such as JIT and total quality, to operate successfully?
3. What are likely to be the main obstacles to the implementation of Japanese-style manufacturing organization by established companies in the West?
4. Assess the propositions that Japanese manufacturing methods demand the dismantling of the power of organized labour and result in an intensification of work.
5. What do you consider the arguments to be for and against the take up of Japanese methods by Western companies?
6. Identify the control strategies in use at Ford and Nissan at shopfloor level. In what ways are these similar and in what ways do they differ?
7. You are advising the officers of a trade union who are concerned about the plans of a company (whose blue-collar workers they represent) to introduce total quality control. The plans include an area-working scheme, the establishment of a company council, flexible working and quality circles. How would you advise the union to respond?

## References

Crowther, S. and Garrahan, P. (1988) Invitation to Sunderland: corporate power and the local economy, *Industrial Relations Journal*, Vol. 19, no. 1, pp. 51–9.

Garrahan, P. and Stewart, P. (1991) *The Nissan Enigma: Flexibility at Work in a Local Economy*, Mansell, London.

Guthrie, G. (1987) After Japan and beyond, *Production Engineer*, May, pp. 29–31.
Starkey, K. and McKinlay, A. (1989) Beyond Fordism? Strategic choice and labour relations in Ford UK, *Industrial Relations Journal*, Vol. 20, pp. 93–100.
Wickens, P. (1987) *The Road to Nissan*, Macmillan, London.
Womack, J. P., Jones, D. T. and Roos, D. (1990) *The Machine that Changed the World: The Triumph of Lean Production*, Rawson Macmillan, New York, NY.

## Additional Reading

Child, J. (1984) *Organization: A Guide to Problems and Practice*, Paul Chapman, London.
Kamata, S. (1982) *Japan in the Passing Lane*, Allen & Unwin, London.
Oliver, N. and Wilkinson, B. (1992) *The Japanization of British Industry*, Blackwell, Oxford.
Pfeffer, J. (1981) *Power in Organizations*, Pitman, Boston, Mass.
Schonberger, R. (1982) *Japanese Manufacturing Techniques*, Free Press, New York, NY.
Wilkinson, B. and Oliver, N. (eds.) (1988) *Industrial Relations Journal*, Vol. 19, no. 1, pp. 7–10 (special issue on 'Japanization').

# CASE 3

## The Implementation of High-Performance Work-Teams

### Sharon K. Parker and Paul R. Jackson

## Organizational Setting

Norahs & Luap, Inc (N & L) is an electronics company in the East Midlands that manufactures control equipment for such process industries as chemicals, nuclear power and oil. It is part of an American-owned corporation that has sites throughout America, Europe and Asia. N & L contains the manufacturing facility, which produces standard components and sub-assemblies. There are also a number of staging facilities, one of which is located at N & L, where the equipment for customers is installed to their detailed specification.

N & L employs 412 people, of whom 200 are based in manufacturing and the remainder in staging. The workforce is stable, with an average length of service within the company at the start of our involvement of five years. There are five trade unions on site, although management prefers to communicate directly with the workforce rather than through union representatives.

In 1987, the company moved to a purpose-built site on an industrial estate on the outskirts of the city. However, by 1988, pressure from three much larger competitors was highlighting areas of poor performance and eroding the sustainability of the UK manufacturing operation. For example, the company was hitting target delivery dates only one third of the time. Following results such as these, the US parent company was considering moving manufacturing out of the UK and into the Far East. Not surprisingly, everyone within N & L felt very vulnerable.

The US management began to put heavy pressure on UK manufacturing to improve performance, and the first step taken was to restructure management to give a team reporting directly to the Manufacturing Director. This team consisted of people responsible for production (Peter Hardy), personnel, manufacturing engineering (Graham Liddell, responsible for the design of new products), purchasing and traffic (responsible for liaising with component suppliers and with customers), production and inventory control (responsible for production scheduling), site services and quality assurance.

The management team developed a number of strategies designed to ensure survival of the manufacturing facility in the UK. This case study focuses on one of these, the implementation of product lines within the production area.

## Background to the Case

Every process control system is unique to an individual customer, both in terms of hardware and software. The initial stage therefore is a complex and lengthy period of specification by design engineers working closely with the end customer. However, most systems can be specified in terms of a common core of hardware components, such as main processor boards, input/output (I/O) units and visual display unit (VDU) consoles — with the one-off elements being confined to a number of discrete sub-assemblies, idiosyncratic wiring or system software.

The manufacturing facility is responsible for the production of printed circuit boards (PCBs) and standard sub-assemblies. Production is characterized by relatively low volume and high variety: about 100,000 boards are made per year, for around 200 different products. Once combined in sub-assemblies, these products are supplied worldwide to operations (or staging) sites for integration of the final assembled system to suit the customer.

## *The Production Process*

The layout of the production area is shown in Figure 3.1. It is organized functionally. The figure shows the production flow for an example board type.

The first stage is *kitting* within the computer-controlled stores department, where all the components required for a job are assembled according to the specification produced by a works-order program. Some passive components (mainly resistors and capacitors) are assembled onto paper-tape using a sequencer, which places them in the correct order for the next stage. This is *auto-insertion* of components using machines that place passive components (such as resistors, capacitors and diodes) and semiconductors on the board.

From there, work goes on to *first-phase manual assembly*, where unusual components (too low volume to pass through auto-insertion) are placed by hand. Boards are then transferred on a trolley to the *flow-solder* area, where solder connections are made. Boards return to the manual assembly benches for *second-phase manual assembly*, where large components that cannot pass through the flow-solder machine are inserted and soldered in place.

An initial *quality audit* is conducted at this stage by inspectors, checking that all components have been placed correctly. The next stage is an *in-circuit test* using automatic test equipment to check for continuity in the circuitry, followed by *high-potential testing* to ensure that the board is grounded properly. The board is then exercised within the *run-in* area by repeatedly powering it on and off and performing customized tests at an elevated temperature of 50°C. *Functional tests* are then completed using automatic and/or manual test equipment. Finally, boards are moved to *final quality audit*, then either stored or transported to customers.

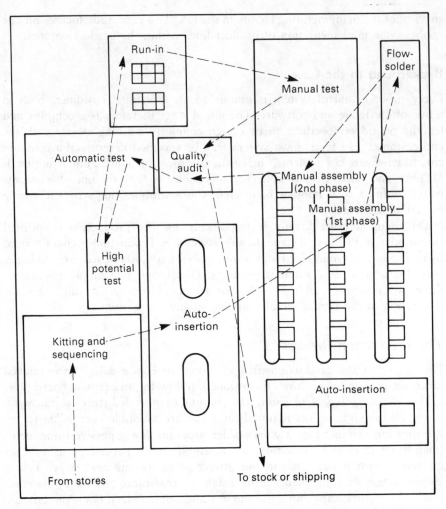

**Figure 3.1**  Original layout of the production process at Norahs & Luap, Inc.

## Manufacturing Personnel

The age distribution of the workforce in manufacturing at N & L is mixed: 25 per cent are less than 25 years old, 38 per cent are between 25 and 35 years old and 37 per cent are aged between 35 and 60 years (the average age is 34 years).

Two thirds of employees are women. They do most of the work in kitting, insertion and manual component assembly, in jobs which are low in problem-solving demands but high in the degree of manual dexterity required. Personnel for these jobs are mostly recruited from other local electronics companies who pay slightly less than N & L. The main criterion for selection of assembly operators is basic experience with electronic assembly. The personnel manager described it thus: 'can they breathe and use a soldering iron?'

Assembly operators require about 3–6 months of on-the-job training, and fit into the grade-1 classification of the four-grade pay structure. Personnel performing these jobs cannot move into grade 2 without obtaining a formal qualification.

Routine testing procedures, such as loading program cards into run-in machines, are performed by test examiners. These are also employed at Grade-1 level, but can move onto grade 2 with experience and a formal qualification (usually a two-year diploma). Test engineers who perform more complex fault-finding and live electrical testing are employed at grade-2 level.

## Problems Facing Manufacturing

Three problem areas faced the management team in 1988: conflicting priorities between production and manufacturing engineering, problems between manufacturing and staging sites and poor performance within production itself.

**Production and manufacturing engineering** A key problem facing manufacturing from a scheduling point of view is the evolutionary nature of the design process. Customers working with the company's manufacturing engineers repeatedly change their minds about what they want; indeed, part of the company's role is to educate the customer in understanding what their real needs are. As a result, systems design and production overlap, and changes are frequently made during production itself. There may also be changes made in the specification of the product or changes to account for design faults encountered during product development.

This ongoing design process often results in conflicts between production and manufacturing engineering. The engineers want to be able to change specifications during production itself in order to accommodate the availability of new components or to bring about improvements in design that do not alter functionality. The production manager is concerned primarily with maintaining production schedules and delivering a functional product by an agreed target date. Consequently, the design engineering manager often finds it difficult to obtain approval for production to be halted in order to bring about specification changes.

**Manufacturing and staging sites** Conflicts between manufacturing and its customers (the staging sites) are particularly marked for the staging facility at the same location. As internal customers, they resent the fact that they tend to get lowest priority from manufacturing compared with the demands of staging sites elsewhere. However, they in turn cause problems for production when they take advantage of their position by making direct requests to different areas within production for urgently needed parts when their requirements change. This, of course, increases the disruption in work schedules within manufacturing. It also creates personal resentments within manufacturing since

staging workers see themselves as more highly skilled than those in manufacturing: 'we don't have a routine, do-the-same-all-day job like most people
in manufacturing. Our job is complex as we do the one-off aspects of a
product to fit it for a customer's needs.'

**Production**  By early 1988, manufacturing was experiencing many problems
in production. The quality yield of products (the percentage of fault-free
products) was about 70 per cent, totally unacceptable to management in a
product which relied on guaranteeing to the customer a high level of fault-free
performance. The build lead time was around eight weeks for most products,
and customers were increasingly demanding a quicker response to orders.
Delivery integrity (getting the right product to the customer at the right time)
was getting ever harder to attain. The causes of these problems were many,
some of them hard to pin down precisely.

Work flow through the factory was not balanced in that there were often
large stocks of work awaiting completion at different stages in the manufacturing process. For example, on a number of occasions there were over 800
boards piled up on trolleys next to one of the in-circuit test machines awaiting
either functional tests or fault diagnosis, an obvious bottle-neck in the process.
Part of this stock of work-in-progress also resulted from the reworking of sub-
assemblies that had failed the inspection process, largely as a result of simple
operator errors, such as inserting components the wrong way round, or dry
solder-joints for manually inserted components.

Board testing was undertaken by specialist testers in a separate section of the
shopfloor. Consequently, assembly operators saw the identification and recti-
fication of faults as the responsibility of the test section rather than that of the
assembly area that had generated many of the faults in the first place. This
tendency was compounded by the enjoyment that many test engineers got from
fault-finding: 'I get a real buzz out of tracking down a particularly obscure
fault. You feel a bit like a detective trying to solve a mystery!'

More fundamentally, most production workers had no sense of ownership
of the product or of the production process as a whole, apart from doing their
set tasks in accordance with the company's standard manufacturing procedures.
A supervisor described what happened when the chargehand was on holiday
and information was needed about the master production schedule: 'None of
the operators knew how to access the computer system so I said to them "how
do you know which jobs are priority?" The girls said, "Well they're the ones
on the top of the pile". They had no idea, and no interest, beyond that.'

Most of the operators were not cross-skilled and had worked on the same
small range of tasks since before the move to the current site. For example,
Syoti is 32 years of age and had spent the previous nine years fitting connectors to
the end of wires cut to length. She said: 'Wiring is a hassle-free job. I like it,
I'm damned good at it, and I plan to do it till I retire.'

Once a task was completed, any faults that there might be on a board were
seen by operators as the domain of the quality inspectors, whose job it was to
detect faults and send the board for reworking. Individuals within manufacturing

tended to identify with their own function or department (assembler, kitter, storeperson, tester, inspector) rather than with the product they helped build. Thus there was no feeling of common cause among groups of workers; rather, each group sought to deal with production problems by finding another group to blame and pass the problem on to. Production supervisors spent most of their time chasing late orders and reacting to problems.

## The Problem: The Implementation of Product Lines

In response to these production problems, Peter Hardy and the group reporting directly to him in production prepared a document on a manufacturing strategy for N & L based on reorganization into product lines. A product-line form of organization was expected to improve communication, reduce inventory costs and allow much greater responsiveness to changes in customer demands. The specific goals defined by the strategic plan were

- zero defects at every stage in the production process;
- reduction in lead time;
- 100-per-cent delivery integrity;
- removal of non value-added processes; and
- a culture with employee ownership of quality and customer service.

This plan was presented to the manufacturing management team. Although accepted by all team members, several managers of indirect areas gave what amounted to only a nominal approval, seeing product lines as not particularly relevant to their areas. 'We're quite happy to let them go ahead with it,' said Graham Liddell, the manufacturing engineering manager.

### Forming a Pilot Team

A key first element of the strategy was the creation of a multi-skilled team to manufacture a specific product, the PX Unit. This team would perform tasks previously undertaken within manufacturing and staging. Applications for the PX Unit team were called for in July 1989. Major interest initially arose from workers in a number of areas of production, although no test engineers or examiners put their names forward for consideration. Given the sense of superiority held by workers in staging, it is perhaps not surprising that they were almost all scathing about the idea that assembly workers could ever do a job as complex as theirs. Many also felt threatened that management seemed to be taking part of their work away.

During August, the team was constituted as Mike (an experienced member of the staging facility who had responded to some pressure to move into the new team — management felt that there should be one person at least from staging), and four relatively unskilled members (one white female, two white males and one Asian male) drawn from the assembly, kitting and stores areas of manufacturing. The selection of membership for the PX Unit team was based on obtaining a mixture of skills within the team rather than on the compatibility of team members. (To choose the 'ideal' mix of personalities was felt to be dangerous in the long term because it would allow others in manufacturing to dismiss a successful pilot as rigged in its favour from the start.)

## The Early Days of the PX Unit Team

Team members, all at the grade-1 salary level, were enthusiastic about the prospect of working flexibly within their own team, and being the pilot for the implementation of the manufacturing strategy for the company as a whole. Management expectations were that, following one month of intensive training in both technical and team-development aspects, the team would be able to build five PX Units per week. The PX Unit team was managed by Peter Hardy, the production manager, and supported by a group consisting of two manufacturing engineers (including Mukesh, who eventually became the supervisor of the PX Unit team), an assembly supervisor and the test supervisor. Members of the support group retained their original positions, giving assistance only on request. After the first few months, such requests became less frequent and Mukesh effectively ran the group alone and made most key decisions.

Although there was a great deal of enthusiasm and commitment from the support group, their commitment was not matched by that of others on the site as a whole. In particular, the attempt to streamline production by creating a team that cut across manufacturing and staging (but responsible to the manufacturing manager) led to problems in both areas.

The PX Unit team needed support from Janice Mannering, the manager in staging, who was uncertain about the extent of her responsibility. Other workers within staging were often hostile and not supportive, partly because they felt work was being taken away from them but also because they believed PX Unit team members were incapable of working to their level of skill. This was indeed a difficulty for PX Unit members as the standard of wiring in staging took a long time to learn.

From the manufacturing side, the PX Unit team were now treated as a separate customer and given the low priority afforded to staging. Boards from production were thus frequently late in delivery, and the tight schedules set by management for production were impossible to meet despite constant overtime worked by team members. Manufacturing groups who were not part of production were also unresponsive to the PX team. For example, requests for urgent parts were often treated by purchasing as low priority, and manufacturing engineers saw the whole initiative as 'nothing to do with us'.

The team members themselves became demoralized very quickly, feeling that they could meet neither management targets nor their own initial expectations. The first PX Unit system they built took 7 days rather than the target of 3.5 days, a 'failure' that weighed heavily on the team. In fact, Peter Hardy was very pleased since the system would have taken 10 days to build with the old production methods, but did not communicate this to team members in case it reduced the credibility of future targets.

Team members realized that the technical skills most of them had lacked when the team was set up could not be acquired in a few weeks. As well as the difficulty of learning the complex wiring for staging, testing was problematic in two ways. First, none of the PX team had ever done it; and, second, test technicians were reluctant for inexperienced people to enter their department and use their equipment.

Team-building sessions within the PX team were the scene for constant bickering and personality clashes. Mike emerged as dominant, both because of his pushy temperament and because he already possessed many of the skills needed by the team as a whole. He felt that much of the responsibility for the team's success depended on him, and effectively recreated the role of chargehand, which had been removed when the team was set up: 'Every football team needs a captain and if you ain't got a captain you stray a bit. He's not there to tell them what to do or make major decisions, just to control them. I class myself as this sort of captain, I'm a natural leader.' Other team members resented his position but their relative lack of skill and experience made them reticent to do anything about it.

In February 1990 (four months after the team was set up) the team was still not meeting the production target of five PX Units per week, and results from an opinion survey at this time showed that the PX Unit team members were among the least satisfied workers in manufacturing.

They were unhappy with management's commitment both to the manufacturing strategy and to their team's place in its implementation. They did not see themselves as working well together and were beginning to doubt whether there really was a need for change in the direction of team working. They felt themselves constantly hemmed in by constraints from other parts of the site, and unable to meet their production targets as a result of lack of direction and support from elsewhere.

Mukesh was also feeling frustrated, finding that the move from a passive, reactive culture to one of employee ownership and involvement required lots of persistence from supervisors. He described an instance where a team member asked him how he could improve his performance appraisal rating. Mukesh told him he needed to 'use his initiative more'. When asked what he meant by this, Mukesh explained that using initiative meant doing things that were not already being done, and he gave some examples of things a person could do. A few weeks later the team member came back to Mukesh claiming he had 'done the things you suggested' and 'what next?' Mukesh often had to fight the temptation simply to tell people what to do rather than go through the painstaking process of getting people to learn for themselves.

## The PX Unit Team Settles Down

A year later when the opinion survey was repeated in January 1991, the performance of the team had improved considerably, and they were now regularly meeting revised targets of 10 PX Units per week despite persisting problems of supply of internal components.

This was partly a consequence of becoming more proficient in the technical duties they performed, but also through becoming more self-managing. In Mukesh's words

> Initially they were bewildered and didn't know what was expected from them. I kept pushing it into them that I am not a boss, but a resource. I say to them, 'You don't get work given to you on Monday to finish by Friday that you sit down and do. I want you to know why you're doing it, where it's going, is there any better way of doing it, all kinds of things ...' Slowly they've learnt to make their own decisions – often better decisions sometimes than I could have made!

Similarly, team members felt more valued by management: 'In the last 8 to 9 months they've started to treat us like adults. We've got more freedom as well, you don't have to follow one particular rule, if you think you can do something easier in your own way, they let you do it.'

This freedom extended beyond individual jobs to encompass responsibility for administrative and managerial tasks. For example, some members were in charge of ordering components and tools, some set the group's production schedules and targets, and others were involved in monitoring and displaying objective measures of performance.

As a result both of broadened responsibilities and of a clearer understanding of what was expected of them, most team members had become more confident in their abilities. One member stated:

> I never had any interpersonal skills when I came into the PX team. I did, but not in the way I've got now. Now, I speak my mind, I'm good in meetings, and I'm good at meeting people like customers ... I've been speaking at a conference with 68 people from this company. I was nervous, but I did it ... five years ago, I could never have done that.

Most team members felt confident enough to liaise directly with manufacturing engineers and with production control – and some were talking directly to customers.

Team members were also more satisfied with each other, one member remarking: 'We're brilliant now compared to what we used to be. We still have personal clashes which you're always going to get, ain't you, but the good thing about our group is that now most of them don't hold back on what they think.'

Although individual team members were taking on responsibility for more tasks, Mike was still making most of the key group decisions, and this tended to generate friction. Mukesh was frequently called in to resolve these interpersonal conflicts, and his success in doing so was acknowledged by the team: 'I'd go as far as saying Mukesh is the best supervisor. He can sort out things without shouting, he treats everyone the same, and he gives you the space to work things out yourself.'

Overall, members of the PX Unit team much preferred their new way of working despite the hassles involved. The PX Unit team was also successful in meeting management's objectives, including reduced lead time (from 7 days for one system to 10 per week), reduced defects and improved delivery integrity (from delivering the right products on time about 33 per cent of the time to about 80 per cent of the time).

Some non-value-added processes had been removed, although the team felt that the biggest improvement would come with replacing final inspection with ongoing quality checking. This was not likely to occur for some time: management in quality were happy for PX Unit team members to 'look at' but not 'inspect' their own products.

Regarding the final goal of a new culture, team members appeared to feel ownership for the products, the production process and meeting the targets. Mike stated: 'My actual goal is customer satisfaction. It's my personal goal, and I pump that into the team because that's what's been pumped into me. I'll do anything to make sure the job goes out on the day it's meant to – I'll put pressure on people, I'll stay late, whatever.'

Encouraged by the success of the PX Unit team, manufacturing management decided to proceed to the next stage in the strategy – the implementation of product lines across the whole of manufacturing.

## Beyond the PX Unit Team

Plans for product lines were put together by the team responsible for the PX Unit, with Peter Hardy as the key driving force. Peter announced these plans at a meeting with all manufacturing personnel:

As you may have heard on the grapevine, there are going to be some fairly radical changes in the way work is organized in production. You're all aware of the PX Unit team? Well, that was our 'guinea pig', and we'll be using experiences from it to shape what happens in production as a whole.

We are going to reorganize production into five product-based cells, called 'product lines', with 7, 8, 10, 20 and 24 people in each. Each product line will manufacture a specific type of product – four will deal with current products and one line will be responsible for a new product that we'll be launching soon.

This is how the shopfloor will look with product-lines. [*Peter showed them an overhead of the new layout – see Figure 3.2*]

Each line will be a 'factory within a factory', with stores, kitting, assembly, quality audit/inspection and test being performed by cross-skilled workers within each cell. This means people will have the opportunity to learn new skills. For example, a kitter might learn assembly skills and even test. Of course, because of the cost, there will only be one flow-solder machine and this will be shared between the lines.

Q: Does this mean that us quality people are going to be working in a line?

A: No. We'd like people in the lines to be responsible for their own quality checking and inspection. So the *functions* of quality audit and inspection will be devolved to the product lines. The role of QA will change and they'll become responsible for monitoring the quality of the manufacturing process rather than product quality. So you'll be doing

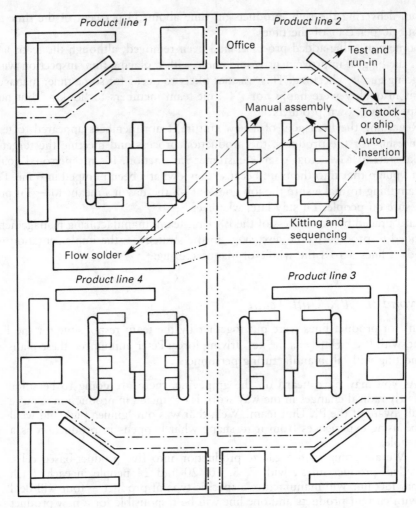

**Figure 3.2** Planned layout of four product lines (the product line for the new product will be located closer to engineering)

things like putting in statistical process control charts to monitor the process.

In a similar way, people in the product lines will be trained in routine maintenance. Maintenance engineers will then be freed up for more complex jobs, like designing simpler process operations. Training and goods-in/despatch will also be retained as separate groups outside of product lines.

Q: I hope we're going to have damned good supervisors to help us people in the lines learn all these extra things!

A: Each line will operate like the PX Unit team — as a self-managing work group supported by a 'team manager' rather than controlled by someone who tells you what to do all the time. It will be the team manager's job to make sure you have what you need to take on these extra responsibilities.

As a member of a product line, you will share responsibility with the others for meeting targets, so you will get training in things like setting targets, working out schedules to meet the targets and analysing the process to make it more efficient. We believe that your job will become much more satisfying and you'll have greater opportunities for development.

After announcing these plans, Peter suggested that people took time to think about all the information he had presented. People's thoughts and concerns could be passed on to members of a focus group set up to work through issues that would arise from the implementation of product lines. This focus group included volunteers from the shopfloor, as well as an independent consultant, so that all perspectives could be taken into account.

## Case Study Tasks

1.  You are an independent adviser to the management team. Prepare a report or verbal presentation for the management team about the implementation of high-performance work-teams within N & L. Consider the human resource implications of product lines for each of these areas:

    - Work roles for operators, supervisors and specialists (such as technicians and engineers).
    - Training.
    - Recruitment and selection.
    - Appraisal and reward systems.

    For each area consider (in both the short and the long term) the following:

    - What sorts of problems/issues/changes might arise.
    - How they might be prevented or overcome.
    - What changes to existing practices and structures need to be made.

2.  How might the transition to product lines be made easier than it was for the PX Unit team? In particular, think about the cross-functional issues and problems that might arise with product lines, and give your recommendations about how these might be dealt with.
3.  *Evaluation exercise* As an independent adviser, you have been asked to monitor the impact of product lines. What criteria would you consider for deciding whether the innovation had been successful? What data sources could you use?
4.  *Role-play exercise* A focus group has been set up to consider issues concerning the introduction of product lines. The ultimate aim of the group is to put forward a list of recommendations about the implementation of product lines to manufacturing management.

    The team consists of

- an experienced test engineer;
- a production supervisor;
- an assembler;
- a quality inspector;
- a member of the PX Unit team; and
- an independent consultant.

The role-play exercise unfolds as follows:

(a) Carefully read the case study and the 'Essential Reading' references.
(b) Allocate a role to each person within your group. Note that the role of the independent consultant is to facilitate the discussion, making sure all views are heard, as well as to contribute his or her own expertise. Make sure each person's name and role are visible to everyone in the group.
(c) Each individual should make notes on the general human resource implications of the introduction of product lines, and issues specific to their own role. Information from the text, personal experience and reading can be used (notes from the *Teacher's Manual* also might be useful). Consider questions such as: What concerns might the people I represent have about product lines? How could these be addressed? What are the lessons from the experiences of the PX Unit team for the people I represent?

Hold the meeting for a set time limit (suggested 35–50 minutes). The objective of this first meeting of the focus group is to determine the key issues to be discussed in subsequent meetings.

Suggested steps for the meeting are

(a) as a group, brain-storm (i.e. list issues quickly, without any evaluation) as many issues and concerns as possible;
(b) prioritize and select 5–6 key issues that will be explored in depth in subsequent meetings;
(c) for each key issue, generate as many solutions as possible. For example, a concern held by operators might be a perceived lack of incentive for taking on more responsibilities. The possibility of linking skill acquisition to pay might thus be an option to explore, as might ensuring jobs are designed such that they are intrinsically motivating.

5. Come out of role and have a class discussion with the tutor about the outcomes of the role play.

## Essential Reading

Grey, S. M. and Corlett, E. N. (1989) Creating effective operating teams, in R. Wild (ed.) *International Handbook of Production and Operations Management*, Cassell, London, pp. 554–66.

Oldham, G. R. and Hackman, J. R. (1980) Work design in the organizational context, in B. M. Staw and L. L. Cummings (eds.) *Research in Organizational Behavior*, Vol. 2, JAI Press, Greenwich, Conn., pp. 247–78.

## Further Reading

Carnall, C. A. (1982) Semi-autonomous work groups and the social structure of the organization, *Journal of Management Studies*, Vol. 19 pp. 277–94.

Cummings, T. G. (1978) Self-regulating work-groups: a socio-technical synthesis, *Academy of Management Review*, Vol. 3, pp. 625–34.

Cummings, T. G. (1981) Designing effective work-groups, in P. C. Nystrom and W. H. Starbuck (eds.) *Handbook of Organizational Design*, Oxford University Press, pp. 250–71.

Denison, D. R. (1982) Sociotechnical design and self-managing work groups: the impact on control, *Journal of Occupational Behaviour*, Vol. 3, pp. 297–314.

McCalman, J. and Buchanan, D. A. (1990) High performance work systems: the need for transition management, *International Journal of Operations and Production Management*, Vol. 10, pp. 10–25.

Oliver, N. and Davies, A. (1990) Adopting Japanese-style manufacturing methods: a tale of two (UK) factories, *Journal of Management Studies*, Vol. 27, pp. 555–70.

Pearce, J. A. and Ravlin, E. C. (1987) The design and activation of self-regulating work groups, *Human Relations*, Vol. 40, pp. 751–82.

Peters, T. J. (1988) *Thriving on Chaos: Handbook for a Management Revolution*, Macmillan, London.

Wall, T. D., Kemp, N. J., Jackson, P. R. and Clegg, C. W. (1986) Outcomes of autonomous workgroups: a long-term field experiment, *Academy of Management Journal*, Vol. 29, pp. 280–304.

Walton, R. E. (1985) From control to commitment in the workplace, *Harvard Business Review*, Vol. 63, no. 2, pp. 77–84.

## CASE 4

# Valleyco: Total Quality on the Shopfloor

## *Rick Delbridge and Mike Noon*

## Organizational Setting

Valleyco is a subsidiary of a large multinational, Eurocomponents, which manufactures parts for the motor industry. The plant is situated in a South Wales valley, populated by close-knit family communities, from which it draws its workforce of 250. The overwhelming majority of shopfloor operators are women who have worked at the plant for at least five years. There has been a factory on the site for over twenty years but during that time five different companies have run operations — the takeover by Eurocomponents two years ago was therefore treated with some suspicion. The plant is heavily unionized with the majority of unskilled operators belonging to the GMB and skilled workers in the AEEU.

## Background

During the 1980s the motor industry in the West has been put under considerable competitive pressure. The Japanese in particular have introduced a new manufacturing style — the just-in-time (JIT) system — which is designed to be more efficient than the old-style mass-production techniques of the West. The overarching principles of the system are the minimization of stocks and a reliance on demand 'pulling' products through the system rather than production pushing them; the reduction of set-up times to improve flow and responsiveness to the market; employees' flexibility to work where required at any given time; and a drive for continuous improvement.

The JIT system is reliant on good-quality components and so total quality control (TQC) is a prerequisite in operating JIT. The theme of TQC is to 'make them right first time' with an emphasis on defect prevention and responsibility for quality resting with the makers of that part. Quality standards are set to customer requirement and a 'quality ethos' is imbued throughout the whole organization.

A large proportion of a motor car is manufactured by component suppliers, with final assembly by the auto manufacturer. Traditionally, in the West, negotiations for contracts between suppliers of components and the final assemblers were based on price. To compete these days quality (to meet TQC standards) and delivery (to meet JIT requirements) are of equal importance, so both these developments have been pushed down the supply chain and have been 'forced' upon component suppliers. The major motor manufacturers are very powerful and will not tolerate substandard quality or late delivery of their bought-in components.

Consequently Valleyco has undergone considerable change. When Euro-components took over two years ago it kept virtually the same management personnel and structure, but imbued them with the ethos of quality through training courses and visits to other businesses in the group. The current plant manager is Phil Evans, who has worked his way up from the shopfloor. Phil and his managerial colleagues have presided over the move to producing 'what is needed, when it is needed'. Employees have been encouraged to think about two sorts of customers: the 'external' customers – the car companies – to which their assembled components are delivered, and the 'internal' customers, who are their work colleagues at the next stage of the assembly process. The removal of the costly buffers (high stock levels) has emphasized the need to ensure production/assembly is 'right first time', so there has been a move to 'building quality in' as assembly takes place, away from the traditional method of 'inspecting it out'. This has meant a decrease in the number of shopfloor inspectors with a concomitant increase in individual operator responsibility. JIT and TQC have put both workers and managers under more pressure because, with less production slack, any hold-ups or poor-quality operations will mean a greater likelihood of failing to deliver to the customer on time. In the short run this is costly as late-delivery penalties will be incurred, while in the longer term it may encourage the customer to look elsewhere for their component supplies.

In the years before Eurocomponents took over, Valleyco enjoyed little in the way of investment, either in new technology or in training. The new owners, however, have begun to spend some money on new machinery to replace some of the outdated equipment. In addition there have been some intensive training courses, introducing the workforce to statistical process-control techniques – SPC – which is a key characteristic of JIT systems.

More recently Valleyco has begun to introduce business units, whereby a single manager takes sole responsibility for a team of about twenty workers. These are to be oriented around customers, and the first one operational is a cell manufacturing components for a Japanese assembler with a plant in the UK, Japcarco.

The plans for the new business units were presented to the workforce as a *fait accompli* and the unions have had no role in the design or implementation of any of the changes. At the time of the takeover, Eurocomponents instructed both the managers and the workforce that there would need to be some radical changes in the subsequent years or the plant would close. Threat of closure was powerful rhetoric in an area already suffering relatively high rates of unemployment; consequently the unions were compliant, although sceptical of JIT as a system.

## The Problem

Recently Eurocomponents have become concerned about the performance of Valleyco. There seems to be an unhealthy variability of quality evident from complaints by some of the customers. As a consequence, Eurocomponents have hired a management consultant to spend a few days at the firm to complete a quality audit that will examine six elements typically present in total quality systems:

- Training.
- Team-working.
- Application of statistical methods.
- Quality culture.
- Management support/attitudes.
- Identifying and caring for the customer (internal and external).

What follows are a series of key extracts from the management consultant's notes on Valleyco. In addition, Figure 4.1 shows the layout of the shopfloor, with the arrows showing the workflow.

## Extracts from the Consultant's Notes

*Shopfloor Assembly Areas*
The pattern of change in the assembly areas has left two distinct groups: the Japcarco lines and general assembly.

*The Japcarco lines*   This cell is run as a separate business unit; it receives all subcomponents from just two suppliers and ships daily to Japcarco. There is virtually no stock held for these products. There are 25 operators and 2 module controllers (shopfloor supervisors) working in this unit. Those operators working on the Japcarco lines have received extra training for the new jobs they are carrying out and have been lectured face to face by management on the need to maintain quality standards. The two module controllers spent a week in Japan watching a supplier run an identical line there. The manager with responsibility for all aspects of the two Japcarco lines is Mike Phillips. He is supported by Peter Williams, a production controller.

The Japcarco lines have received some new technology investment in the form of automated assembly equipment, which guarantees 'zero defect' assembly. The customer (a representative from Japcarco) regularly inspects these areas and quality standards are known by all involved as 'Japcarco requirements'.

There are no quality inspectors on these two lines, but each has a quality engineer attached. The module controllers carry out SPC checks on new, digital read-out testing equipment. This required a 10-week programme with each controller spending 2 hours per week working with computer software training material.

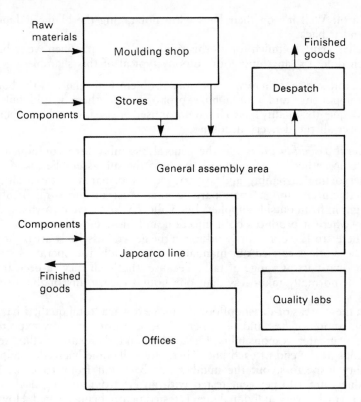

**Figure 4.1** Valleyco Shopfloor layout

The operators work for a group bonus based upon what actually goes out of the door of the factory. This typically results in pay levels equivalent to the earnings of the rest of the shopfloor workers. However there is a great deal of team spirit, and they help each other out when the need arises. They are left to organize themselves into teams co-ordinated by the module controllers.

Since the assembly process is automated the operators simply load the machines, checking the quality of the subcomponents as they do so. They seem very conscious about quality, so I asked about quality standards on the line. The following is typical of the responses:

**Carol** (*operator*): Look at the state of these arms – all this bubbled paint on them. I said to Mike, 'Are these OK?' and he checked with quality and they said 'No'. Then Peter came over and said, 'Send 'em'.
**Julie**: Yeah, well that's because Japcarco are screaming for 'em, isn't it?
**Carol**: Well, I wouldn't want this on my car I can tell you! It's a bloody disgrace. What happened to 'Quality comes first' like it says on all these posters on the wall, eh?
**Julie**: Hah, that's production control for you – 'ship it and sod it'. They don't care what it's like as long as it's shipped on time.

**Carol**: Well it's on their backs. I'm not taking the blame if Japcarco send it back.

**Julie**: Yeah, so much for all this total quality crap. When we're behind schedule it's 'anything goes'. Bloody typical of this shambles.

Peter told me that there was a serious problem with many of the bought-in components and that a huge proportion of them would fail SPC. Consequently, quality has to be compromised or else it would be impossible to meet all the delivery deadlines.

*General assembly areas*  In the general assembly area components are made up, either by machine or hand, into the sub-assemblies, which then undergo final assembly and are packed for dispatch to three large car manufacturers and a spare-parts chain. Most of the components are bought in from outside suppliers but Valleyco does have its own moulding shop where it produces both injection and blow mouldings.

There are 120 operators working in the general assembly area. Virtually all the work is carried out manually and typically the operators stick to their own narrow range of tasks because 'that's all they've been trained for'. It normally takes less than one hour to learn any of the assembly jobs.

In these areas of the shopfloor the move toward 'total quality' has been rather more *ad hoc* and piecemeal. The operators are now expected to take a greater responsibility for quality and there are quality testing stations at the end of each line. There are still some 'viewers', shopfloor quality inspectors, but the number has been cut from 16 to 5. Some products are 100 per cent tested with an electronic testing device — in other words, every individual item is tested before being packed. However, for others only a sample of each delivery undergoes anything more than a visual scan to check all the components have been fitted.

The operators in these areas are working to individual piece rates for bonus set against standardized timings for each job. The quality tests also have standard times attached. The wages are very low, similar to those of a shop checkout operator, but an extra 30 per cent can be earned if maximum bonus is achieved. The bonus, or more specifically, how to increase it, was a frequent topic of conversation among the operators, for example:

**Jean** (*operator*): How much bonus have you earned today?

**Mary** (*operator*): I'm behind on my number. I've been testing all day and it's a right sod of a target.

**Jean**: You wanna do what old Lynne used to in the old days, remember her? She'd be sat at the end of the line testing and packing. The red fail light would be going on and she'd still be chucking 'em in the box like there was no tomorrow. She'd say, 'Well, it's no bloody skin off my effing nose is it, eh? I don't give a toss, I just want my bonus.'

**Mary**: These bought-in parts are most of the trouble. They buy in the cheapest there is and then moan about the reject rate of the final assembly. Here we are running SPC but none of the subcomponents is quality assured.

**Anne**: The stuff made in our own moulding shop's just as bad, if not worse.

**Jean:** That's because they're an idle lot in there. I know for a fact that they spend half the time fiddling with the machines instead of making the parts. It's all very well for them, but it holds us up. If they fart around, then I take home less money on Friday.

**Mary:** I spend half my time spotting defects. You can't just chuck it out now, because FrancoCars or whoever will send it back. They're red hot on quality these days. Mind, I could do with the extra cash.

**Jean:** And only one of the these bloody electronic testers is working again. It takes a bloody age to make up its mind if the part's OK or not. It's slowing me down, I can't wait around for it to make up its mind.

**Mary:** I reckon we'd be better manual testing those but they don't want to know about it [*pointing to quality lab*]. I tried to tell Phil [*the Plant Manager*] about it last week but he just didn't listen.

**Jean:** He can be an arrogant sod. He's never interested in what we have to say even though he used to be one of us. I remember him when he was on the shopfloor and he was a lazy bugger.

### The Moulding Shop

The moulding shop contains two new and very expensive blow-moulding machines. It also has about 20 injection-moulding machines of different types and sizes; many of these machines are more than 15 years old. The plant runs two shifts; each has a foreman, either Dai or John, who is left in charge day to day, five operators and two machine setters. There is also a quality inspector on each shift, either Brian or Ivor.

I was told by Dai that it is difficult to mould plastics to a consistent standard, particularly with such old machinery – the joke on the shopfloor is that the machines are still insured against Viking raids. The setters regularly struggle to place the new tools in the old machines. The machines are so unreliable it is a ritual for the setters to cross themselves in imitation prayer before testing. One of the them told me

> We spend half our time looking for clamps and blocks round here. Trying to fit the new tools in these old machines. We're always having to cut corners just to get the stuff out. It can take three hours or more to set some of 'em. We tried some special variable clamps and they were dead handy, really saved time and trouble. But when it came down to it management said they couldn't afford it. I mean, how much is a bloody clamp anyway?

The finance manager told me the clamps had been priced at £50 each and the moulding shop had ordered 40, which he considered an unnecessary expense. The purchase of these clamps was therefore blocked.

Several of the machines need constant operator supervision but the number of operators in the shop was recently halved. The other operators move from machine to machine disconnecting the mouldings from the discarded stems and 'finishing' them if necessary. This process involves the operator using a scalpel to remove any 'flash' from around the component.

At regular intervals the quality inspector wanders through the shop visually inspecting a handful of the previous hour's work. Brian and Ivor carry out the same function – a watch-dog over production – but Brian is particularly unpopular with the setters and operators in the moulding shop. I asked about the quality inspection and was told:

**Jeff** (*setter*): That Brian is bloody hopeless, he knows sod all. He's always sticking his nose in where it's not wanted.

**Dai** (*foreman*): Ah, well that's his job, I suppose. Still he is a right dickhead.

**Jeff**: He came over yesterday and wanted me to start 'fiddling with knobs'. He just doesn't understand. It's not that easy. I'm sure he thinks that if you turn a switch then all the components you've already made will be alright as well! At least Ivor knows about machines.

**Kevin** (*setter*): I tell you, he's gonna get himself in deep water soon, the way he's going on. He'll find a knife in his back if he's not careful.

**Dai**: That's right enough. Still we'd turn out any old rubbish without a quality bloke here.

**Jeff**: Yeah, but still, some of these quality standards are ridiculous. Those quality engineers sit in that office and just make these things up. What do they know about actually making the stuff? They should bloody try and manage some of their requirements on these heaps of junk.

The animosity towards Brian is widely held. Apparently he has been jumped twice by the setters and labourers and tied up and gagged 'for a laugh'. Once the security guard found him in a box in the back of a lorry that was about to take a delivery to the West Midlands and, on another occasion, he was found in a skip just before the last of the shopfloor were packing up for the Christmas break. He seems to be a laughing stock and is known by the shopfloor as 'Jobsworth'.

Ivor, the other quality inspector, commands more respect and is more popular:

**Susan** (*operator*): That Ivor's alright, isn't he? He knows where these bloody bits are off to and whether they'll do or not.

**Eileen** (*supervisor*): Yeah, he'll let through more than most, but he knows if they'll really be alright or not. He don't just go by the drawings.

**Susan**: Well, he's got the experience, he knows more about the end-product than that other wally.

**Eileen**: Mind you, if there's one faulty one in a big bag he'll find it!

In reality the testing methods used by both Brian and Ivor are identical. Ivor and Brian have detailed engineering drawings of over 300 different types of component, each indicating the customer's tolerable variations from the set lengths, widths and angles. Along with the visual check they carry out more detailed examination of the first batch from each machine and run SPC charts on the blow moulders. The inspection is to ensure the products are within the customer's specifications.

The manager in charge of the moulding shop, Lee Jones, wants production to be geared to 'internal customer' demand – in other words, what is required by the assembly areas, in accordance with JIT principles. However, due to the age of equipment and lack of other small tools, the set-up times on the injection moulders make it impossible to run off small batches. He also finds difficulty in redeploying the operators. The following is typical of the sort of verbal exchanges I heard regularly:

**Lee:** I want the operators that are left to work full time on the machines that need manual operation. The automatic machines can be left to run on their own.
**John:** What about all the flash on the parts coming off the automatic machines? We'll still need operators to deflash those parts or they'll all be rejected by quality control.
**Lee:** OK. Anything that requires deflashing is not to run.
**John:** In that case everything will be off.
**Lee:** I don't care, just do it.

The next day Lee had to return to the moulding shop because the assembly area was short of a part:

**Lee:** Why have you shut down the Boston Matthews [*machine*]? That was producing 15977s [*components*] and we need those desperately. The customer is screaming down the phone for them.
**John:** Well, it was flashing so I turned it off, like you said.
**Lee:** If we stop the line up there [*pointing to assembly*] we get fined £2,000 a minute. We'll be out of business by the end of the day!
**John:** So, I'll start it up again, shall I?

*Quality Department*
The quality department includes 10 engineers and they work closely with the engineering department to develop processes that allow quality to be built in. These employees work in offices next to the accounts and personnel departments. There is also a quality laboratory where the products undergo rigorous testing for periods of several hundred hours. These tests include exposing the components to extremes of temperature and inducing artificial ageing.

The quality engineers seem dedicated to TQ. I was told:

**Keith:** We're firm believers that production should control quality. We have to put the responsibility back on the shopfloor. At a broader level quality should be incorporated at the design stage.
**Graham:** Yes, we should decide where quality checks are needed and the form they should take, but then it's down to production to carry them out.
*Andy:* You become very cynical — what can go wrong will. If an operator can find a wrong way to do something they will. Education must come from above. If the directors and top management are dedicated to a policy of quality products then that filters through. There must be training from the top down. Every level of labour must have quality in their job, right down to cleaning the floors.

*Phil Evans, Plant Manager*
Phil is a large and personable man. He has worked at the plant for 20 years and knows all the employees by their first names. He told me:

I can't speak highly enough of my workers. They've been tremendous. We've had to withstand tremendous pressures and these workers have seen us through. We've come through the difficult years and I really believe we're on the up from here. Now we've got JIT and TQC installed it'll be plain sailing.

My plan from here is to make this plant the major source of these components in the UK and to make it the biggest and most profitable Eurocomponents factory in Western Europe.

The way things are going, I do not think Phil will achieve his goal without some major changes.

## Case Study Tasks

There are four options designed to suit different circumstances. Your course tutor will tell you which one will be used.

## *Option 1: Suitable for Two-Hour Teaching Sessions*

**Stage 1 (20 mins.)**   Divide into three small groups (max. 3 people in each). For larger classes, split into two or more teams. Each group represents a working party from one of the following sections:

- Japcarco line.
- General assembly.
- Moulding shop.

In these groups assess the problems *as they affect YOUR section*. Then formulate a number of proposals that would improve the working of your department. If there is time, give some thought to how other sections might improve their operations.

**Stage 2 (50 mins.)**   The groups join together for a large meeting. Each team has five minutes to present its case and proposals. The meeting is then opened up for general discussion and has the following objectives:

1.   To identify the general problems associated with quality at Valleyco.
2.   To devise a short-term and long-term action plan that could be implemented at Valleyco.
3.   To elect representatives who will present the action plan to the plant manager, Phil Evans.

**Stage 3 (20 mins.)**   Presentation of action plan. The course tutor will role play Phil Evans. (Where more than one team has been established, the 'alternative' action plans can be presented, and teams can be invited to criticize each others plans — in which case it will be necessary to allow more time for this stage.)

**Stage 4 (20 mins.)**   Feedback and general discussion.

## Option 2: Suitable for Teaching Sessions of up to One Hour

**Stage 1 (30 mins.)** Divide into small groups and consider the following questions:

1. What are the problems associated with quality that Valleyco faces?
2. What are the main causes of these problems?
3. What action could be taken to remedy the situation? (Consider both short-term and long-term interventions.)

**Stage 2 (30 mins.)** Reconvene to discuss the issues. Each group will be invited by the course tutor to present one problem and its probable cause, which will be recorded on the board/ohp. This should continue in a 'round robin' fashion until all problems have been added to the cumulative list.

Each group in turn will then be invited to present its short-term and long-term action plan. The other groups can ask questions and offer criticism.

## Option 3: Free-Form/Problem-Solving Techniques

(This option can be used irrespective of time constraints – but a long time slot means more problems are addressed.) Divide into groups of between five and ten people.

**Stage 1** *Brainstorm* the problems faced by Valleyco. (Brainstorming involves each person in turn forwarding one problem, which should be listed on a board/flipchart. Continue in turn until no more problems can be forwarded. *No comments or discussion* about the problems is allowed at this stage.)

**Stage 2** *Problem selection* – each group member privately ranks the problems from 1 to $X$ (1 being the most important; equal ranking is not allowed). The rank values for each problem from each group member are then added to provide a rank 'score', which is noted next to the problem. *Remember* the lower the 'score' then the *more important* the problem, because it has been ranked highly by group members.

**Stage 3** For *each problem in turn*, starting with the most important (i.e. lowest 'score') complete (1) and (2) below, then move on to the next problem:

1. Perform a *cause-and-effect analysis* by generating a list of causes under the 4Ms categories – machines, manpower, materials and methods.
2. Generate an *action plan* to remedy the problem.

**Stage 4** Reconvene as a large group and feedback the action plan. Discuss and criticize the different remedies.

## Option 4 (Individual Written Work)

Imagine you are the management consultant sent into Valleyco. Write a report of 1,000 words outlining the key problems at Valleyco in relation to quality. Suggest a short-term and long-term action plan to remedy these problems.

## Background Reading

For a discussion of quality in a nutshell, see Income Data Services (1990) Total quality management, *IDS Study*, no. 457, May. For an examination of JIT, and what have become known as 'Japanese management techniques', see N. Oliver and B. Wilkinson (1988) *The Japanization of British Industry*, Blackwell, Oxford.

## Additional Reading

Also look at one of the 'classics':
Collard, R. (1989) *Total Quality: Success through People*, IPM, London.
Crosby, P. (1979) *Quality is Free*, McGraw-Hill, New York, NY.
Deming, E. W. (1982) *Out of Crisis*, MIT Press, Cambridge, Mass.
Schonberger, R. J. (1982) *Japanese Manufacturing Techniques*, Free Press, New York, NY.

# A Greenfield Site: Cableco

## Helen Newell

## Organizational Setting

Calendarco is a diversified multinational company that has 135 plants in 16 countries throughout the world. It employs some 69,000 employees and, in 1987, had sales of £5.6 billion, its electrical cables business accounting for some 39 per cent of total turnover. Cableco, the electrical cable business of Calendarco, was founded in the UK in 1914. It produces a comprehensive range of power and telecommunications cables at four different factories. By 1987 Cableco's turnover had risen to nearly £135 million and the workforce to 2,200 employees. Cableco makes a range of different cables and had been producing building wires, a relatively basic range of 'low-tech' electrical cables primarily used for house wiring or domestic appliances at its plant in Southampton. The plant, established in the 1930s, had enjoyed a good relationship with its employees for many years, based upon four important elements:

1. Labour segmentation with employees recruited into various grades with little chance of promotion. Manual staff work for 39 hours per week and non-manual staff work for 35 hours per week. The manual group is made up of process workers (semi-skilled), skilled mechanical trades and skilled electrical trades. The non-manual group is divided between supervisory, clerical, technical and managerial grades.
2. Job-evaluated payment systems graded by skill, with a productivity bonus paid invariably each month and with overtime working on Saturdays.
3. Recognition of six trade unions covering various grades of manual worker and staff.
4. Nationally agreed terms and conditions of employment determined by the Joint Industrial Council (JIC) for cable making, covering all companies in the industry.

## Background to the Case

Over-capacity within the industry and fierce competition from the UK and abroad meant that the domestic cable division had been making a loss for some time. In 1984 the company was faced with a choice, should they continue in the business or get out completely? If they were to stay in the business, how could they become more competitive?

The technical director argued that an investment of £20 million in a green-field site, attracting a development grant from the government and utilizing modern process technology, could produce a profitable return on investment within 24 months if, for the same tonnage, the number of employees could be reduced from 350 to 150. He argued that this was possible with the adoption of new technology provided there was full flexibility of labour. Calendarco subsequently decided to build a new plant that would house the latest in computer-integrated manufacturing (CIM) systems. The system would be based upon three fundamental concepts:

1. A CIM system to plan and direct every phase of the business.
2. Flexible manufacturing involving the application of machine technology that allows different areas or zones within the plant to achieve a fast response to varying business needs.
3. Just-in-time (JIT) production techniques with computerized monitoring to schedule and sequence the supply of raw material and work-in-progress, thus eliminating expensive stockholding.

The main board decided that the project would have a greater chance of success if it was developed away from the company's other sites and that the new factory should replace the existing plant in Southampton. Furthermore, the board insisted that, within the environment of advanced technology and the latest techniques of computer integration, it was essential that the personnel policies of the new factory should also reflect 'an equivalent degree of advanced thinking in the human resources area'.

The site chosen was in South Wales, some distance from Cableco's other plants and in a development area attracting government financial aid. It was also in an area of high unemployment, promising a plentiful supply of labour.

## Devising Appropriate Human Resource Policies

A small project team consisting of two members of Cableco's divisional personnel department and the new plant general and personnel managers, was given the task of developing the new policies in the human resources area. They began with a period of research, visiting companies the team members believed to be innovators in their field and taking part in discussions with the Work Research Unit of the Arbitration, Conciliation and Advisory Service (ACAS).

The new plant personnel manager, recruited from outside the Calendarco organization specifically for the job, had firm views about the way in which employees ought to be managed in the new plant. In particular, he believed that the policies adopted should reflect 'best practice' in the UK. He was the driving force behind the company's new philosophy. Instead of the rigid job demarcation, repetitive tasks and traditional supervisory systems in operation at Cableco's other plants, the project team wanted employees in the new factory to work in small, highly adaptable teams. The project team developed plans to create what they called a 'model working environment' based upon flexibility and involvement, where all employees would be equal, with no distinction between office and factory.

This model working environment was based upon the principles of single employee status and co-operative team-working, aimed both at motivating employees and ensuring their commitment to the success of the new plant. All staff would enjoy similar terms and conditions of employment, which would include a salary structure based upon an annual rather than a weekly hours contract, and which would reward adaptability and achievement. However, all senior specialists and managerial staff were to be excluded. They would be treated as a corporate rather than a plant resource liable to be transferred to another part of the Calendarco organization at some time in the future.

The CIM system that had been chosen had certain implications for the type of employee who would be needed to use it. In the first place employees would need to be computer literate. The type of skills they would require were diagnostic rather than motor related, with only a minimal degree of manual skill required. The process was not going to be high speed but it would involve constant operator attention requiring the application of detailed production schedules as shown on the visual display units with little, if any, supervision. Employees were going to be required to work flexibly not only in relation to the performance of tasks but also in relation to skills (for example, operators carrying out day-to-day maintenance tasks) as well as flexibility in relation to hours worked. From this a profile was developed of the characteristics future employees would be required to possess.

The project team saw recruitment as critical to the successful running of the plant. They endeavoured to select only those employees who would be suited to the different work requirements and ethos of the plant. They wanted employees who had the 'right attitudes', people who would be flexible, who were anxious to develop their own potential and who would accept responsibility: they wanted the 'best' employees available. The recruitment procedure was time consuming, expensive and sophisticated. It included the assessment of personality profiles and computer aptitude testing as well as conventional interviewing techniques. Interviews were held not only by the potential employee's immediate manager within the plant but also with at least two senior members of the management team.

The various functions within the plant (production, maintenance and administration) were divided up into a number of skill modules each of which would require a different combination of skills and knowledge. All employees would acquire skill modules across all functions, each skill module requiring between four and eight weeks' training. Employees would be paid a basic salary and an increase of £250 for each skill module they obtained. Calendarco was anxious that pay levels should be kept within reasonable limits and the decision was taken that the level of basic salary should be determined by reference to salaries paid in the local area (a figure that was some £2,000 a year less than at the Southampton plant). Since salaries would increase quite quickly as new skill modules were acquired, Calendarco decided to set levels just below the average for the area.

A key feature of the motivational aspect of the policies was to be comprehensive communication and involvement informally through the free exchange of information, opinions and ideas on operational matters, and formally through joint consultation in the form of the Business Review and Consultative Committee (BRCC). Rather than adopt a non-union position the project team was persuaded to maintain a policy of union recognition well established in the rest of Calendarco. However, copying other forward-thinking organizations opening new ventures on greenfield sites, they decided to withdraw from the JIC and (after holding a 'beauty contest' where a number of unions were invited to make a presentation to the company as to their suitability for recognition), a single union, no-strike agreement was signed with the Managerial, Administrative, Technical and Supervisory Association (MATSA). Among other things, the agreement stressed the importance of operational objectives and arrangements including complete flexibility and active co-operation in all elements of change and an undertaking to accept training, as well as an obligation on the part of the company to provide training as necessary.

## The Problem: Implementing the Human Resource Policies

The original time-scale was for the Southampton plant to close by December 1988. The plant was still open in December 1989. The development and design of Cableco's advanced manufacturing technology were fraught with problems that, in turn, had serious implications for the type of employee policies Cableco had decided to implement. Many of the suppliers had been asked to make significant advances in the development of their equipment, advances that had not been attempted before. They delivered the machinery to the plant only to discover that it did not perform the tasks Cableco required of it. Attempts by Cableco's technicians to modify or repair the new machinery themselves prior to official acceptance by the company would have led to a breach of the manufacturer's warranty. This meant that Cableco employees (who had not been involved in the original design process) were also excluded from the modification process.

Two major factors affected the operation of the company's reward system. The details of the skill modules could only be drawn up once the plant was operating. This could not be done without machinery that worked. In addition, more and more new plants (also attracted by government financial aid and a ready supply of labour) opened up in South Wales, all requiring skilled maintenance workers. The salaries being paid by Cableco quickly became uncompetitive. This led to the introduction of new hierarchical levels within the maintenance department linked to higher salaries, as attempts were made to recruit and retain staff. Twelve months after the opening of the new plant, the union and management were involved in what the management referred to as 'conventional and at times fairly confrontational' negotiations, which led to the nominal award of one skill module, regardless of whether the necessary skills had been acquired. In the mind of employees, skill modules became associated with length of service rather than with skill acquisition and flexibility. This distortion of the payment system and infringement of the single-status principle created much resentment among the production workers.

The plant personnel manager, the driving force behind the new policies, left Cableco in October 1988 to pursue a career elsewhere. With his departure the emphasis on consultation and communication was almost forgotten in the face of the increasing pressures to meet production targets and close down the Southampton factory, and informal communication systems did not develop. The general manager, aware of the substantial difficulties facing the plant, made attempts to keep employees informed but felt that, if they knew how serious the plant's position was, they would revert to 'traditional adversarial behaviour'. The employees argued that they knew things were going badly and they did not believe the information they were being given about the plant's performance was accurate. After the personnel manager's departure the plans for formal communication and information systems were ignored.

## Case Study Tasks

Depending upon the time available, the first two sections of the case study (organizational setting and background to the case) can be used to present students with the opportunity to devise their own human resource strategy for a greenfield site.

1. Why did Calendarco decide to open a greenfield site? Could Calendarco have introduced the same type of human resource policies in its Southampton factory?
2. What were the factors that influenced the design of the new plant and its human resource policies?
3. Why did the employees at the plant feel that working there was not what they had been promised it would be? When were these promises made and how were they broken? Do you think that things would have been different if the personnel manager had not left when he did?
4. Why did Calendarco want to set pay levels only slightly above local labour market rates? What was the effect of this? Could anything have been done to avoid this situation?
5. Do you think that Calendarco's greenfield site was successful? What is it about a greenfield site that makes it 'green'? Is it too late for the plant to recapture its 'greenfieldness'?

## Essential Reading

Beaumont, P. and Townley, B. (1985) Greenfield sites, new plants and work practices, in V. Hammond (ed.) *Current Research in Management*, Pinter Publishers, London.

*Industrial Relations Review and Report* (1986) Nissan: a catalyst for change?, November, no. 379.

Lawler, E. E. (1978) The new plant revolution, *Organizational Dynamics*, Winter.

Rousseau, D. (1990) New hire perceptions of their own and their employers' obligations: a study of psychological contracts, *Journal of Organizational Behaviour*, Vol. 11, pp. 389–400.

## Additional Reading

Beaumont, P. B. (1985) New plant working practices, *Personnel Review*, Vol. 14, no. 1, pp. 15–19.

Incomes Data Studies (1984) *Study No. 314, Group Working and Greenfield Sites*, May.

Guest, D. (1989) Human resource management: its implications for industrial relations and trade unions, in J. Storey (ed.) *New Perspectives on Human Resource Management*, Routledge, London.

Whitaker, A. (1986) Managerial strategy and industrial relations; a case study of plant relocation, *Journal of Management Studies*, Vol. 23, no. 6, pp. 657–78.

# PART II

## The Flexible Firm, Manpower Planning and Bargaining

# CASE 6

## The Permanent Search for Temporary Staff

### Dorothy Wong

## Organizational Setting

Home Cosy is a major mail order shopping company in the UK. It is geographically divided into two main operations: a head office and a distribution centre. The head office houses such departments as marketing, sales and computing; it is linked to the distribution centre by an online computer network. Orders received directly from its customers are passed on from the sales department to the distribution centre where individual items are fetched from the on-site warehouse, packed and dispatched to the customer.

Despite the close liaison between the two operations in terms of information sharing, there are significant differences in terms of the organizational functions and personnel problems encountered. This case study will concentrate on the problems at the distribution centre only. Within the distribution centre, there is a variety of jobs in terms of seniority and skill requirements. Hierarchically, this case study will focus on the unskilled and semi-skilled shopfloor employees performing mainly warehouse and manual work.

The distribution centre employs an average of over 2,700 people. Because of the widely fluctuating demands in the product market, the actual number of semi-skilled and unskilled shopfloor workers in the distribution centre could vary in the order of hundreds from one week to another. The recruitment and redundancy of such large numbers of staff are carried out regularly by the on-site personnel department, headed by a divisional personnel manager, according to the various peaks and troughs of customer demand during the year.

In early 1990, at the peak of national publicity of the 'demographic time-bomb' in the 1990s, a study was commissioned by the Home Cosy personnel department to investigate the problem and possible solutions concerning the recruitment and retention of shopfloor staff at the distribution centre.

## Background to the Case

A major competitive advantage of the company over its competitors is the speed of its delivery. Under normal circumstances, merchandise will be delivered to the customer within 48 hours or two working days from the time the order is placed. In order to maintain this competitive advantage, the distribution centre plays an important role in responding speedily to the widely fluctuating and unpredictable customer demands. As a result, it has developed a tradition of using part-time and temporary staff extensively to achieve numerical labour flexibility at a relatively low cost. In order to ensure a continuous supply of temporary staff, the company has made temporary work a prerequisite for a permanent job in the distribution centre.

## Organization of Work

The jobs involved in this study belong to three broad categories: the picking of individual items from the warehouse; the packing of various items that are ordered by a single customer; and the processing of returned items. All these jobs form part of a carefully designed work system, where orders are divided into individual batches to be processed in a twenty-minute cycle. Similarly, returned items will be examined, recorded, repacked and taken back to storage in a parallel twenty-minute cycle.

## Characteristics of the Jobs and the Jobholders

Most of the jobs require a great deal of walking around and sometimes heavy lifting. To the management, it is not physical strength, or age, but physical fitness and dexterity that are essential requirements of the job. As a result, women are generally considered as better at the job because of their good hand and eye co-ordination. Nevertheless, there is no overt gender preference with regard to recruitment. In the absence of any formal company statistics, it is estimated that about 70–80 per cent of the jobs in the study are occupied by women. Many of the female employees are housewives with either young or grown-up children.

Because the intake of full-time shopfloor staff has been frozen for the last couple of years, the majority of the jobs in the study are part time in nature. Yet most of the part-time jobs involve 25–31 hours working per week or an average of 5–6 hours per day.

## Payment System

Every job in the work system has undergone time study by independent assessors. Based on the time study, a performance-related pay system was introduced with the union's consent. Under this system, a new recruit will start from a basic training grade, and then progress through an eight-grade pay scale according to individual performance. The actual performance level of each grade is programmed in the main computer, which will automatically allocate work to individuals according to their grade.

## Functional Flexibility

Under the present work system, each job is composed of several simple tasks, and the skill level of each job is kept to a minimum. As a result, a certain amount of functional flexibility can be easily achieved. The progression up the performance-related scale is mainly a measure of speed rather than skill achievements. As individual performance is continuously monitored by the computer and the supervisor, one can expect to go up or down the grades, either voluntarily or involuntarily, according to one's speed. However, in case one is assigned to a different job at a lower grade for the sake of functional flexibility, one is still paid at the rate of the higher grade achieved previously. For example, when a grade-8 picker is packing at the speed of a grade-3 packer, she will still be paid at the top rate.

## Working Environment/Company Image

Built in the Sixties, the distribution centre has the typical layout of a warehouse, with few windows, poor ventilation and little natural lighting. The majority of shopfloor workers actually call it a factory, and regard themselves as factory workers. For the more qualified worker, the stigma attached to the factory image is evident. When asked how she would describe her working environment, a lady who used to work as a typist in another firm but is currently working as a return processor (whose job is to open returned items and to enter the product codes into a computer terminal) sounded very offended: 'This is a factory. But I am not a factory worker. I am a VDU operator.'

## The Problem

The Home Cosy distribution centre is situated at a newly developed town surrounded by some rural and agricultural areas. In the last two decades, the company has been able to recruit temporary staff with relative ease. Quite often, it used to be a case of people ringing in to ask for work. In the boom years of the late 1980s, the recruitment and retention of staff has become increasingly difficult.

After some preliminary discussion with management, it is found that the problem of recruitment and retention is largely restricted only to the temporary and Saturday staff. Yet the problems with these two groups of staff are quite different.

## Saturday Staff

The Saturday staff comprise mainly A-level students and, to a lesser extent, housewives and people who have a full-time job during the week. According to research interviews conducted with supervisors and a random sample of Saturday staff, most of the students will certainly leave in a year or two's time to either go to a college or to find a full-time job. Many housewives and people with full-time employment take on Saturday work at Home Cosy in order to pay for a holiday, home improvement or other luxury items. They are not very likely to stay on once their objectives are met. Only a small number come to work on Saturday to supplement their basic income to support their family. This last group provides a small core of relatively stable Saturday staff for the company. Yet the necessity for them to work on Saturdays is closely related to the general economy, the career opportunities and the amount of overtime work offered by their own or their partner's full-time job.

In sum, the volatility of the Saturday staff is extremely high. Although no formal labour turnover statistics are kept, according to the management and supervisors, very few will stay in their jobs for more than a year. Most of the Saturday staff will leave in a matter of months or even weeks.

However, the problem with the Saturday staff is not one of recruitment – even in the spring of 1990, when the shortage of young people was supposed to hit British industry hard, Home Cosy still had a seven-months-long waiting-list of students applying for Saturday work. The problem, according to the supervisors, is mainly the waste of time, effort and money in training new recruits whose turnover rate is so high (though the only training offered is on the job and lasts, on average, from a couple of minutes to a couple of hours). Also, during the first few weeks, a new recruit is not only too slow to meet the required speed but also more likely to make mistakes. Worst of all, most Saturday staff, especially the students, do not take their work seriously, and are therefore more difficult to control.

Although Saturday work is classified as permanent work within the company, paradoxically, it is often treated by the employees as a temporary part-time job as reflected by a high voluntary turnover rate.

## Temporary Staff

The temporary staff at Home Cosy cannot be categorized as easily as the Saturday staff. However, except for students seeking temporary jobs in the summer and those who want to save up for luxury items, most temporary staff come to work with the hope of eventually obtaining a permanent job with the company. While the volatility of the first two groups of temporary staff has been demonstrated in the last section, the last, and the biggest of the three groups, warrants further discussion.

Temporary staff work on basically the same jobs as their permanent counter-parts on the shopfloor. They are also paid according to the same performance-related scheme as permanent staff. They work the same shift hours and have access to such facilities as the staff canteen, the sports and social club and the staff shop. The major benefits denied to temporary staff are the company pension scheme and paid sick or casual leave.

A great deal of temporary staff think the present entitlement of a maximum of three days' no-pay absence throughout the period of temporary work (after which one will be dismissed) is unfair and a little too harsh on them. Although temporary staff accrue paid holidays in money before they leave the company, the difficulty lies in the inability to take time off during the entire period of temporary work, which could last for up to six months. In practice, this means an automatic termination of temporary work by the company should the temporary staff be off work for more than three days for whatever reasons (including sickness or any personal and family emergencies). As a result, although most permanent staff are satisfied with their terms and conditions at work, the company's policy towards temporary staff is often described as 'harsh' by both permanent and temporary staff.

More importantly, the lack of job security inherent in temporary work is a major factor leading to the non-retention of temporary staff. The fact that a temporary employee could be laid off with one week's notice has put many people off, because one simply cannot plan ahead in terms of reliable income, availability for other jobs, social engagements and holiday commitments. For those who eventually want to obtain a permanent job with Home Cosy, it is often a test of their patience. Some of the temporary staff interviewed have literally lost count of the number of times they were laid off and called back again by the company.

## Participants' Diagnoses of the Problem/Views on Key Issues

### Management

According to the management, pay is definitely not an issue leading to the problems concerned, because the company is well known for offering some of the best-paid unskilled and semi-skilled jobs in the local area. This is confirmed by an independent local-pay and benefits survey, and by interviews with shopfloor staff. Both management and employees are aware that hard and often physically demanding work is expected in return for the premium rate paid by the company.

Management thinks the company has been fair to temporary staff because they are getting the same terms and conditions as permanent staff – except for pension rights and paid sick or casual leave. While denying pensions is to be expected by temporary staff, management justifies the stringent absence procedures on the grounds that temporary staff are only employed when there is an immediate need for additional workforce. It will defeat its own purpose if temporary staff are allowed to have extended absence.

Implicitly, the lack of job security is not considered a major problem with the non-retention of temporary staff because it has not been a problem in the last twenty years. Rather, the two perceived major reasons for the recruitment and retention problems experienced are as follows:

1. *Increased competition within the local labour market* In the last couple of years, a number of financial, insurance and retail companies have moved into the area. Many of them offer good financial perks, a pleasant working environment, considerable investment in training and have under-taken public-relations campaigns. As a result, the competition for labour within the local area is much intensified.

2. *The new shift system has made the company less attractive*  Eighteen months ago, a new shift system was introduced into the distribution centre to cope with increased customer demand. As a result, a total of ten part-time shifts were created in addition to the traditional full-time, morning, afternoon and evening shifts. The new shift system has extended the morning shift into lunchtime, the evening shift into dinner-time and the afternoon shift possibly into both. As a result, such long and unsociable shift hours are thought of as a major source of recruitment and retention difficulties.

## Supervisors

Most of the supervisors interviewed do not think their company or at least their departments have problems of staff shortages because they always seem to be able to recruit sufficient staff whenever necessary. The turnover of permanent staff has always been negligible, except for Saturday staff. The performance of temporary staff is not much different from permanent staff. Some supervisors remark, from their experience, that temporary staff probably work harder because of their desire to impress the supervisor to recommend them for a permanent job.

## Shopfloor Staff

Most shopfloor staff, both temporary and permanent, regard the company's employment policies as fair. The common view is that 'they work you hard, but they pay you well here'. Many regard their jobs as unskilled and uninteresting. Some remark cynically that they are paid for boredom. Yet a surprisingly high proportion of the staff interviewed actually say they like their jobs being simple and easy, because they do not have to bring home any worries about work. Also, more than half of the staff interviewed think they can do something that requires more skills and qualifications but would rather stay in their current jobs, because many believe that a skilled job in the local area does not always pay as well as their own jobs.

Even those who regard the stringent absence policy towards temporary staff as 'harsh' realize the company has been fair in the sense that all the terms and conditions have been set out in the contract and explained to them when they first started working. Even so, some think the company is a little 'crafty' in this respect. When a temporary employee is laid off after less than six months' continuous employment, the company will not have to pay any redundancy allowance. After a couple of weeks, the same person can be employed as temporary staff again without the company being obliged to make any long-term commitments.

On the other hand, many of the 'weekday' permanent staff have worked at Home Cosy for a long time and have no intention of leaving until their retirement. As a whole, they represent a group of loyal and satisfied staff, highly regarded by the management as the stable core of their workforce.

## Case Study Tasks

1. Based on the above information, identify and analyse the problems facing the personnel department of Home Cosy. Some suggested areas of discussions are

   (a) product market characteristics;
   (b) labour market characteristics; and
   (c) possible mismatches within the employment system.

2. In what way does the use of delivery time as the company's competitive advantage constrain its recruitment and retention policies?
3. What are the fundamental problems in the permanent use of a temporary workforce?
4. What is the possible sub-optimization available to the personnel department faced with the above problems?
5. Does Home Cosy fit into Atkinson's (1985) model of 'the flexible firm'? If yes, identify the 'core' and the 'peripheral'.
6. How useful are the core/peripheral and permanent/temporary distinctions in the discussion of this case?
7. Are repetitive jobs necessarily dissatisfying? What is their impact on performance?
8. Is Home Cosy's personnel department practising human resources management or personnel management at the distribution centre?

## Essential Reading

Atkinson, J. (1985) Flexibility: planning for an uncertain future, *Manpower Policy and Practices*, Vol. 1, Summer, pp. 26–9.
Collinson, D. (1987) 'Picking women': the recruitment of temporary workers in the mail order industry, *Work, Employment and Society*, Vol. 1, no. 3, pp. 371–87.
Guest, D. (1989) Personnel and HRM: can you tell the difference?, *Personnel Management*, Vol. 21, no. 1, January, pp. 48–51.
National Economic Development Organization (NEDO) (1986) *Changing Working Patterns: How Companies Achieve Flexibility to Meet New Needs*, London.
Wood, S. (ed.) (1989) *The Transformation of Work*, Unwin, London.

## Additional Reading

Farnham, D. (1990) Personnel managers or human resources managers? Responses and change in the personnel function, in *Personnel in Context*, IPM, London.
Pollert, A. (ed.) (1988) The 'flexible firm': fixation of fact?, *Work, Employment and Society*, Vol. 2, no. 3, pp. 281–316.
Storey, J. (ed.) (1989) *New Perspectives on Human Resource Management*, Routledge, London.

## CASE 7

# Finding New Employees for High-Reliability Operations

## Gary Brown

## Introduction

The research upon which this case study is based is ongoing and therefore pseudonyms have been used throughout. The author is grateful for the financial support of the Economic and Social Research Council.

## Organizational Setting

Air traffic controllers (ATCOs) ensure the safe, orderly and expeditious flow of aircraft in the skies and on the ground by means of such remote technology as radio communications, radar and VHF navigational aids. Controllers work for a variety of State, military and commercial organizations. In the civil aviation sector these range in size from the semi-governmental United Kingdom Air Directorate (UKAD), with some 1,500 ATCOs serving both all the major UK airports and also the 'area radar centres' that deal with navigation in the high airways, through to such companies as Air Navigation Services Ltd – a subsidiary of a major telecommunications company – with around 160 ATCOs at seven UK airports, down to single-site operators, such as Melthorpe International Airport with its own staff of 21 ATCOs.

All UK air traffic control (ATC) operations have a safety record second to none. While machine and computer systems have a substantial and increasing part to play, human reliability is still central to the operation of the system. Indeed, it is a legal – and eminently practical – requirement that controllers and pilots have safe 'rulebook' procedures to fall back on in the event of partial or total technical failure. It is therefore essential that all operators of ATC can find and secure new staff of sufficient quality and in adequate numbers. All have had somewhat different methods of doing so, from 'poaching' trained staff from other employers at home or abroad, through to large-scale *ab initio* recruitment and training programmes, to a 'craft apprenticeship' approach of developing the best of ATC assistants – a support role that requires only a relatively short period of on-the-job training – into fully qualified controllers.

## Issues and Problems

Under government pressure, UKAD cut back its ATCO cadet-recruiting programme between 1982 and 1987, and shed non-operational staff. However,
the volume of air traffic worldwide increased beyond industry expectations
leading to a manpower crisis throughout ATC, UKAD having been by far the
major provider of 'new blood' to the whole UK civil ATC industry. All ATC
organizations must now tread a delicate line between the need suddenly to
increase their intakes and drastically to shorten their training programmes (in
order to get ATCOs in front of consoles in the shortest possible time) and the
necessity of continuing, absolute reliability of the system. This case study
examines developing patterns of recruitment and early training for these high-
hazard operations.

## What is Air Traffic Control?

ATCOs have a favourite description of their work: long periods of extreme
boredom interspersed with a few short, sharp moments of sheer terror. The
statistical risk of failure in UK ATC is extremely low – indeed, there has been
no accident attributable to ATC error for forty years – yet the consequence of
any single failure is likely to be catastrophic in terms of always spectacular and
perhaps heavy loss of life. Organizations operating in these 'low-risk/high-
hazard' areas need extremely high reliability from both people and technology.

All ATC operations in the UK are legally required to have at the core of
their objectives 'the securing of a safe, orderly and expeditious flow of air
traffic within the airspace over which they have control' (UK Civil Aviation
Authority). With few exceptions all aircraft are legally obliged to follow
instructions given to them by ATC and, for this reason, all ATCOs must have
a licence issued or approved by the Civil Aviation Authority (CAA). Before a
new controller may handle live traffic, this licence must be 'validated' by the
CAA after a further period of training specific to the unit where the controller
is posted. Many of the daily procedures followed by controllers are embodied
in aviation law; criminal as well as organizational sanctions may follow errors
or failures. In addition there are strict, career-long retesting, training and
medical requirements. The actual job of controlling aircraft is generally regarded
to be highly demanding on powers of concentration, communication and
reaction to the vagaries of fast aircraft in congested airways; and work periods
are short, but intense and sometimes stressful. However, controlling is a secure
and (in recent years) well-rewarded profession, and the majority of ATCOs
seem to regard the core task as more of a 'hobby or obsession' than a 'job'.

Before introducing the three organizations that are the concerns of this case
study, it is necessary briefly and simply to outline the different types of ATC
work carried out by ATCOs. Many readers will be familiar with the glass-
topped visual control-room on top of an airport ATC tower. In here sit
*aerodrome controllers*, who line up arriving and departing aircraft both on the
ground and in the air within about three miles of the runways. They usually

operate visually and by radio contact with the aircraft and with other controllers. In a darkened suite lower down the tower sit *approach controllers* using radar and radio to move aircraft between the runways and the high airways within about a thirty-mile radius of the aerodrome. ATCOs working at aerodromes alternate between these jobs, which at busy airports are often further subdivided between a large team. The third type of ATC — and run in the UK by UKAD alone — is *area radar control*, which is concerned with traffic high in the skies, some of which will be departing from or heading to UK airports and others of which will be over-flying UK airspace. The area radar centres operate wholly by radar, radio and telephone and are not necessarily located near airports.

Eyesight and voice, radar and radio are clearly the key technologies of ATC. All are continuously backed up by a pen-and-paper 'procedural rules' system designed to ensure that aircraft are kept horizontally and vertically separated by prescribed distances. In addition, ATCOs need detailed knowledge of meteor-ology, standard radio communication practice, radar capabilities and ATC and aviation navigation rules, laws and practices. The many oddities and unique characteristics of the aircraft and pilots under their control lead controllers to stress the need for creativity, flair and good humour in handling the traffic patterns. In all this work controllers are supported by assistants whose task is primarily to handle paperwork and pass messages from unit to unit. The training required for this job is short and relatively uncomplicated, and the operating ATCO is held directly responsible for ensuring the work is carried out properly. Nevertheless, a capable and experienced assistant makes a valuable contribution to the smooth running of a unit.

## The Pressures on ATC in the 1980s

### Demand

The volume of air traffic worldwide has grown continuously, and at a rate usually well in excess of any forecast, resulting in severe congestion and widespread delays. The congestion is particularly severe in and at the intersection of the airways controlled by UKAD's area radar bases, where indeed nearly three quarters of all its controllers work. Throughout Europe there has been a shortfall of ATCOs relative to ever-increasing traffic levels, exacerbated by a 'retirement bulge' as the large number of controllers recruited during the very rapid expansion in commercial air services in the late 1950s and early 1960s near the end of their operational careers.

### Cost and Politics

During the 1980s policies of perceived efficiency and slimmed workforces were strenuously applied, particularly in those governmental or semi-governmental organizations where bureaucratic rather than market forces were considered to prevail. UKAD, being both in the public sector and by far the largest ATC organization, came under severe pressure from its political masters in the Department of Transport, the Monopolies and Mergers Commission, and its direct paying customers − the airlines and airports − to cut payroll costs. In the mid-1980s UKAD bowed to this pressure. Staff were shed from administrative functions, and the total number of ATCOs was slightly reduced by a combination of natural wastage and a reduction in the recruiting effort. However, the number of operational controllers was further reduced by the need to redeploy some of them into essential support and development positions previously held by non-ATCO personnel. Although some internal operational efficiencies were generated by new working practices, by 1987 it had become clear to UKAD that it had allowed itself to be pushed into serious error; the public, the travel industry and − somewhat ironically − the airlines all railed against increasing 'air traffic control delays'. (In fairness to UKAD it should be said that delays were often caused by congestion outside UK airspace, and that 'ATC delay' announced to passengers often hides breakdowns in airlines' own operations.) In 1988 a House of Commons Select Committee severely criticized past UKAD senior management − and, by implication, that of other commercial ATC operators − for errors of planning and judgement in forecasting demand and capacity. UKAD promised to address the capacity problem vigorously over the next five years, in large part by increasing massively its recruiting plans.

## Problems of Demography and Skill Shortage

A further, and industry-wide, failure with regard to 'manpower planning' may also be seen by looking at the age composition of the labour market. Although the labour force in the UK is predicted to rise by some one million over the next decade, government statistics based on the birth rate, year on year, predict that the number of 16−19-year-olds will fall by 850,000 (Cassells, 1990). Competition for young blood is therefore going to be extremely tough at exactly the time when ATC is trying to remedy past planning errors. While ATC offers a challenging, secure and well-paid career, its training is demanding and lengthy, as well as being very specific to the task. It has also been widely perceived as predominantly a male career. As regards skills, working ATCOs regard the learning process as being difficult less in its content than in the sheer amount of detail that has to be mastered. Many ATC instructors regard current trainees as ill-equipped by modern school-education methods for 'old-fashioned, hard, fast learning', and also feel that new entrants are too often deficient in the basic skills of mental arithmetic and clear verbal expression, which are a vital part of everyday ATC work.

For all these reasons, in mid-1988 ATC operations in the UK found themselves desperately short of controllers and with an insufficient number in the pipeline to meet even the most conservative estimates of demand for their services over the next five or six years. We shall now turn to the three companies and their responses to this challenge.

## UKAD

A semi-public body, UKAD runs all area radar control and supplies approach and aerodrome services to twenty airports, including the three busiest: Heathrow,

Gatwick and Manchester. Although area radar operations are likely to remain in UKAD's control for 'reasons of national security', it may — and does — bid for other aerodrome contracts as and when they come up for renewal, and its own current aerodrome contracts are similarly contestable. During the 1980s its board had adopted a mission of 'moving from an administrative to a managerial culture' but found its old civil-service links to run deep among its scientists, technicians and operating professionals.

UKAD owns and operates its own training college for ATCOs and, in the past, has trained not only its own cadets but also those of more than fifty overseas countries, as well as employees of other UK organizations. Until 1987, for the purposes of maintaining its own strength, it placed an annual advert in a specialist aviation magazine announcing that 'applications for cadetships would be received' between certain dates. Thirty to forty cadetships were commonly on offer and UKAD expected around sixty applications, almost all of which would come from aviation enthusiasts or ex-military controllers wishing to be retrained in the rather different, and more demanding, skills of civil control. In addition, controlling was widely seen as a male job and only small numbers of women ever applied, although those who were successful enjoyed a high reputation among their colleagues. Selection was by means of interview by operational ATCOs followed by a stiff medical. Numbers were selected on the basis of an expected 15–20-per-cent failure rate on the 136-week training course. On-the-job training was interspersed with classroom modules for the various ATC skills. Success on the course gave cadets an array of ATC 'ratings', each of which had then to be 'validated' by further training and examination at the actual operational site to which the cadet was posted. The emphasis on safety in all air traffic operations necessitated annual revalidation and medical examination as a permanent feature of a career in ATC.

## UKAD's Response

Two solutions were immediately available to the problem. The first involved restricting the flow of traffic within the system — a measure that was highly unpopular with the public and the air travel industry, but that was designed to maintain safety and some degree of predictability of departure times. The second solution was to go all out to recruit large numbers of new cadets and to rethink the training system in order to make them operational in the shortest practicable time. Some efforts were also made to attract fully experienced controllers to UKAD but these were never in plentiful supply before the crisis struck. Within the civil-service-like culture of UKAD, there was also a strong hierarchical division between assistants and controllers, which led to a widespread reluctance to regard the assistants as a potentially plentiful source of future controllers, although small numbers had always managed to cross the barrier. The prime source of new recruits was thought to be young people aged 18–22, either fresh from school or dissatisfied with a first job. Their career-long service would provide the best return on the large training investment. However, good success rates had been obtained in the past with more mature students when applications up to the age of 27 were allowed.

From 1988 to 1990 recruiting targets were continually revised upwards but settled at, 1988 – 80 cadets, 1989 – 140 cadets and 1990 – 240 cadets. Thereafter the target was intended to be 240 cadets for each year until the mid-1990s. UKAD's personnel department – not staffed by ATCOs – decided the 'typical' applicant of previous years was simply not available in sufficiently large numbers. It would be necessary to launch a much wider recruiting campaign than had been done previously, offering attractive salaries while studying – just under the national average starting salary for graduates – with the prospect of a very substantial raise on successful completion of initial training. The near-certain prospect of earnings of nearly double the national average by the age of 40 would be stressed.

As UKAD now faced the prospect of selecting from applicants unlikely to have much knowledge of aviation, it was also thought necessary to establish a psychological profile of current controllers in order to have a method of screening potential cadets. This profile, drawn up by outside consultants, led UKAD to adopt tests principally designed to measure two contrasting traits of 'independence of mind' and 'comfort with democratic settings and practices'. High scores on both of these were thought likely to have good predictive value regarding ability to be a competent controller once fully trained. Although a validation programme was commenced in 1988, UKAD could not of course simply await its outcome but decided to proceed with using the recommended tests as a large part of the selection process. The psychological profile was thought to be a particularly unusual one – reflecting the need for a controller to accept high personal responsibility for his or her actions yet in a necessarily team-work environment – and it was therefore decided to trawl a large number of potential applicants by means of extensive advertising and strong presence at careers fairs. Applicants, of whom UKAD hoped to attract between 2,500 and 3,500, would initially be screened by the psychometric and aptitude tests and then be further probed by a panel consisting of a senior personnel manager and two ATCOs. They would look for evidence of maturity, strong motivation, a flexible yet decisive mind and clarity of expression. Using this new system, UKAD found it had little difficulty in meeting its new recruiting targets.

UKAD also saw that it would have both to expand its college to deal with the rise in cadet numbers and to look at ways of shortening the training courses. The first objective could be partly achieved by discontinuing all training for non-UKAD cadets for the foreseeable future. Nevertheless it was still necessary to expand the facilities physically and to find many more qualified instructing staff. Attractive salary offers were made to instructors within and without UKAD and a number of recently retired or medically disbarred ATCOs were also re-employed. Even then successful applicants faced delays of up to a year before a training place became available. Shortening the training course proved more problematic, particularly in a setting where absolute safety and reliability were key organizational objectives. After protracted negotiations between ATCOs and management, often in an atmosphere of mutual distrust and poor communication, it was agreed that the cadet intake would be streamed into either aerodrome and approach controllers or aerodrome and area radar controllers. This enabled the formal course content gradually to be reduced from the previous 'all-skills' length of 136 weeks training to only 72 weeks. On-the-job training was virtually eliminated from this initial training. However, when implemented, this shortening led many ATCOs to be concerned that standards of overall awareness of the complexities of air traffic were being eroded, resulting in both an increasing failure rate in practical examinations and a need for much longer periods of practical training at the unit to which the successful cadets were posted.

By 1990 the manpower picture for UKAD showed some signs of improvement as large numbers of newcomers to ATC were certainly being recruited. However, there remained substantial cause for concern: the debate over the quality of these new recruits continued and their failure rate in initial training remained very high. Whether the manpower crisis was really in the process of swift resolution remained a highly contentious issue.

## Air Navigation Services Ltd

Air Navigation Services Ltd (ANS) was formed in 1947 in order to provide technical and support services along the 'imperial' air traffic routes in those places where existing ground services were inadequate for rapidly expanding international air travel in the post-war years. Up until the early 1970s, ANS held only overseas air traffic contracts, which it staffed primarily with small communities of expatriate controllers trained at its own UK college. This college also held contracts for the training – but not the recruitment or selection – of ATCOs for civil and military clients worldwide.

However, in recent years, ANS has concentrated on training local staff to assume responsibility for its overseas contracts. The expansion of air traffic and associated facilities in the UK and Europe led ANS to compete for ATC contracts at UK airports, which it was able to staff with its returning expatriates, 'topped up' as necessary with fully qualified controllers recruited from UKAD and other employers. For most of the 1970s and 1980s, ANS felt that it did not need to recruit and train complete newcomers in any significant quantity. Nevertheless, it did allow very small numbers of its ATC assistant population to apply for places at its own college when these became available – for example, because an overseas client failed to fill completely a course it had booked. In these cases the chosen assistant – almost certainly from a unit where there was an ATCO due to retire at a time that matched this 'accidental' training vacancy – would be trained only for the ratings needed at his or her home unit, and would also receive a large amount of on-the-job training between each module of the ratings courses. This procedure was comparatively rare and indeed had been the cause of some dissatisfaction in the past as assistants with an ambition to train as controllers were never certain of ANS's commitment to allow them opportunities.

### Response

Faced with the growing realization of the coming controller shortage, from

1988 onwards ANS intensified its recruiting efforts among fully trained ATCOs. However it faced the problem that its overall size did not enable it to recruit except in anticipation of specific vacancies at its operational units. ANS also took steps to try to ensure that its salary packages were seen to be competitive, although it was reluctant to make this its main recruiting and retention tool. Instead it preferred to stress the 'family feeling' it believed to exist throughout its ranks in marked contrast to the hierarchical and bureaucratic atmosphere that was widely reported to dominate daily life in UKAD. Yet ANS felt that in reality their prized 'family atmosphere' had perhaps become somewhat diluted over the years as fewer and fewer of its domestic controllers had been trained with the company at the very outset of their careers.

Although it was not economically feasible to recruit student controllers in any great numbers, ANS decided it would regularly make places at its college available to its own assistants. Assistants, frequently recruited locally, of two or three years standing at operational units, could be recommended by their station manager if he or she felt they had potential for more advanced training. They would then be interviewed by a senior company manager – always an ATCO – principally to probe their motivation to stick at formal periods of intense classroom and simulator training. ANS wished to structure this training along the lines of an old-fashioned craft apprenticeship, with formal learning interspersed with practical training at the 'home' operational unit. It was felt that a good student would obtain the necessary aerodrome and approach ratings in about nine months and then go on to validate at an already familiar site in three to six months. Nevertheless, fully trained controllers from other employers would still be the prime recruiting target for some years to come, as initial training was costly and not necessarily predictable in its outcome.

## Melthorpe International Airport

Melthorpe Airport is jointly owned by seven local authorities in the North of England and has its own staff of 21 ATCOs and 19 assistants. In common with all UK regional airports, throughout the 1980s it handled substantially increasing amounts of traffic in all areas of its activities. Situated in an area where many military training flights are carried out, it also has a wider and more sophisticated radar coverage than is usual, making it an attractively challenging operational unit to controllers. As Melthorpe has no initial training facilities of its own, and places at the UKAD or ANS colleges are very costly, it has usually preferred to recruit fully trained controllers as and when necessary. Of the current establishment, 16 ATCOs were 'poached', mostly from UKAD. The remaining five, however, worked as assistants at Melthorpe and had been sent by them (over a fifteen-year period) for further training, usually after five to eight years' service. These assistants had all had to fight hard for the opportunity to obtain higher training, the onus being on the individual to persuade his or her superiors to make a 'cadetship' available. Assistants were usually recruited through advertisements in a national aviation magazine.

*Response*

In common with other operators of ATC, Melthorpe had not anticipated the coming shortage of controllers and indeed suddenly realized that the average age of its own staff was in the mid-40s. Staff turnover seldom ran above one controller per year, with medical problems − by far the majority of which would be relatively trivial in other occupations − accounting for almost all losses. Recruiting fully experienced controllers to deal with both the future traffic levels and a retirement 'bulge' was becoming increasingly difficult as other employers sought to retain staff, in any case traditionally not very mobile, with competitive salaries. Indeed, senior ATCOs at Melthorpe felt the quality and number of applications for anticipated vacancies owing to retirement or expansion was increasingly disappointing. As a result they decided to experiment with holding an 'open competition' among those assistants who had at least five years' experience and who wished to aim at advanced training. This would consist of an interview by two ATCOs and the airport Director of Operations − himself an ATCO by training − which would primarily test those powers of 'rapid, flexible decision-making under pressure' that were considered essential to operational ability. This would be done by presenting the assistants with 'scenarios' taken from current affairs − for example, the progress of a prison siege − and interrogating them on possible courses of action. Applicants who were successful would be ranked in order of ability to go forward − medical permitting − to a training college when a vacancy at the unit looked likely to arise. However, Melthorpe was concerned that the overall manpower problems in the industry meant that training places would be in very short supply for independent operators.

Melthorpe's ATC unit training manager was also investigating whether there were available any psychometric tests that would assist the selection process, particularly in view of the high cost of a failure at training. He also felt that any early use of a valid test would help to prevent the raising of false hopes of advancement among existing and future assistants. In the meantime, Melthorpe would also continue to sell itself hard to any good-quality, fully experienced ATCOs who applied for a vacancy, stressing in particular its busy and varied workload, its independence and small size and its attractive rural location.

## Case Study Tasks

This case raises a large number of issues, some to do with approaches to recruitment and initial training and others to do with the context in which decisions are made and, indeed, research done. Users of the case will be able to draw up their own list of pertinent questions. The following list is intended to offer some useful starting points:

1.  What are the organizations doing to address the problem of acute manpower shortages? What pressures are limiting their options?
2.  Although the three organizations are performing similar functions in a

highly integrated system, they are of greatly differing sizes and histories — could they nevertheless learn from each other?
3. What other types of operations may face these types of problems?
4. How might organizations select and train new members to make judgements on the nature of acceptable risk?
5. How many levels of analysis may usefully be applied to this case?

## Essential Reading

Alston, J. P. (1985) *The American Samurai*, De Gruyter, Berlin (esp. pp. 47–8).

Atkinson, J. (1989) Four stages of adjustment to the demographic downturn, *Personnel Management*, Vol. 21, no. 8, August, pp. 20–4.

Cassells, J. (1990) *Britain's Real Skill Shortage*, Policy Studies Institute, London.

Drabek, T. E. (1986) *Human System Responses to Disaster: An Inventory of Sociological Findings*, Springer-Verlag, Berlin (esp. Chap. 8, Hazard perceptions).

Fincham, R. and Rhodes, P. S. (1988) *The Individual, Work and Organization: Behavioural Studies for Business and Management Students*, Weidenfeld & Nicolson, London.

Van Maanen, J. and Barley, S. R. (1984) Occupational communities: culture and control in organizations, in B. M. Staw and L. L. Cummings (eds.) *Research in Organizational Behavior*, Vol. 6, JAI Press, Greenwich, Conn.

Weick, K. (1987) Organizational culture as a source of high reliability, *California Management Review*. Vol. 29, no. 2, pp. 112–27.

## Additional Reading

Benton, P. (1990) *Riding the Whirlwind: Benton on Managing Turbulence*, Blackwell, Oxford.

Berg, P. O. (1982) Seven trends in contemporary organizational theory, in P. O. Berg and P. Daudi (eds.) *Traditions and Trends in Organizational Theory*, Studentlitteratur, Lund.

Gill, J. and Johnson, P. (1991) *Research Methods for Managers*, Paul Chapman, London.

Hutchins, E. (1990) The technology of team navigation, in J. Galegher, R. E. Kraut and C. Egido (eds.) *Intellectual Teamwork: Social and Technological Foundations of Cooperative Work*, Lawrence Erlbaum Associates, Hillsdale, NJ.

Orton, J. and Weick, K. (1990) Loosely coupled systems: a reconceptualization, *Academy of Management Review*, Vol. 15, no. 2, pp. 203–23.

Perrow, C. (1984) *Normal Accidents: Living with High Risk Technologies*, Basic Books, New York, NY.

Sills, D. L., Wolf, C. P. and Selanski, V. B. (eds.) (1982) *Accident at Three Mile Island: The Human Dimensions* Westview Press, Boulder, Colo. (esp. Part 4, The interaction of social and technical systems).

Timperley, S. and Sisson, K. (1989) From manpower planning to human resource planning, in K. Sisson (ed.) *Personnel Management in Britain*, Blackwell, Oxford.

Watson, T. (1989) Recruitment and selection, in K. Sisson (ed.) *Personnel Management in Britain*, Blackwell, Oxford.

# CASE 8

## The Open Door?
## Women and Equal Opportunity
## At ComCo (North)

### Janette Webb

### The Employer

ComCo (North) is a manufacturing division of a US-owned multinational corporation. The division was founded in the 1960s and employs approximately 1,000 people out of the 82,000 worldwide ComCo (CC) employees. CC is an international supplier of commercial and technical computing and tele-communications test and measurement products. CC (North) has an R & D facility and designs and markets its own products as well as manufacturing US-designed products for European markets.

The corporation is known worldwide for its progressive management, which is underpinned by a US-style corporate philosophy known as the ComCo Way. The philosophy is based on a carefully elaborated, systematic human resources approach to the management of the workforce. It is committed to growth through continuous technical innovation, with profit as its primary objective. People are regarded as the key resource through which technical innovation is maintained. The goal of maximizing profit through continuous innovation is regarded as compatible with the goal of maximizing individual growth and the fulfilment of individual potential. The corporate ideology seeks therefore to establish the groundwork for shared values and ideals and to emphasize a unity of purpose among all levels of the workforce. This is succinctly stated in the following extract from corporate promotional material designed to show CC's commitment to equal opportunity:

> We believe our diverse workforce helps CC realize its full potential. Recognizing and developing the talents of each individual brings new ideas to CC. The company also benefits from the innovation that results when CC people work together who have differing experiences and perspectives. In this way, a well-managed diverse workforce expands our base of knowledge, skills and understanding. It also enables us to be more responsive to the needs of our customers.
>
> In order to reap these benefits, we need extra attention and commitment

from every individual. Managers, in particular, play a critical role and are responsible for creating a work environment in which the contributions of all people can be recognized. To do this they need to understand how best to utilize individual talents so that people's special attributes can be used to achieve company objectives. Managers must also communicate this attitude to our people who should reflect it in working with fellow [*sic*] employees, customers, vendors and the general public.

CC needs to continue to identify and attract a workforce of the best talent available in each location where we operate. Our ability to use our diversity to realize our full potential will be an important factor in achieving future success in the global marketplace.

The corporate philosophy is reinforced materially by single-status terms and conditions of employment, above-average pay rates, share ownership and private health-care schemes, and a high level of other social benefits inside and outside work. The majority of the workforce has security of employment, but not job security: people are expected to be flexible and to accept job transfers according to requirements defined by periodic restructuring. CC has always been a non-union employer. The belief is that the management style, performance appraisal procedures, training provision and level of remuneration obviate the need for trade unions. As far as managers are concerned, any problems are dealt with on an individual basis and pay is negotiated annually between supervisor and employee, according to individual contribution to the company (albeit within established grade boundaries).

The main carriers of the CC Way are the managers and supervisors who are trained in communication skills and expected to be accessible and approachable at all times. This is facilitated by open-plan factory design, with integrated 'production' and 'office' areas; managers are routinely visible to their staff, and cafeteria and coffee areas are shared. Status differences between levels are minimized by the use of first names and by the deliberate 'informality' of a dress code in which shirt sleeves dominate and those reluctant to take their jackets off are likely to be seen as stand-offish. The company emphasizes the value of 'management by wandering around' as a means of keeping in touch with feeling at the grass roots. Hence casual conversation is encouraged, rather than seen as time wasting. The aim is to create an ethos whereby any individual can approach their manager to discuss a problem, or proceed to the next level manager if no resolution is forthcoming. In theory any individual can carry their problem forward to the highest level: metaphorically, the door is always open.

Labour turnover at CC (North) is very low and company loyalty is high. This is reinforced not only through a high level of material benefits and responsive, accessible management, but also through the development of an internal labour market. Once selected, individuals will generally be redeployed, with retraining and counselling if necessary, if their existing job disappears, or if they do not meet the performance requirements of the job. At higher levels, it is unusual for managers to be appointed from outside CC, although geographical mobility is frequently necessary to attain promotion. CC also discourages 'poaching' of its engineers, through a commitment to continuous development, as well as high levels of remuneration. The main forum for discussion of career moves is the annual performance review, carried out by each employee's supervisor or manager. It is, however, emphasized that it is up to the individual to take the initiative in identifying a career path and to set agreed performance objectives along this path with their manager. Subsequent rewards will be tied to the attainment of these objectives. Overall the belief is that security of employment, training and promotion opportunities and good financial benefits will generate good employment relations and the conditions necessary for continuous technical innovation.

In return for a high level of personal and financial investment in each individual, the company expects high levels of commitment, effort and continuous improvements in performance. A major plank in the production arrangements that seek to ensure high-quality goods and continuous improvement in manufacturing processes is the use of just-in-time (JIT) and total quality management (TQM) techniques. JIT is a minimum inventory production system, which aims to build products to order, rather than for stock, cut work in progress and reduce product completion times. TQM aims to make everyone responsible for the quality of the finished goods, at each stage of production, and to improve or eradicate errors and product failures. Operators stop building products when the daily requirement is met and they are expected to work instead in TQM groups to identify and correct problems with the production process and to work towards zero defects. Because there is little work in progress in a JIT system, any problem quickly results in production grinding to a halt: to make the system work, everyone (managers, engineers and operators) has to be willing to stop their work and solve the problem before production can continue. Life is more precarious than it is under a batch production regime and operators need to maintain a high degree of vigilance, attention to detail and the flexibility to use diagnostic skills when required. Production managers in CC regard manual employees as a very important source of knowledge about the production process and seek to extract such knowledge through TQM groups in order to make process improvements. The substantive content of most assembly work, however, remains monotonous and the requirement to switch between these two areas of activity has been a hard one to sustain. Participation in TQM activities is therefore rewarded through an element of pay, but the job itself has not been upgraded. The use of JIT production has been accompanied by increased use of subcontracting of work previously done in-house. CC is concentrating increasingly on high-tech electronics and buys in mechanical and electro-mechanical sub-assemblies from contractors. The number of jobs for manual staff has declined through subcontracting, increased automation and decreased need for fault finding and rework on products that are increasingly error-free.

## CC and the Individualistic Ethos

CC has a sophisticated human resources model of the employment contract, which emphasizes the individualistic character of the relationship between the company and the employee. The employment structure and management practices discourage the expression of common causes in a number of ways. First, pay is negotiated annually between each individual and his or her manager, on the basis of the performance review. Second, managers claim to make themselves available and accessible at all times to discuss, and diffuse, grievances quickly. Third, security of employment and a developed internal labour market sustain the belief that opportunities for improved pay and status are dependent not on collective action but solely on the individual's motivation, ability and achievement. The ideology is strictly meritocratic: in theory anyone can get to the top, if they show themselves willing and able and have the drive to complete appropriate training. Lastly, all individuals are regarded as having a valuable contribution to make to the company, whatever their job.

Conversely, no one is expected to come to work simply to pass the time and there is considerable peer-group and supervisory pressure on individuals to fall into line, or move on. Thus any problems are firmly located with the individual, not the company, and counselling will be directed to this effect. By implication, the individual carries the blame for their own relative failure and since there are in reality a very small number of promoted posts, most people will be relative failures. It is typically those in middle management who experience the contradictions between the espoused ideals and the reality of restricted career mobility most strongly, particularly when recession means little or no growth in jobs and little movement up the ladder.

In many ways there is, of course, little to complain about, since pay and benefits are relatively high, many people have intrinsically interesting jobs and there is a high degree of acceptance of the CC Way: 'the opportunities are there, it's up to the individual to take them', is an often-heard comment. In terms of the prevailing norms, therefore, it is difficult for anyone to articulate a 'common cause' and even more difficult to suggest that, far from being a matter of individual choice and opportunity, there may be very real structural constraints that work to the systematic disadvantage of one group in comparison with another.

## The Sexual Division of Labour in CC (North)

Structural constraints are, nevertheless, evident in the unequal division of labour between men and women. The company has a workforce consisting of 60 per cent qualified engineers, most of whom are men. Even outside these categories, most higher-level jobs are occupied by men (for example, in accountancy, commercial sales and information technology). Women are concentrated in the lower manual grades, while men dominate the technical, graduate engineering and managerial grades. Even at manual level, staff are divided into two main groups: production operators (a semi-skilled grade) and test engineers (a skilled grade). While production operators are 90 per cent female, test engineers are 90 per cent male.

Women are well represented in clerical and secretarial roles, either as personal secretaries, departmental secretaries or as clerical staff in such areas as accounts, personnel or purchasing. They have limited internal mobility, because they lack technical or professional qualifications. At graduate engineer level, CC (North) has approximately 16 per cent women. The highest-graded woman in the division is in R & D, and has an electronics Ph.D. She has been with the company since qualifying. There are no women line managers in production, despite the concentration of women at lower levels, and no senior women in manufacturing engineering or technical marketing roles. Personnel employs eight women, out of a staff of thirteen, although this is also headed by a man.

## Equal Opportunity in CC (North): Some Views on Policy and Practice

CC's approach to equal opportunity is determined by the individualistic employment-relations ethos, as illustrated by the following extract from its personnel policies and guidelines:

EQUAL OPPORTUNITY
The company objective of 'Citizenship' requires that CC take positive action to seek out and employ members of disadvantaged groups in each of our facilities throughout the world. CC recognizes that this positive action promotes social and economic progress within local communities where CC operates while it also provides a stable and productive workforce.

CC is committed to providing each of its employees with opportunities for advancement at all levels based on individual initiative, ability and accomplishment. Equitable employment decisions made without regard to race, colour, religion, creed, sex, age or handicap are the cornerstone of this world wide policy.

Although CC's Affirmative Action and Equal Opportunity programmes are primarily centred around our US entities, those outside the US should review and extract any portion of the policies and guidelines for their use that would be appropriate to ensuring that our corporate objectives are met.

The guidelines apply to all employment practices as they pertain to any position for which an employee or applicant is qualified. All other personnel actions including (but not limited to) transfers, promotions, compensation, benefits, education and training, recreation and social programmes, will similarly be administered in conformity with the objectives of this policy and philosophy of non-discrimination.

The approach to policy can be characterized overall as 'the open door': the opportunity is there, if the individual is willing and able to use it. The statement above also makes clear that CC is responsive to the local legislative framework. Hence it has a stronger, more elaborated version of policy in the USA (affirmative action and contract compliance), and a weaker version in the UK where the legislation makes discrimination against an individual illegal, but relies heavily on voluntaristic compliance. In CC (North), separate pay structures were operated for men and women, until the advent of the Equal Pay Act forced the creation of a common pay scale. In practice men remain heavily concentrated in the higher-pay grades and women in the lower.

## Summary of Main Differences between US Affirmative Action and UK Equal Opportunity Frameworks

In the USA, legislation requires employers to act to redress the effects of past inequality; positive action is thus inherent in the approach. In the UK, legislation assumes voluntary compliance by the employer and refers only to present discriminatory acts against an individual. Positive action is permitted only in relation to targeted advertising or the provision of special training, where a group is absent or under-represented in a specific job category. In the US courts, claims can be heard, and redress sought on behalf of an entire category or group of people. The UK legislation is dependent on an individual bringing a case to an industrial tribunal and proving their claim of discrimination. In theory the individual cases of all other claimants have to be assessed on their own merits and the employer is not obliged to change those structures that produced the discriminatory consequences. 'Case law' created through individual claims is, nevertheless, regarded by the UK Equal Opportunities Commission as significant in combating sex inequalities. In the USA, a contract compliance provision requires employers in receipt of public funds to satisfy state and federal officers that they are making additional efforts to recruit, employ and promote qualified members of groups formerly excluded. Failure to comply could result in the loss of a contract. In the UK contract compliance is currently illegal. As a consequence of contract compliance, many US employers set recruitment and promotion targets; this is the exception in the UK. Within US enterprises, direction of affirmative action is generally from a specially created office, staffed by expert personnel. Equal opportunity policy in the UK tends to be part of the remit of a personnel manager who may be more or less expert, or it may emerge from a grass-roots-led campaign, orchestrated through trade-union bargaining procedures. In the USA procedures for monitoring the composition of the labour force, in relation to hiring, promotion and termination decisions, are often standard. In the UK such procedures tend to be piecemeal and statistics on labour force composition may not be readily available.

## The Perspective from CC (North) Personnel Group

The personnel group in CC (North) plays an active role in promoting good practice in recruitment, selection, training, assessment, pay and counselling. One of the managers, Donald Bell, is the site representative for equal opportunities. He is part of a small UK team, set up eighteen months ago, to look at CC's equal opportunity activities. The aim is to help develop a flexible environment and a positive attitude in managers and employees, to ensure that all opportunities are open to all groups and to understand through discussion what lies behind the current pattern of inequality. The team has so far met infrequently and there has been little substantive action. It is aiming to collect UK data on CC's employment of women, ethnic minorities and disabled people. This would be used to identify areas for specific initiatives.

Donald sees equal opportunities as part of the good-citizenship objectives of the company. He does not see equal opportunities as a burning issue for the division, either among managers or staff, although he is aware of a few rumblings of discontent among some women. He aims to set up some focus groups, with women and men, in order to obtain more input on workforce perceptions and to generate information for use in the UK-wide equal opportunities team meetings. In practice he believes that recruitment and selection is broadly fair and non-discriminatory. The philosophy is 'best person for the job'. There is no targeted recruitment advertising to attract under-represented groups. Indeed, in the context of a recession, and very limited new recruitment, most vacant jobs are filled either through a waiting-list system, drawn up on the basis of people writing in, or through small-scale graduate recruitment. Internally all jobs are advertised on the noticeboard and most applicants are interviewed, unless there are more than about six candidates. The formal criteria for selection decisions are knowledge, experience and potential. Interviews for manual and intermediate non-manual jobs are generally one to one, with the line manager or first line supervisor. For more senior posts, two or three interviewers, generally from the same department, would be involved. Personnel has no direct role. Those required to interview would, however, generally have received one-and-a-half to two days' training on selection and interviewing.

All recruits receive induction training, as well as job-specific training. There is no special training provision for women, although Donald believes that an interactive video course on US-style affirmative action has proved popular with women staff. Managers generally receive some training on equal opportunities as part of a modular management-development programme.

In Donald's view, CC (North) would welcome more female supervisors, engineers and managers: 'it would be more healthy for the company ... But they're not coming through from the schools and colleges'. CC is, after all, an engineering company, so the low proportion of women with technical qualifications excludes women from the majority of management posts. There is nothing CC can do about it, other than get its women engineers out to schools and colleges to talk to girls about engineering careers.

Nevertheless, Donald also feels that 'nothing is impossible' in CC, if the individual has the right motivation and the ability. Study for qualifications through day release or evening classes is supported. There is some movement out of manual jobs into clerical and secretarial roles and some production operators become supervisors. Donald believes that a move from production operator to line manager is possible, for the right individual, but no woman has yet managed this. There is virtually no movement from operator to test-engineer grades, but 'women operators are being trained to do the simpler testing things', as test engineering becomes a smaller part of total production and is simplified through automation. Quite a few women are coming into the low-level test-engineering jobs, but there is an excess of male test engineers. They are gradually being redeployed, through counselling, generally into maintenance or information technology roles, using their electronics skills. They also receive updating and retraining to help them move into new jobs. Donald does not foresee a general decline in manual jobs for women, because of the steady demand in the printed circuit-board area. There is currently some anxiety, as manual jobs are in a state of flux: no one likes change or the disruption caused by retraining for a new job.

In terms of the workplace environment, Donald believes that CC spends a great deal of time making sure people know their problems will be sorted out. There is, however, no separate route for complaints of sexual harassment from the general open-door policy. There are a few examples of incidents known to Donald. These are usually resolved by the personnel manager, if not by the line manager. It is up to the individual to approach someone appropriate, but Donald is aware the majority probably do not feel happy going above their immediate manager.

Some general provision is made for working parents. Women are entitled to up to six months' maternity leave, with the right to return to the same job or one of similar status. At the discretion of the woman's line manager, she may be allowed to return part time for the first six months. The arrangement may be extended, again subject to the manager's discretion. There are no job sharers at present. There is also a provisional entitlement to three days' paternity leave, again subject to managerial discretion. Lastly, an employee may take a career break of up to a maximum of three years throughout their career, but no guarantee of employment is given at the end and the arrangement is again subject to discretion. Some flexibility over hours of work is available, with start times of 7.00 to 8.30 a.m. and, accordingly, variable finishing times. There is no childcare provision. Women returning to work after maternity leave receive a sum of £750 as a one-off payment to help meet initial costs. Donald sees no likelihood of facilities being provided at the workplace: 'it's not the business we want to be in'. He is aware of some demand for crèche facilities or childcare allowances, and for more flexibility of hours of work, and feels that CC has gone some way towards meeting these.

## A View from a Line Manager

How do the managers in CC (North) feel about equal opportunities issues? Let's take a line manager in production, Will Smithson. He feels there is basically no problem. He hears occasional grumbles from a few of the operators, but in his view 'the girls' are mostly happy with their lot. Their orientation is primarily to home not work, and he detects a degree of complacency in the women (as well as some of the men): they don't want to take on new challenges and the prospect of change in their job makes them feel insecure. Anyway, they are fortunate to have jobs here: there is always a queue of people waiting to move from other local employers and the work environment there is a great deal harder on women. For a start the women here are not ordered about, they are not the target of verbal abuse, they get time to chat with their mates and the place is not covered in nude pin-ups. There is far more mutual respect between managers and operators, and you have to persuade the women to change working methods, not tell them what to do. This makes his life more difficult: he spends much of his time persuading them about the new production methods, but the operators still remember the changes as having been imposed. Once they were involved, there was however a period of a year or so of enthusiasm for JIT and TQM methods, but Will now finds it hard to motivate them to keep going on TQM activities. He feels the attitude is 'just leave me alone and let me build the product'. He does not see the division between female operators and male test engineers as an issue. He feels it is quite natural that women aren't interested in technical work. They have the kids and the shopping to worry about, and they are happy as long as they can do their work and get away promptly at the end of the day. He mostly feels quite comfortable about the way CC treats its workforce and believes that problems get dealt with. When it comes to selection and promotion decisions, he looks at applicants on their merits. He does not see any need for more proactive equal opportunities policies and thinks it is up to the individual if they want to move into a non-traditional job.

## A View from a Production Operator

Janet Findlay, a production operator, sees things slightly differently. She is well aware of all the advantages of a job with CC and she finds the workplace friendly and relaxed. Realistically she knows her prospects for internal mobility are limited to obtaining a job as supervisor of other women assemblers. She does not particularly want to move into clerical or secretarial work. She now carries out some of the test-engineering work previously carried out by men and believes that the women will increasingly be expected to take on more of the test-engineering role, as automation progresses and testing becomes more routinized. She is doubtful women will receive the same recognition as the men, in terms of pay and grading, for acquiring the new skills. She thinks that, if she had been a man, the company would have taken it for granted that she would get day release for electronics training. As a women it is harder to raise these issues with her manager, because he sees women as uninterested in technical skills and he assumes that she will marry, have children and stay at home for a good few years, so why should she want training? Despite the 'open door' policy, she feels hesitant about approaching managers outside her area, because of how it might be seen, and feels that the lack of women managers in production, who might have a better understanding of her views, is a problem.

## A View from a Purchasing Clerk

Susan Bates, a friend of Janet's since school-days, started working for CC as a production operator when she left school at 16. She took a night class in touch typing, on her own initiative, and moved into a secretarial job, when a suitable one was advertised. She likes the flexibility of the company, which allowed her to move progressively out of secretarial work into an office automation support role, training other women on word-processing and graphics packages, and setting up new office procedures. A great deal depended on having a sympathetic boss. She felt she was fortunate in having someone who was genuinely willing to renegotiate her job description at her annual performance review and hence facilitate her promotion. She feels a different manager might have prevented her moving on via the performance-review mechanism, preferring to monopolize her secretarial and organizational skills for the benefit of his own department.

The support work in office automation, however, has become increasingly technical and has been taken over by the already-existing technical support function. Susan has no technical training. She wonders whether being female made a difference: would the company have assumed that technical training was the next step, if she had been a man? Susan moved into a clerical job in purchasing, but is unlikely to gain much further promotion, because higher-level jobs in purchasing are now going to graduates. This is a consequence of the increasing status and role of purchasing, resulting from the change to a JIT production system. It is very unusual for CC to sponsor women through college or university, but Susan is aware that she needs some external qualification if she wants to progress further at work.

## A View from a Manager in Manufacturing Engineering

Andrew Thomas began his career with CC as an electronics graduate twelve years ago. His career has progressed well up to middle-management level. After a spell in R & D he moved into manufacturing engineering and has since gained promotion to manager. He still enjoys coming to work and he likes the people-oriented aspects of his management role. Life is never easy, however: the JIT production system keeps you on your toes. When there is a problem on the line, you cannot put it in the 'too difficult' category until tomorrow, because production stops. The operators realize that all your engineering qualifications do not count for much if you can't get production going again. You certainly lose your engineering mystique! And you have to develop your skills at working with people.

He started work at the same time as a few women engineers and knows there is some dissatisfaction among them, as they start to think about having a family. None of them have children, though some of them have steady partners. He is married and has recently become a father. His wife works in the NHS, which has, he would admit, better provision for women with children. He does not see himself taking a career break to spend time looking after the children, but is beginning to understand for the first time the sorts of pressures faced by dual-career couples, when they become parents. He is not sure about whether the CC women engineers really have any more to complain about than their male peers, however: there is generally a restlessness about the people in their 30s who have been here for ten years or more, as they start to see that the corporate philosophy of individual growth does not coincide with rapid promotion to more senior jobs, especially in the current recessionary climate. In his view it would be very unfair to take any special measures to support women engineers, just because they are in a minority. They would not want this anyway: everyone wants to be here on their own merits.

## A View from a Woman Engineer

At graduate-engineer level, women face a different set of problems. They also feel that CC is a very good employer and they enjoy their work. Potentially they can progress to high-level jobs, and they know women have some advantages, because the company is keen to be seen to be promoting competent women.

Sara Drysdale is a marketing engineer in her late 20s. While keen to emphasize that she personally has never had any difficulty, she is also aware of her 'token woman' status and feels relatively isolated. She likes the men she works with, and is usually treated as 'one of the boys'. Still, she is excluded from some of the informal chat, because she does not share their enthusiasm for rugby and other sports. There is no woman manager she could discuss her future career with, so she has to rely on the understanding of her male manager. She respects him and knows that he is very supportive of her in general.

Nevertheless, CC are not, in her view, providing positive support for women to enable them to develop a career in areas where they are presently under-represented. She feels it is very dependent on individual managers and their willingness to support competent women engineers. Given a supportive boss, career prospects are reasonable as long as she works as an 'honorary man':

> I think the difficulty is still being able to actually sit down, map out your career and possibly say that at a certain time you may well wish to have a family. There is still that feeling that it is a very difficult thing to sit down and say that.

In Sara's view this is unlikely to change in the absence of a stronger UK legislative framework, which would force a more proactive approach to such issues as parental leave and flexible arrangements for return to work. She is aware that the US affirmative-action framework provides a stronger framework of rights and thinks that CC is slightly hypocritical about this: they take great care to transfer the North American management style to Britain, but they adapt their equal opportunity policy to the local context. In a British context, this means losing out on some provisions and contradicts the CC commitment to leading the way for other local employers in standards of good practice.

Sara also finds the company's stance on childcare, parental leave and part-time working paradoxical, given the espoused commitment to a good working environment and, in other areas, the provision of considerable welfare benefits. The CC concept of 'welfare' is, she feels, based on the individual, disconnected from family and domestic circumstances. This is okay for the men, as long as they have their domestic support, but the reality is that, for women (who are still expected to provide the domestic support), a good working environment means provision for family responsibilities, in the form of flexible leave arrangements, the ability to vary hours of work and help with childcare whether through crèche facilities or through financial support to the parent. She is also aware of women in the company who have felt under pressure to return to work quickly, and to return full time when they would prefer part time, because of the perceived threat to their credibility as serious engineers. In the present economic context such women feel that arguing for more flexibility would mean risking their jobs.

In the absence of stronger legislation, she thinks little is likely to change, unless men also change and start to take on a bigger role in childcare and at home. She knows that management jobs in CC are still structured around men and conventional male career patterns. Managers not only have to be geographically mobile but many also work long hours and spend significant periods of the year visiting other CC divisions and customers all over the world. The increasingly global nature of the business is making this aspect of the job more intense. The assumption appears to be that a manager has a wife at home, or at least a wife with a secondary job, who runs the house and looks after the children. She does not see how women with children could live up to the 'company man' ethos, and she doubts whether her male peers will speak out, in case they are seen as lacking commitment. It is hard to challenge most of this as a woman, because the work norms are tacit and not generally open to discussion. Anyway she feels she would be labelled as the 'typical female', lacking the necessary drive to succeed. The lack of women to talk to at her level means she is also uncertain about whether most of this is simply her problem, or whether other women share her views. Company culture makes it difficult to have any sort of women's support group. Male colleagues might feel threatened and, anyway, it is not generally the sort of activity that is seen as acceptable in CC. There is no problem about taking individual initiatives, because that is the culture of the company, but this generally means giving talks to girls at schools or colleges and perhaps having some external involvement in government initiatives to encourage girls and women to study technology, and is part of the CC good-citizenship objectives.

Sara finds the work itself very rewarding and intrinsically interesting. She wants to be able to progress but not at the cost of having to choose, in the way that male colleagues do not, between family and career. She faces a more complicated work situation than her male peers, particularly in relation to her credibility as a woman engineer. Other people's reactions may be sceptical, so Sara has to convince them that she knows what she is talking about and can deal with them as an equal. She rarely works with other women. She also feels she has to be careful about her personal conduct, because she has occasionally been the subject of harassment, usually from outside the company. Although she feels fortunate that her boss takes her seriously when she raises such problems, and has dealt with offenders, she is nevertheless aware that she faces constraints in doing her job male peers do not. She is not surprised that, for the majority of women, an engineering career seems like the difficult option. In her view it is not a problem of technical competence or lack of interest on the part of women, it is more to do with men treating women as 'naturally' unable to cope with technology and excluding women from the technical sphere.

In relation to the company, its corporate philosophy embodied in the CC Way has many strong points and advantages. The individualistic ethos is very powerful and makes it difficult to explain why, for women as a group, it seems to work to their disadvantage, particularly in the face of a management convinced that it is doing its best for every individual. The consequent lack of legitimacy for 'women's issues' is therefore something of a problem for women graduates. It is also, in her view, difficult to imagine the company adopting a more formal equal opportunities policy, because it does not fit the ethos of the CC Way, which relies on informality, managerial discretion and guidelines rather than hard-and-fast procedures. As far as she is aware, most 'model' equal opportunities policies in Britain stress formalization of procedures and increased bureaucratic controls to limit managers' use of discretion.

## Case Study Tasks

### Role Play

Members of the group should each be assigned to roles as indicated in the case. Depending on numbers in the group, there could be more than one personnel manager, etc., or the group could be split into subgroups, for separate discussions, with a plenary session to compare notes. Another variation on the role play would be to have some members of the group acting as observers. Observers would be called on to give a commentary on the group discussion in a final feedback session.

For the role play, you should imagine that the personnel manager, Donald Bell, has asked for volunteers to join a focus group on equal opportunity issues. For different reasons, each of the above people have responded. Donald has made it clear that what people say will not be personally attributed outside the meeting and he hopes that participants will feel relaxed enough to speak openly. He also makes it clear that participation does not have any implications for the individual's status in their department and, in fact, none of the participants has direct managerial responsibility for any of the others.

During the discussion, each participant should be invited by Donald to air their views on equal opportunity issues in the division. Donald should also give a summary of the perspective from personnel and explain his views. Subsequent discussion should aim to produce an agreed statement listing areas where the group feels that an equal opportunities initiative is warranted. It should prioritize areas for action, set out what the first step should be in each case and decide who is responsible for carrying action forward in each area. The group should bear in mind that resources are at present limited and should therefore consider how necessary resources could be generated. The discussion should also take into account the context at CC (North), including the individualistic ethos, the human resources model of management, the engineering orientation and the recessionary climate in electronics. In other words, the participants need to be able to distinguish between what ideally might be done and what is feasible in practice.

### Subsidiary Questions

1. How would you describe the current approach to equal opportunities

policy and practice in CC (North)? Can you identify areas of employment practice that might be perpetuating the existing sexual division of labour? Could these be changed to improve opportunities for women?

2. Is it the case that an engineering company can do little about gender inequality in the workplace, until more women qualify as engineers and start to apply for technical jobs?

3. Does the human resources model of management and an individualistic employment ethos overcome inequalities between men and women at work?

4. What kind of equal opportunities initiative would be appropriate for CC (North), given the corporate culture and the preference for guidelines rather than hard-and-fast rules and procedures?

5. If the company were to implement its US affirmative-action policies in the UK, what action would have to be taken in CC (North) to bring employment policy into line?

6. To what extent is the equal opportunities framework, in use both in the UK and USA, limited in its implications for change in the overall distribution of jobs between men and women?

## Essential Reading

Cockburn, C. (1988) The gendering of jobs: workplace relations and the reproduction of sex segregation, in S. Walby (ed.) *Gender Segregation at Work*, Open University Press, Milton Keynes.

Cockburn, C. (1991) *In the Way of Women: Men's Resistance to Sex Equality in Organisations*, Macmillan, London (esp. Chapters 1 and 7).

Pearson, R. (1989) 'Women's employment and multinationals in the UK: restructuring and flexibility', in D. Elson and R. Pearson (eds.) *Women's Employment and Multinationals in Europe*, Macmillan, London.

Webb, J. and Liff, S. (1988) Play the white man: the social construction of fairness and competition in equal opportunity policies, *Sociological Review*, Vol. 36, pp. 532–51.

## Supplementary Reading

Dawson, P. and Webb, J. (1989) New production arrangements: the totally flexible cage?, *Work, Employment and Society*, Vol. 3, pp. 221–38.

*Equal Opportunities Review* (periodical carrying summaries of equal opportunity initiatives, policies and court cases).

Stamp, P. and Robarts, S. (1985) *Changing the Workplace for Women*, NCCL, London.

## Acknowledgements

Thanks are due to staff at CC (North) for their time, their interest and patience. Financial support from ESRC for part of the case study material used here is gratefully acknowledged.

# CASE 9

# Multi-Plant Industrial Relations: Fast Foods

## Nicholas Kinnie

### Organizational Setting

Fast Foods is part of a large multi-plant group, Waterfields, which has interests in milk products, food processing, transport and industrial services. Waterfields, which acquired Fast Foods around ten years ago, made pre-tax profits of £40 million on a turnover of £1,500 million in the last financial year.

Fast Foods operates in a highly competitive product market, which is volatile and fluctuates depending on the weather and holiday seasons. It produces several hundred lines for its branded goods and for supermarket 'own labels'. Three quarters of its products are fresh, with a shelf life of around five days, and the remainder are frozen. Predominantly a sales rather than a marketing organization, it has recently been experiencing a decline in market share. In the last financial year, Fast Foods made pre-tax losses of £4.2 million on a turnover of £97 million, although it has previously been profitable.

Fast Foods was originally established in the nineteenth century as a single plant based in Sussex. A family firm for much of its history, it developed a highly paternalistic approach towards its employees. Around twenty years ago, Fast Foods started buying up successful regional companies to bring them under a single brand-name and to develop a national distribution network. Work is exchanged between the plants and new technology is being employed extensively. At present, the work is labour intensive with a high proportion of part-time female employees.

Unions are recognized widely throughout Fast Foods, with workplace representatives in each of the plants. Employees belong to different unions, as follows:

| | |
|---|---|
| Production workers | TGWU |
| Drivers | TGWU |
| Maintenance workers | AEU |
| Van sales | USDAW, TGWU |
| Clerical workers | ACTSS |
| Supervisors | MSF |
| Managers | Management Association |

# Current Plants

There are now seven plants within Fast Foods, and details of their employment and levels of unionization are given in Table 9.1.

The head office and largest processing plant are based on the Sussex site. This is the original site and currently the most important. Both managers and employees on other sites tend to look to the Sussex plant to take the lead on industrial relations matters. Details of the other plants are as follows:

*Dorset*   The first plant acquired by Fast Foods outside the Sussex plant just over 20 years ago. It was relocated to a greenfield site around three years ago, and produces mostly frozen foods.

*Cheshire*   The second plant to be acquired 17 years ago. The plant itself is 35 years old and has poor working conditions. There has been some investment in equipment, but the plant is struggling to survive.

*Hertfordshire*   This plant was purchased 11 years ago. It is the largest plant outside Sussex and produces the same range of products as Sussex.

*Gloucestershire*   The plant was purchased at the same time as the Hertfordshire plant and has been owned by a variety of companies over the years. It produces a similar range to Sussex and supplies the Midlands.

*Lincolnshire*   This was purchased only three years ago by Fast Foods with the Northumberland plant. It is a modern plant and has enjoyed a high level of investment in equipment, but is presently under utilized. It processes the standard range of goods.

*Northumberland*   This plant has recently expanded its output and employment by some 50 per cent. It does not process the full range of products and concentrates instead on meat products.

Fast Foods has been through a whole series of reorganizations of its management structure in the last few years. For example, as recently as a year ago a regional

Table 9.1   Fast Foods – current plants

| Plant | Total employees | Female (%) | Part time (%) | Unionized | | |
|---|---|---|---|---|---|---|
| | | | | Manual[1] | Non-manual[2] | Management[3] |
| Sussex | 1,275 | 31 | 17 | 100 | 83 | 65 |
| Dorset | 381 | 43 | 17 | 93 | 60 | 5 |
| Glous. | 346 | 34 | 15 | 96 | 72 | 10 |
| Herts. | 466 | 42 | 14 | 97 | 76 | 20 |
| Northumb. | 311 | 34 | 9 | 100 | 81 | 60 |
| Lincs. | 187 | 46 | 6 | 100 | 82 | 58 |
| Ches. | 281 | 45 | 11 | 100 | 86 | 62 |
| *Total* | 3,248 | | | | | |

*Notes*
(1) Manual – average for production workers, drivers, maintenance and van sales. (2) Non-manual – average for clericals and supervisors. (3) Average for eligible junior and middle managers; senior managers are not unionized.

structure was set up with managing directors for the West and Wales, Midlands, North, and London and the South East. This has since been abandoned because it was soon realized it added an unnecessary layer of management, which duplicated the work of managers at head office. Consequently, a number of senior managers and directors have recently left the company.

The present organization structure simply has a Board of Directors at head office with the Directors of Finance, Production, Marketing and Sales, and Personnel reporting to the Managing Director. Each site has a plant manager and a small functional team including a personnel manager.

This study looks at Fast Foods at a time when further changes are planned, and concentrates on possible alterations to the balance between the centralization and decentralization of its industrial relations institutions. In particular, senior managers at Fast Foods are considering making changes to the levels at which collective agreements are made and industrial relations decisions are taken.

## Background to the Case

Until around three years ago, a senior personnel manager, based at head office, carried out the negotiations in all the plants (with the exception of Northumberland and Lincolnshire, which were not then part of the company). He visited each plant and negotiated with local shop stewards. The agreements made were unique to each plant, and unknown to managers and stewards in the other plants.

These arrangements were changed when the senior personnel manager left Fast Foods. The directors decided to strengthen the personnel function at both the head office and plant levels to improve the performance of the company by reforming the approach to industrial relations. Subsequently, two senior appointments were made, Guy Davies as Personnel Director, and David French as the company Industrial Relations Manager. Personnel managers were also appointed, where they did not already exist, in each of the plants. Negotiations were devolved to each plant and, with one exception, conducted by local managers. These plant agreements were formal and written and negotiated by the newly appointed plant personnel managers. Each plant was to take greater responsibility for its own actions.

However, plant bargaining was to take place within the constraints set by head office. Most importantly, head office issued a 'model' agreement that set the standard for all the plants.

The model included

- target pay increases for each group of employees;
- proposed changes to the make-up of total pay, including bonuses;
- targets for changes in conditions of employment, including sick pay; and
- costings on the proposed changes to the total wage bill.

In addition to this model, various other changes were introduced. An industrial relations manual was issued to each plant personnel manager giving guidance on how day-to-day issues should be handled. Meetings were called of all plant personnel managers to discuss issues of common interest. Information was circulated on current industrial relations policy and possible future changes. Advice and guidance were 'made available' at head office and plant personnel managers were expected to consult 'where appropriate'. David French, the Fast Foods Industrial Relations Manager, regularly visited the sites, and actually conducted pay negotiations at the Gloucestershire plant.

Under the new arrangements, pay and conditions agreements at each site were virtually the same even though they were negotiated separately. For example, pay rates for production workers on all the sites were within 1 per cent of those negotiated at Sussex, and differences in pay were attributed to special local circumstances. Holiday entitlements were common, and sick-pay arrangements virtually the same.

This situation existed not only because of the existence of the model agreement but also because of the links between the workplace representatives at each site. These links were strongest for the manual workers and centred on the Senior Production Steward at Sussex. He kept in close contact with the other stewards via the telephone, and acted as a clearing house for pay-and-conditions information. He collected information from each plant, collated it and then circulated it to all the stewards.

Although all the plants were moved to a common settlement date, November, in practice, the timing was different. Effectively, the Sussex plant made the master agreement that set the pattern for the others to follow. Negotiators often waited for Sussex to settle before they made their own agreement. Indeed, negotiations were often held up to await the outcome of a vote at Sussex, a situation that brought an element of unreality to the proceedings.

## The Problem

This pattern of bargaining worked well for the first year, but the strains began to tell in the second year. Some of the plant managers felt the system was too constraining and that company-level involvement was becoming a sensitive issue. They argued they had been given their independence and were held responsible for managing their plant, but felt they were not completely free to handle their industrial relations in the way they saw fit. Indeed, they feared their credibility could be undermined in the long term if they were seen to be at the beck and call of head office, and wanted a loosening of the ties. This issue came to a head as a result of the events described below at the Cheshire plant.

The Cheshire Plant Manager, Paul Johnson, was carrying out negotiations locally with the production workers' senior steward over pay and conditions. Johnson had taken charge of the negotiations because he was unhappy about the way his personnel manager had conducted last year's pay negotiations. He was very anxious to achieve an agreement since he was the last to settle and head office were keen to tie things up. In order to clinch the deal he made an offer to increase the holiday entitlement for those employees with long service. The steward found this attractive but would not commit himself, and asked, instead, for time to consult his members. Following this, Johnson rang French, the Industrial Relations Manager at head office, to check that all was well.

French told Johnson, 'You've stepped outside the brief, you can't do that, we'll have read-across all over the place ... you've got to take it back from them'.

Johnson refuted this forcefully, saying, 'This is the only way we can get a deal, and in any case what does it matter?'

French reminded Johnson that the model agreement had the Board's support and, eventually, after a 'frank exchange of words', Johnson agreed, under protest, to withdraw the offer.

In the next set of negotiations he told the steward he had made a mistake and withdrew the offer, with much loss of face. Immediately, the steward saw what had happened and started asking to see the 'organ grinder rather than the monkey'. He went on saying, 'this whole situation is a farce ... every time we have an adjournment you're on the phone asking what to do ... you can't even have a —— without asking'.

Johnson insisted, 'this plant is independent and must stand on its own two feet ... pay and conditions are based on what we can afford rather than what other plants get'.

The steward replied, 'You must be joking, you can't move an inch without their say so, we want a meeting with people from Head Office'.

Johnson replied, 'What purpose would that serve? We manage this plant, not them' and, for good measure, added, 'You should spend less time worrying about details like these and more time on getting a good deal for your members!'

This had the effect of making the steward think and, eventually, agreement was reached after Johnson made concessions on the timing of holidays.

The next day Johnson telephoned head office. He was furious and told French to 'get off my back ... leave me to run my business without your interference'. French replied that the plants were free to make their own settlements. 'Yes, free when you say so', replied Johnson, 'you can keep your so-called advice ... I'm going to solve my own problems in future'.

French was aware that Johnson was in a position of some influence since he knew the Managing Director of Fast Foods well and could count on his support for this kind of argument. On similar occasions in the past, the Managing Director had put pressure on Davies, the Personnel Director, to weaken the central ties. He also knew that while the Hertfordshire and Northumberland plant managers held the same views as Johnson, the remainder felt the current head-office role strengthened their position.

Those supporting Johnson argued that the head-office role became intrusive at critical times, such as during wage bargaining, and felt this threatened their authority on other matters. Indeed, the stewards became so sensitive to outside intervention that this actually restricted the role head office played in other areas. They believed they should have greater freedom, with the minimum of control from the centre, and were, in effect, saying 'give us the bag of money and let us deal it out', even to the extent of removing parity on grade rates.

The other plant managers argued that the head-office role was helpful. They claimed the model agreement and guidelines stopped anomalies appearing, but allowed for minor differences. Indeed, they believed that having Sussex settle first actually made it easier to negotiate their own agreement. In addition, they could argue to union negotiators that some issues, such as the grading structure, were 'sacred cows' that 'we dare not touch'. They also found head-office advice on employment legislation and other issues helpful and liked to draw on their experience when considering any 'knock-on' effects of changes they were making. Overall, they claimed the current system was basically working apart from a 'few mutterings and grumblings' at the time of wage negotiations. They were quite happy to continue with the current arrangements.

There were similar differences within the employees, and these were most noticeable among the manual shop stewards. Four sets of views existed. First, there were those who were very parochial with no real idea of the centre's role in industrial relations. In the words of the Dorset Senior Production Steward, 'My first priority is to the people who elected me ... I'm not concerned about what's happening 50 or 100 miles away ... in any case there's not much brotherly love in this company'.

Indeed, some stewards, for example in the Northumberland plant, quite enjoyed being king, or queen, of their own particular castle and, like the Gloucestershire stewards, argued 'We're getting the best of both worlds ... we're getting the same as Sussex and we're negotiating locally'. Bargaining comparisons were made internally, for example at the Lincolnshire plant, between maintenance engineers, production workers and drivers.

This group were quite content to allow the current arrangements to continue as long as they did not receive less than Sussex. However, they were astute enough to realize that a shift to genuinely independent plant bargaining would probably leave them worse off, because of their relative lack of negotiating experience and bargaining muscle. If there was to be a change they would not be averse to a move towards company-wide bargaining to safeguard their interests.

A second view was that head office had a role to play in industrial relations, but that this was less than it was two or three years ago because local factors were now more important. In the words of the Hertfordshire Senior Production Steward, 'They're much freer now than they were a few years ago. Once, the same bloke used to do all the negotiating, but not any more. We look after ourselves now'. Experiences of this kind meant they were very reluctant to give back any of their new-found freedom by moving to company-level bargaining.

A third, small group had a clear idea of what was going on and, for them, company-level intervention was a very sensitive issue. Stewards at Cheshire resented the role played by head office and argued that, if the current arrangements continued, 'we want to talk to the guy who's pulling the strings, not his puppet'. If there was to be a change they wanted plants to become genuinely free, feeling confident they had the ability to negotiate a good deal for themselves. At Sussex, however, the Senior Production Steward was not pressing for a change, even though he knew better than most what was going on. The current arrangements gave him considerable power, power that would probably decline under either company bargaining or plant bargaining in a different form.

A final small group of stewards were volatile and unpredictable. They used any argument they could in order to get the best deal for their membership. For example, the Hertfordshire drivers used local pay arguments to make gains, but were not afraid to make comparisons with Sussex if they felt it would help their case.

## Case Study Tasks

This case provides examples of the issues surrounding the determination and change of bargaining and decision-making institutions within a multi-plant organization. It is particularly concerned with the levels at which agreements and decisions are made. The task involves examining the causes of the problems, considering alternative arrangements for industrial relations and putting forward proposals for change.

Imagine you have been called in by the board of Fast Foods to give advice on possible future changes to their industrial relations institutions.

Consider the following questions:

1.  Why have the problems described emerged?
2.  What are some of the possible different collective bargaining arrangements, and what are the advantages and drawbacks associated with these?
3.  What actions might be taken by line and personnel managers at the head office and in the plants to control industrial relations under these different collective bargaining arrangements?
4.  When making your recommendations consider the following:

    (a)  What changes would you make and why?
    (b)  How might you introduce these changes?
    (c)  What difficulties would you expect to encounter when making these changes?
    (d)  How might you overcome these difficulties?

This case can also be used as a role-play exercise. Using this method, a 'live' debate is set up between students role playing presenters/consultants to the company and line and personnel managers from the head office and plants in Fast Foods. Further details of this teaching method and an extensive set of detailed role-play briefs can be found in the *Teacher's Manual*.

## Essential Reading

IPM (1990) *Determining Pay: A Guide to the Issues*, London.

Kinnie, N. J. (1985) Local managers' control over industrial relations: myth and reality, *Personnel Review*, Vol. 14, no. 2, pp. 2–10.

Marginson, P., Edwards, P. K., Martin, R., Purcell, J. and Sisson, K. (1988) *Beyond the Workplace. Managing Industrial Relations in the Multi-Establishment Enterprise*, Blackwell, Oxford.

Marginson, P., Edwards, P. K., Purcell, J. and Sisson, K. (1988) What do corporate head offices really do?, *British Journal of Industrial Relations*, Vol. 26, no. 2, pp. 229–46.

## Additional Reading

ACAS (1983) *Collective Bargaining in Britain: Its Level and Extent (Discussion Paper No. 2)*, London.

Edwards, P. (1987) Factory managers: their role in personnel management and their place in the company, *Journal of Management Studies*, Vol. 24, no. 5, pp. 479–501.

Kinnie, N. J. (1983) Single employer bargaining: structures and strategies, *Industrial Relations Journal*, Vol. 14, no. 3, pp. 76–81.

Kinnie, N. J. (1987) Bargaining within the enterprise: centralized or decentralized?, *Journal of Management Studies*, Vol. 24, no. 5, pp. 463–77.

Marchington, M. (1990) Unions of the margin, *Employee Relations*, Vol. 12, no. 5, pp. 1–24.

Marchington, M. and Parker, P. (1990) *Changing Patterns of Employee Relations*, Harvester, Brighton.

Winkler, J. (1974) The ghost at the bargaining table, *British Journal of Industrial Relations*, Vol. 12, no. 2, pp. 191–212.

# PART III

## Developing Cultures
## of Quality in the
## Service Sector

# CASE 10

## Culture and Commitment: British Airways

### Heather Hopfl

## Organizational Setting

At the beginning of the 1980s British Airways faced serious difficulties. In the financial year 1981–2, financial journalists claimed the airline was losing money at the rate of £200 per minute. It was confronting a serious downturn in the market. Moreover, the over-staffing that had resulted from the dissolution of the distinction between the British Overseas Airways Corporation (BOAC) and the British European Airways Division (BEA) had not been resolved. The organization had a bureaucratic style of management, damaging industrial relations and a poor reputation for customer service. The Conservative government sought to privatize the airline and, under the direction of Lord King, the newly appointed Chairman, a dramatic turn-around was initiated. There was a drastic reduction in staff numbers from 60,000 to 38,000. This was achieved by a combination of voluntary severance and natural wastage. Unprofitable routes were abandoned and surplus assets, particularly aircraft, were sold off. Within two years the strategy had brought the airline into profit but, in order to ensure this was maintained, the board recognized that a radical change was needed in the way the organization worked. Primarily, it was thought that the airline needed to shift from being operationally driven to being market led.

Significant reductions in costs were achieved but the airline was finding it increasingly difficult to compete on the basis of cost alone. Moreover, many costs, such as aviation fuel and airport charges, were outside the company's control. Customer service was seen as 'the critical factor that could give a competitive edge but could not be easily duplicated' (Bruce, 1987, p. 21). Colin Marshall, who was appointed Chief Executive of British Airways in February 1983, recognized the problems as those of an organization that had become demoralized and that lacked any real appreciation of what the customer wanted. Marshall saw the need 'to create some motivational vehicle with the employees ... [to raise] their morale, and in turn ... customer service' (Young, 1989, p. 3). Marshall believed in visible management and his personal style reflected this. There is a story in the airline about how Marshall demonstrated this on the first day of the new Super Shuttle service when hot breakfasts and newspapers were provided for the first time. With huge queues building up at the desks and no relief or assistance forthcoming from the supervisory grades, Marshall rolled up his sleeves and began to help (*ibid.*). His senior managers were given specific goals and expected to achieve them. At all levels, he emphasized individual responsibility and risk-taking.

In the cost-cutting of the early 1980s, training in British Airways had been cut back. In March 1983, Marshall announced, 'We may need to put people through refresher courses to really concentrate on teaching staff how to sell the airline and its services'. Eventually, this led to a campaign that became known as 'Putting the Customer First'. Passenger research followed and, in November 1983, an event, 'Putting People First' (PPF) was held. The event sought to bolster self-esteem. It said, 'if you feel OK about yourself you are more likely to feel OK about dealing with other people'. It was an enormous campaign. It aimed to put 12,000 customer-contact staff, in groups of 150–200, through a two-day course in the newly renovated Concorde Centre. Over the two days the staff experienced a range of exercises, group discussions and presentations. They were given the opportunity to review their experiences of dealing with customers:

> They were introduced to concepts of setting personal goals and of taking responsibility for getting what they wanted out of life. There were confidence-building exercises ... simple techniques of behaviour modification were also taught to help staff to develop new approaches to dealing with upsets, coping with stress and developing a more positive attitude to themselves.
>
> (Young, 1989, p. 7)

The importance of the PPF programme was in what it said about management attitudes and intentions. It represented a considerable investment of time and money and gave force to the notion of service. It tried to provide an 'emotional context' for people to respond to and to change. There was, apparently, a great deal of cynicism in the first few weeks, but after about two months this had disappeared. 'PPF, and the recognition by the highest levels of management of the importance of staff that it communicated, had a strong effect, both on the level of cynicism and on the needs of the non-front line staff to "belong" to what was going on' (*ibid.*).

A further aspect of PPF was that staff became actively involved in developing ideas for improving customer service. Customer First Teams, using the techniques of quality circles, were formed in many departments across the airline. Profit sharing encouraged staff to have a stake in the company's future. Two significant events occurred in 1984. A new corporate identity was introduced and Nick Georgiades was appointed Human Resources Director. This heralded a fundamental change in what had previously been the personnel department. Administrative procedures formerly attached to the personnel role were handed over to line management. The extent to which Nick Georgiades was responsible for all such changes is open to question, but human resource management was to take on a considerable role in supporting and nurturing organizational change.

All human resource management staff were offered a week-long residential programme, which focused on consultancy skills in the context of change.

Initially, the changes that took place in the airline were directed at improving customer service but it was recognized that managers needed to alter their style if they were to support the change programme effectively. The dominant style of the organization was seen to be bureaucratic with an emphasis on the rationality and dependability of the system. In 1985, however, a week-long residential programme for managers was introduced: 'Managing People First'. This was originally targeted at middle managers but was later extended to junior managers and supervisory grades. The programme directed the organization towards a more open, visible and dynamic approach to management. It sought to underscore a number of key themes. These were urgency, vision, motivation, trust and taking responsibility. These themes were reinforced by the course activities and rhetoric. 'Managing People First' ran for five years and, during that time, 2,000 managers attended the course. At the same time, the culture change programme was sustained by a number of interventions throughout the 1980s. PPF, and 'Managing People First' concentrated on the individual but, in November 1985, a third major corporate programme was launched, 'A Day in the Life'. The purpose of this intervention was to give emphasis to the benefits of collaborative working. The programme consisted of ten presentations characterizing all aspects of work across the airline. It was designed to give staff a greater appreciation of the function and operation of the principal departments in order to break down some of the trans-functional barriers that exist in large organizations. Unlike PPF, this event was run entirely by British Airways staff for British Airways staff. In every programme, a significant feature was the appearance of the Chief Executive or one of the directors to endorse the commitment of top management to the programme.

In 1986 Terminal 4 was opened at London Heathrow Airport and a new British Airways advertising campaign was launched to raise the public visibility of the airline. 1987 saw the privatization of British Airways and higher-than-expected pre-tax profits for shareholders. In order to sustain the commitment and achievement of the staff, 'To Be The Best' was launched in 1987 against a background of growing competition. This reinforced the message of the importance of the service ethic and of pride in the company's achievements. The year 1988 saw the merger of British Airways with British Caledonian, with the attendant problems of cultural reconciliation.

Staff surveys and customer feedback suggest that these initiatives have had a considerable impact on the culture of the organization and this impression is reinforced by financial results, which have been substantial and impressive. Even in the post-Lockerbie period, the Gulf War and serious economic recession, British Airways have been able to demonstrate a commendable ability to remain in or to return to profit.

However, the reaction to the past decade of change has not all been positive. Some staff found it difficult to reconcile the values promoted by the culture change with their experiences in the workplace. There was some frustration and disillusionment as a result of the conflicts between caring values and profits, and between espoused values and the need for workplace expediency. The emotionally charged programmes of the 1980s have now been superseded by more commercially focused and strategic programmes, such as the 'Fit for Business' programme launched in 1989. At the same time, the theme of caring for the individual and corporate pride has been carried forward. In 1992 a new suite of programmes is to be introduced to revitalize and augment the change programme.

## The Problem

The scene is a new art-deco-style hotel just off the M4 and within a fifteen-mile radius of Heathrow Airport. It is 8.30 a.m. and a group of about thirty middle managers have arrived for a three-day workshop, 'Visioning the Future'. In the conference room the trainers are busy adjusting their equipment, making sure their speakers are properly positioned, checking the large screen and playing with the lights. This event requires a level of stage management that would not be unfamiliar to a touring rock-band. Outside in the lounge area the participants are milling around drinking coffee and waiting for the workshop to begin. One of the trainers stands at the door to ensure that no one gets in early to 'spoil' the experience. Nine o'clock. The doors to the conference room are opened and the managers are ushered in. From the speakers the opening music from 'Also sprach Zarathustra', the 'Fanfare for Common Man', blasts out a triumphal welcome. People find their seats and focus their attention on the large screen. The lights dim and the corporate logo appears before them. Three days of management development have begun.

Somewhere in the darkness, Mike Riley, Flight Crew Scheduling Manager, turned to Deborah Davies, Cabin Crew Training, and whispered, 'I think I've seen all this somewhere before'.

'Yes, the Live Aid Concert, I think. It's all Save the World stuff ... British Airways togetherness ... like Coca Cola.' Deborah gave Mike a knowing but invisible smile. 'Well, yes, but I meant on one of the earlier programmes – Making it Happen, We Can Be Heroes, We are the Champions ... something like that'. Mike turned back to the screen. At that moment a Concorde was taking off towards them and the music soared with it. 'You can't help it, you know, it definitely makes you feel proud to work for a company like this – it just gets you right there'. Mike patted his chest in the region of the heart. Deborah gave him a sidelong glance. She was not quite sure whether he was serious or not.

'I wonder if all those who left the company earlier this year feel like that,' she said cuttingly, 'I'll ask you again in the break.' In the one and a half hours of images, music and uplift that followed, Deborah's mind was torn between the evident sense of pride she felt working for such a successful company and an uncomfortable feeling that her emotions were being played on in a rather manipulative way.

At coffee time, Deborah made a point of finding Mike to ask him what he made of 'all the corporate hype'. 'Are you really taken in by it all?' she asked uneasily. 'Do you remember that thing we had on one of the early programmes, I can't remember now which one – there seem to have been so many – but I think it was called "The Love Bath" or something like that. I remember it sounded very "hippy" and I was embarrassed to tell my husband about it when I got home.'

Mike pondered for a second and then smiled, 'Oh God, yes. It was dreadful. It was excruciating. Can you remember it? "The Love Bath", is that what it was? It was supposed to make you feel better about yourself. It was embarrassing. We all had to sit round in a circle – groups of us – and each of us in turn had to sit in the middle. It was really humiliating. Then everybody in turn had to say something nice about the person in the middle. It was dreadful, it makes me cringe just to think of it. Sometimes the only thing you could think of saying was "Nice Jumper, Jim". It was unbelievable – so unEnglish. One day I got back to the office and I was telling an American woman who was working with us what had gone on. She just looked at me in amazement and said, "Say, why don't you just tell these guys to f—— off!"'

Gillian Roper, a Purchasing Manager in her early 30s, had come over to join them. She listened to Mike's remarks and laughed. 'Come off it!' she sneered. 'It was wonderful. One of the best experiences of my life. If you're trying to tell me that things were better before you must be joking. If it weren't for the changes, I'd have been gone long ago. Can you really remember how miserable it was in those days? We were abysmal at customer service and arrogant. Nobody understood the business or what anybody else did. The public were made to feel we were doing them a favour if they chose to fly with us. I don't think I'd ever met an engineer let alone anyone from flight crew. "Managing People First" was a tremendous opportunity and it gave everyone the chance to meet other managers with similar problems and to talk through ways of motivating people. When I came back from that programme I felt as if I'd seen the light. I knew the company was committed to change and would support managers who were prepared to take risks. It was a new approach and I honestly don't like to hear you talking like this. There's no place for cynicism if you want to bring about change and you've got to admit we needed change ...'

Mike admired Gillian. She was a natural enthusiast and enjoyed a good relationship with her staff and the other people on the course. 'Look, I know you felt like that and I know that a lot of other people did as well but, you know, there were other people who were far from happy with the changes and, in particular, the style of the changes. I mean, at the end of the day, it was all about increasing motivation and commitment not about making us "better" people. I'm glad you're more motivated and committed but don't you accept that a lot of this – like this morning – is just evangelism. I don't mind putting myself out for the Church, but for BA? Well, it's asking a bit much! I've worked for this company now for nearly twelve years and I've seen the whole lot. I can't say it actually makes me feel more committed. You know, sometimes over the past few years, especially with "visible management", I've felt quite the reverse. It's caused quite a few rows at home. My wife says she never sees me these days – into the office before seven in the morning sometimes not home until nine or ten in the evening. Your husband works for the airline so you know what it's like. You have the same compromises to make.'

'As a matter of fact so do I,' this time it was Deborah who spoke. 'I'm 32 now. I feel I'm getting a bit old but Bob and I still want to start a family. I'm afraid that once I go out on maternity leave I'll never get back and, well, there's the money. I'm not sure I can afford to give up work. It's a terrible dilemma and yet it's not one that can be deferred forever. The company says a lot about encouraging people to consider the family and it claims that it does a lot for women, but I just don't trust that message. I feel I'll be up the creek if I do decide to take maternity leave.'

'That's nonsense and paranoia.' Gillian's response was ardent. 'You are the company – who are all these people that you seem to be afraid of? You do what you want. Don't invent a corporate demon to justify your own apprehensions. The message of all these programmes has been: take responsibility for your own actions.'

'The Demon King,' Mike looked at the others for approval, 'Lord King – get it? – corporate demon.' The approval was not forthcoming. 'In fairness,' Mike continued, to retrieve the situation, 'no one ever said that the culture-change programme was philanthropic. At every turn we were told that the company needed to change to survive. "Putting People First" is just good business practice. It is important that if we want to keep our jobs, we understand the basis of the business, and customer service is a significant part of that. But, as far as taking personal responsibility or risks is concerned, the message isn't borne out by what we all see happening every day on the job. We talk about caring but I see bullies who are very successful. We talk about risk but you try it. I'd be scared enough about making a genuine mistake – I can't see me taking risks and surviving. We talk about valuing the individual and recognizing that people have domestic lives but, in honesty, who does? I'm never at home. Having said that, I honestly don't think anyone was taken in by the culture change. I mean, sometimes when you read some of the things that have been written about it, it sounds like *The Thoughts of Chairman King* and if you believe the sociologists, we're all incredibly gullible and have a pretty moronic level of tolerance to all the corporate messages. I've never felt like that. I do have reservations about the ways in which the change programme was conducted but, on the other hand, the type of change we needed was fairly radical. I hated a lot of the "touchy-feely" stuff and, if it achieved anything, it gave me the experience of shared humiliation rather than shared self-esteem – but we all had that cosy feeling of having survived something together and there's something to be said for that.'

'Yes, but your point about the conflicts with home life, what about the "Fit for Business" programme? What about the posters – they were a bit of a joke, weren't they? I mean, mountaineering, canoeing. Brian said a guy snoring in front of the late-night film would be more like his personal experience at the end of a long day.' Gillian Roper laughed at her own mental picture of getting fit for business.

'The thing that gets me,' Deborah interjected, 'is the fact that we've just shed about four and a half thousand jobs in the early part of '91 and I wonder how those people who have left the company feel about values and caring. It can't say much to them, can it? What price commitment and loyalty when the chips are down? It's all about money or at least survival at the end of the day. Caring about people and making them feel good about themselves is pretty hypocritical in the face of the so-called "outplacements".'

'The company comes first, Deb – these are necessary sacrifices. Would you have preferred to go instead? Gillian gave Deborah a steely look. 'There were a lot of things that were outside the company's control – the Gulf War, for example. What can you expect?'

Deborah was not going to give way on this one. 'Well, yes, but it did give the company a wonderful opportunity for radical surgery as far as getting rid of staff is concerned.'

'Union consultation, generous pay-offs, an Advice and Support Centre, professional advisers and consultants up to six months after a person had left the company. How many companies would go that far? BA's a good company. Name a better one.' Gillian Roper folded her arms and looked squarely at Deborah and Mike.

'It's as I said,' Mike drew the conversation to a close, 'I think that although individuals felt bad about the cuts and may even have felt betrayed, in the main most people I've spoken to – whether they were leaving or staying – felt that the relationship between commitment and values was never such a big issue. We know it's hype – they know its hype. It's okay. It's reassuring. It makes you feel good. But do I believe in it – well that's a totally different question.'

In the conference room the chairs and tables were being rearranged. After the coffee break one of the trainers was running a session on 'Facing up to feedback'. It was to be a long day.

## Case Study Tasks

Imagine you have just been appointed to a new post in human resource management in British Airways. You are asked, with the benefit of hindsight, to review and evaluate the changes of the past ten years and to assess the extent to which desired outcomes were achieved and maintained. The questions and references below are intended to help you to locate your ideas in a theoretical framework and to help you to focus on some of the key issues.

Questions 1–4 are suitable for seminar discussion (one hour) and question 5 is intended to be written up as an essay of about 3,000 words after further personal research and reading.

1. What do you think were the 'desired outcomes' of the culture-change programme in British Airways?
2. What do you see as the main issues in the discussion between Mike, Deborah and Gillian? What views, if any, do they hold in common and

what are the chief differences in their perspectives? What does this suggest about employee behaviour?

3. Views are expressed about conflicts in work and in the relationship between work and non-work life. What are the main areas of conflict and are these alleviated or exacerbated by culture-change programmes?

4. Can the values of the corporate culture–change be reconciled with redundancies? Is Deborah right in suggesting it is hypocrisy or Mike in contending that it is not an issue?

5. To what extent would it be true to say that culture-change programmes change appearances and promote conformity but do not affect the inner experience of employees?

## Essential Reading

Anthony, P. D. (1989) The paradox of the management of culture or 'He who leads is lost', *Personnel Review*, Vol. 19, no. 4, pp. 3–8.

Pascale, R. (1985) The paradox of 'corporate culture': reconciling ourselves to socialization, *California Management Review*, Vol. XXVII, no. 2, pp. 26–41.

Ray, C. A. (1986) Corporate culture: the last frontier of control, *Journal of Management Studies*, Vol. 23, no. 3, pp. 287–97.

Smircich, L. and Morgan, G. (1982) Leadership: the management of meaning, *Journal of Applied Behavioural Science*, Vol. 18, no. 3, pp. 257–73.

## Additional Reading

Ackroyd, S. and Crowdy, P. (1989) Can culture be managed? Working with 'raw' material: the case of the English slaughtermen, *Personnel Review*, Vol. 19, no. 5, pp. 3–13.

Bruce, M. (1987) Managing people first – bringing the service concept into British Airways, *Industrial and Commercial Training*, March/April, pp. 21–6.

Hopfl, H. J. (1992) The making of the corporate acolyte, *Journal of Management Studies*, Vol. 29, no. 1, January, pp. 23–33.

Hopfl, H. J., Smith, S. and Spencer, S. (1992) Values and valuations: corporate culture and job cuts, *Personnel Review*, Vol. 21, no. 1, pp. 24–38.

Kirkbride, P. S. (1987) Personnel management and organizational culture: a case of deviant innovation?, *Personnel Review*, Vol. 16, no. 1, pp. 3–9.

Lorsch, J. W. (1985) Managing culture: the invisible barrier to strategic change, in R. H. Kilmann, M. J. Saxton, R. Serpa and associates (eds.) *Gaining Control of the Corporate Culture*, Jossey-Bass, San Francisco, Calif.

Schein, E. H. (1984) Coming to a new awareness of organizational culture, *Sloan Management Review*, Winter, pp. 3–16.

Schein, E. H. (1985) *Organizational Culture and Leadership: A Dynamic View*, Jossey-Bass, San Francisco, Calif.

Smircich, L. (1983) Concepts of culture and organizational analysis, *Administrative Science Quarterly*, Vol. 28, pp. 339–58.

Waterman, R. H. (1988) *The Renewal Factor*, Bantam Books, New York, NY.

Willmott, H. (1993) Strength is ignorance; slavery is freedom: managing culture in modern organizations, *Journal of Management Studies*, Vol. 30, no. 5.

Young, D. (1989) *British Airways: Putting the Customer First*, Ashridge Strategic Management Centre, July.

## Acknowledgement

Heather Hopfl is indebted to Sheila Smith, HR Development Consultant, British Airways, for her advice and contribution to the historical aspects of the case study and to Shirley Rae, British Airways, for her comments on an earlier draft.

(Note that the material presented in the case problem itself is fictitious and does not relate to an actual course run by British Airways or to actual comments made by British Airways staff.)

## CASE 11

# Culture Change and Quality Improvement in British Rail

*David E. Guest, Riccardo Peccei and Amanda Fulcher*

## Background to the Case

Like many other organizations, British Rail has been trying to change its culture. There are a number of features of the kind of organization British Rail is hoping to become, but one consistent theme is the need to improve the quality of service provided to both internal and external customers. There has therefore been a major investment in programmes to improve quality. However this is only one of a number of changes underway in British Rail as it responds to market pressures and, more especially, to the government's drive for greater cost effectiveness and better quality of service.

British Rail has always been a highly centralized formal bureaucracy. This has been reflected in a complex and extensive hierarchy, considerable attention to rules and regulations and a rather rigid, autocratic style of management. This does not sit easily with the typical approach to quality improvement, which emphasizes greater flexibility, considerable devolvement of responsibility to those who interact with customers and therefore encouragement of local initiative, perhaps through a sense of empowerment. If this logic is pursued, British Rail has to change both the attitudes and behaviour of its staff, long used to a hierarchical system of control, and change the system of control.

The system of control has been changing. For many years British Rail had a powerful headquarters organization, six geographical regions, a number of divisions within the regions and a number of areas within the divisions. At all levels within the organization there were a number of powerful functional hierarchies for engineering, finance, operations and personnel management. In the 1980s, this system was overlaid by a marketing structure, including, for example, InterCity and Network South-East while the divisional level was removed.

A further reorganization, completed during 1991, has moved British Rail towards a kind of holding company for a number of businesses. These businesses include Network South-East, which is responsible for almost all passenger traffic within the South East of England; InterCity, which operates main-line trains throughout the country; Regional Rail, which operates suburban and rural routes throughout the country other than the South East; and Railfreight, which is responsible for movement of goods in wagons. The reorganization, which was called 'Organizing for Quality' in an attempt to maintain a general focus on quality, reintroduced divisions instead of regions. Therefore, for example, the Southern Region has disappeared and been replaced by three divisions, known as the South-East, Central and South-West Divisions. Each divisional manager has considerable autonomy over railway operations within a defined budget.

One of the important elements of the reorganization has been the appointment of an infrastructure manager within each division. He is responsible for all aspects of engineering. This may help to bring together the previously highly autonomous groups of civil, mechanical and signals and telecommunications engineers. The importance of this is reflected in the fact that 45 per cent of operating costs are attributable to infrastructure. Equally important, the reorganization attempts to remove the traditional power bases of the regions and the functions, representing operating and professional power, and to subordinate these to the 'business' of Network South-East.

The reorganization, like those before it, has been highly disruptive, involving thousands of job changes, and has absorbed a great deal of time and energy. It is only one of a number of changes designed to make the railway more business-like in the possible lead up to privatization. Preparations for Channel Tunnel operations have provided an additional competing priority for some senior managers. The aftermath of the Clapham disaster, in which many passengers died following a signalling maintenance failure, has been more widely felt. It has necessitated a major focus on safety including tightening up of procedures and an attempt to reduce hours of overtime work. This in turn has implications for a range of human resource policies ranging from selection and training to work rostering and reward systems. In the midst of all these changes, the onset of economic recession in 1990 created additional pressures for British Rail as for many other organizations.

As noted above, the use of the term 'Organizing for Quality' reflected a deliberate attempt to give coherence and direction to the variety of changes underway within the railway. The increased attention to safety can also be fitted comfortably under the rubric of quality. Perhaps the key integrating factor, and the main pressure for quality improvement, has been the move towards greater commercialization and the recognition that, if British Rail is to sell a service in a competitive market, that service must improve in quality. Certainly that message has been picked up by its competitors, such as the airlines and the motor industry.

When the concept of quality is discussed in British Rail, it means first and foremost improving quality of service to external customers. As market research has shown, for passengers this means a clean and comfortable service running on time and operated by polite and helpful staff. However, to meet the needs of external customers, the needs of a whole host of internal customers have to be considered and additional factors, of which external customers may be only dimly aware, must also be taken into account. These include the maintenance of the infrastructure, such as track and signalling, the complex co-ordination of weekend repair work and the quality of personnel systems to monitor and control absenteeism. On a railway that has generally been starved of investment, much attention has to be paid to these 'hidden' factors before it is possible to have a major impact on quality of service as defined by external customers.

While the reorganization provides a framework within which to improve quality, the main method of obtaining quality improvements has been through training, the intention being to use training on a massive scale to change the attitudes and behaviour of staff. This was initially channelled through a centrally organized training programme known as 'Leadership 500'. This was a week-long off-the-job training course for the top-500 managers in the whole of British Rail. These courses were followed by 'Leadership 5000'. These were training programmes for the next 5,000 senior and middle managers. Both courses gave some emphasis to experiential learning through analysis of re-lationships and problem-solving styles. In addition, 'Leadership 500' provided top management with an insight into total quality management (TQM), and explored company-wide strategies for its implementation. 'Leadership 5000' focused more on local strategies for implementing TQM and also gave more emphasis to problem-solving skills. Furthermore, the organization and im-plementation was delegated initially to the five British Rail regions.

The training programme for nearly 1,000 Southern Region managers was virtually complete when the regions were abolished in April 1991. Responsibility for the final courses and for all subsequent quality improvement programmes passed to the businesses that, in the case of almost all managers who had worked in the Southern Region, meant Network South-East.

The organization and implementation of the quality programmes, initially in each region and subsequently in business units, was the responsibility of a team of quality managers, largely appointed from within British Rail. The training was conducted by external consultants chosen by the region and business unit. On Southern Region the officially stated aim of the course was 'to introduce into the Region both the principles and practices of Total Quality Management'. This was achieved through a series of inputs and exercises designed to inculcate an awareness of the importance of TQM and provide the competencies necessary to act to improve quality. According to the official statement, managers should leave the programme with

- a clear set of objectives in relation to TQM
- a strategic action plan that involves all employees
- the confidence and competencies to implement the plan.

It was expected that by the end of the whole programme there would be 'an observable improvement in the Quality of service provided within the Region to both Internal and External Customers'.

These courses were run on a regular basis over a period of 18 months and were completed by mid-1991. Evidence from end-of-course reactions and from subsequent follow-up discussions indicates that the training programme was highly regarded by participants. As noted above in the statement of course outcomes, course teams were expected to develop programmes to improve quality in their work areas. The course teams were led by quite senior functional managers who had already attended 'Leadership 500'. These functional managers were team leaders for their immediate subordinates in their sections. Often this meant a team of about six managers. Where there were 12 to 14 managers reporting to the same boss, as occasionally happened, they would be split into two teams. Some teams not only drew up general programmes but also identified a specific quality-improvement project. Sometimes these led to the formation of a formal quality improvement team to pursue the project when they had returned to their workplaces. Whether a specific project was actually taken up after the course seemed to depend partly on the reaction of senior management in the area and partly on the level of enthusiasm of members of the potential team.

A fairly typical example of how this was interpreted and acted upon by a course team is a small plant project. This project examined the use of small hand-held power tools, such as saws, drills and impact wrenches, by the Permanent Way Department, which is responsible for maintaining the track. Traditionally, these had been supplied to the Permanent Way Department by the Regional Engineer's Plant Section. The 'Leadership 5000' team decided to look at this customer–supplier relationship. During the course they devised a system whereby the Permanent Way Department hired the equipment directly from the external supplier, thus reducing overall plant holdings and improving service. Authority to proceed with this project was subsequently given by senior local management and a quality improvement team was set up, after the training course, to implement the plan.

While the courses were still in progress, and as part of the activity to promote quality, the quality managers on Southern Region decided to hold a quality fair. In this it was following a pattern adopted by such organizations as Rank Xerox with a well-established reputation for quality improvement. A quality fair is an exhibition at which those responsible for quality projects display the projects, usually through a combination of media and sometimes including models and demonstrations, and explain them to an invited audience. The fair may last from half a day to three days. There were several advantages in holding a quality fair. It provided an opportunity to monitor the quality improvement projects that should have emerged from the training programme. It would make managers at all levels more aware of the issue of quality – in some cases it would prick their consciences and perhaps goad them into action if they had been slow to follow up their training. The successful cases would provide models and lessons for others to emulate. It should reward, enthuse and motivate those who had undertaken successful projects by providing praise, recognition and an opportunity to explain to an interested audience what they had achieved. And finally, it was useful publicity both within British Rail and with a wider audience of the progress British Rail was making in improving quality.

The fair was held in November 1990. (It should be borne in mind that while the reorganization described earlier, which would abolish Southern Region, was in the offing, at the time of the fair Southern Region still existed and was responsible for managing the quality programme.) Thirty-five exhibits were presented, a large number of senior executives attended and the exercise was judged to be a considerable success. The exhibits ranged from those publicizing the staff-suggestion scheme (called 'On Winning Lines') and those dealing with the trackside environment, including how to make it attractive, maintain visibility and care for flora and fauna, to more technical issues of track care and rolling stock and train maintenance. The co-ordinating group of quality managers within British Rail had decided to hold a national quality fair and those attending this Southern Region fair were asked to judge which exhibits they thought were the most successful and should therefore go forward to the national fair.

## The Problem

As part of a wider evaluation of the impact of the quality programme, it was decided to look more closely at those projects that had been judged the most successful by those attending the fair. It was thought that some general lessons about the way in which these projects had originated and been implemented might emerge. Ten highly rated projects from six locations were selected for closer inspection. The aim was to identify how the projects originated, what outcomes had emerged in terms of discernible quality improvements and other benefits, and how the process of change and implementation was handled.

There was considerable variety of project. One sought to produce a Filofax for supervisors. Another was concerned to devise new ways of dealing with graffiti. Two looked at ways of providing improved training. Another explored a specific computer link. Finally, three were concerned with the development of systems that would attract BS 5750, the British Standards quality accreditation based on the writing and monitoring of procedures to ensure quality. It is perhaps worth emphasizing that several of the projects focused on the development of processes to monitor quality rather than on substantive quality issues.

### The Origins of the Projects

Four of the projects emerged directly from the local quality training programmes, but five had been initiated by more senior managers and one by an outside organization. This occurred despite the intention to use the quality fair to follow up the training. One partial explanation is that some of the projects ostensibly presented as follow-ups to the training were put together hurriedly when the request for participation in the fair was issued and reflected an obligation to show some sort of training follow-up rather than any deep commitment to the project.

### The Outcomes of the Projects

All the projects were successful to the extent that they had developed solutions that had been accepted as feasible by senior management. Authorization to proceed with implementation had been given in eight of the ten projects and six had actually been implemented. All of the implemented projects were judged by senior management to be successful in improving quality. The concrete evidence to support this claim could not be provided in most cases, partly because this was the first attempt at systematic evaluation. On the other hand supervisory and junior management staff, while generally positive, were rather less enthusiastic about the outcomes, largely because the projects for which they felt particular ownership had often made little progress. They remained very positive towards the general idea of improving quality but felt let down in particular by poor communications, lack of resources and especially the lack of senior management support.

## The Process of Change

Comparing the projects that were and were not implemented at the time of the fair, the key factor appears to be the process of authorization by senior management and the requirement for some sort of feasibility study. Three of the implemented projects entailed achievement of BS 5750 certificates for particular procedures. Although another was a very specific computer link, it does appear the projects concerned with developing processes and procedures had a greater chance of success than those dealing with more concrete topics. In contrast, the four non-implemented projects have run up against delays within the bureaucracy, usually related to resource shortages and the need to determine priorities, and have fallen victim to poor communication and a lack of urgency. One, for example, has been in train for 18 months and is still at the early-trials stage.

All the non-implemented projects originated in the training programmes. In contrast, the implemented projects were all devised by senior management. There appears to be a link between the source from which the project originated and the speed of authorization and implementation. It may well be that senior managers more wisely identify and select projects with a better chance of implementation. However, far and away the most highly rated project at the quality fair was one emerging from training and it is one that has not been authorized for implementation. The graffiti project originated at a 'Leadership 5000' course and was handed on to a voluntary team of staff to develop and implement. They conducted an extensive survey of all interested parties to diagnose the problem and spoke to all those who had to deal with it including police, contractors and chemical companies. They tested out for themselves various chemicals and various approaches to cleaning graffiti. They took extensive photographs and videos of the results and compiled detailed statistics and graphs. In conducting such a detailed and enthusiastic analysis, they went well beyond their brief. Presentations were made to their steering group, to their colleagues and to the general manager. Despite an apparently compelling case, reflected in support for the project at the quality fair, authorization to proceed with implementation had not been received.

Evidence from the evaluation of the projects raises some questions about the training. On the one hand it is resulting in some promising and highly rated projects; but the projects are facing difficulty in being implemented. On the other hand, quality is clearly on the managerial agenda and a number of encouraging initiatives are being undertaken. However, their chances of success, judged by implementation, are greater if they originate and are controlled and implemented within the traditional bureaucratic hierarchy.

## Case Study Tasks

You are a consultant retained on a long-term basis to advise Network South-East on its quality improvement programme.

1.  On the basis of the information you have here, would you tell Network South-East that training has been a success? What are the criteria you would use to judge success?
2.  They intend to cascade the training down to supervisory levels and eventually to all staff. Would you advise them to proceed with this? If yes, what changes in emphasis should they consider? If not, how should they proceed instead if they wish to change the attitude and behaviour of staff to result in a better quality of service?
3.  If British Rail were to proceed with quality training for ground-level staff, how would you conduct an evaluation of that training and what issues would you focus on?
4.  One of the difficulties facing the quality initiative in British Rail is that so many other changes are going on that there is a risk of quality being squeezed out. How can this be resolved? (Bear in mind the possibility that the other changes will be more or less continuous for the foreseeable future.)
5.  Does the evidence of the success of the hierarchically initiated quality projects in British Rail throw doubt upon the case for greater delegation and empowerment of junior staff? What would you advise British Rail in this respect?

## Essential Reading

Bramley, P. (1991) *Evaluating Training Programmes*, McGraw-Hill, Maidenhead.
Oakland, J. (1989) *Total Quality Management*, Heinemann, London.
Williams, A., Dobson, P. and Walters, M. (1989) *Changing Culture*, IPM, London.

## Additional Reading

Atkinson, P. (1990) *Creating Culture Change: The Key to Successful Total Quality Management*, IFS, Bedford.
Cole, R. (1989) Large scale change and the quality revolution, in A. Mohrmann *et al.* (eds.) *Large Scale Organizational Change*, Jossey-Bass, London, pp. 229–54.
Collard, R. (1989) *Total Quality*, IPM, London.

Crosby, P. (1984) *Quality Without Tears*, McGraw-Hill, New York, NY.

Hill, S. (1991) Why quality circles failed but total quality management might succeed, *British Journal of Industrial Relations*, Vol. 29, no. 4, pp. 541–68.

Kanter, R. (1984) *The Change Masters*, Unwin, London.

Kilmann, R. (1989) A completely integrated programme of organizational change, in A. Mohrmann *et al.* (eds.) *Large Scale Organizational Change*, Jossey-Bass, London, pp. 200–28.

Peccei, R. and Guest, D. (1984) Evaluating the introduction of new technology: the case of word processors in British Rail, in M. Warner (ed.) *Microprocessors, Manpower and Society*, Gower, Guildford, pp. 84–109.

Peccei, R. and Guest, D. (1985) Decision-making in British Rail, in C. Clegg, N. Kemp and K. Legge (eds.) *Case Studies in Organizational Behaviour*, Harper & Row, London, pp. 61–70.

# CASE 12

# Close to the Customer: Employee Relations in Food Retailing

## Mick Marchington

## Organizational Setting

Hiclas is one of the leading food retailers in the UK, employing 70,000 staff in over 300 locations around the country. The company first started trading over one hundred years ago, and has always had a reputation for high-quality goods, clean and efficient stores and a very professional approach to its business. Hiclas has expanded northwards from its southern base, and now has about thirty stores in the North West of England (the location for this study). The company's market share has continued to grow during the last decade, and the industry as a whole is becoming increasingly segmented between the big six (all of which have an emphasis on good standards of customer service, high-quality goods, pleasant shopping atmosphere and wide range of products) and the remainder. Like most retail outlets, the company is highly centralized, not only in terms of employee relations decisions but also in most aspects of management policy — such as buying decisions, store layout, pricing, financial controls and preferred management style.

There is tremendous rivalry between the market leaders both at national level and locally, with new-store openings having an immediate effect upon sales in the area. Close attention is paid to the activities of the competition — in terms of price, product range, store design and developments — and there has been a rush to open new stores in attractive locations, increasingly out of town to cater for the one-stop shopper. Indeed, over the last few years, each of the major multiples has moved further up market, aiming to target the more quality-conscious customer, and this has increased the competition yet more. Customer demand also varies considerably, but usually in a fairly predictable manner, throughout the course of the day, week and year. For example, sales tend to increase during the week, with peaks on Thursday and Friday afternoons and troughs on Monday and Tuesday mornings. This has implications for the number of staff employed at any one time, and it provides a rationale for the high proportion of part-time staff in the stores. The majority of staff on the sales floor are part-timers, and overall about 70 per cent of all employees are part time. A large proportion of the staff are young (in their late teens and early 20s), although those employed on the checkouts are just as likely to be in their 30s and 40s. As with banks, 'key-time' employees provide the numerical flexibility management deems to be appropriate. In a similar vein, the type of products sold also varies over the course of the year, for obvious reasons, although sudden changes in the weather can cause problems with product availability. Furthermore, although there are supposed to be controls on queue lengths, based upon predefined computer programs relating to the number of items that can be scanned in any one period, this is not always achieved in practice. Again, this has implications for the quality of customer service, a point to which we will return later.

The organization structure of Hiclas is fairly straightforward. At head office there are a range of functions − including personnel − whose role is to implement the core policies and offer advice to the stores. At intermediate level, there is skeleton staff employed in several regions, and again this includes a personnel presence. The regional managers are the main point of contact between the centre and the individual stores, visiting each store every two weeks on average. Given the sustained growth rate of Hiclas during the last decade, the regional management teams have assumed responsibility for a growing number of stores, and have been confronted with an increasing number of requests for assistance at store level. Although some managers might have seen little need for an intermediate tier in the structure in the past, this viewpoint has less credence now the number of stores has increased. Each store is run by a store manager, who has a number of deputies working to him or her, and below this there is a series of departmental heads covering such areas as grocery, warehouse, bakery and customer service. Finally, there are a number of junior managers, often supervising no more than a handful of people, for sections such as fresh foods, the delicatessen or the staff restaurant. The departmental and sectional managers spend a large proportion of their time on the same duties as the staff they supervise.

## Managing Employee Relations

Traditionally, Hiclas operated with a somewhat authoritarian style of management, described by some managers as almost autocratic and militaristic. In recent years, this has softened and there has been a drive to create a more 'open' style that encourages managers and supervisors to seek ideas from staff and to operate in a more informal manner. To some extent this shift in approach has been stimulated by the fact that managers are highly dependent upon staff for consistent high-quality service to customers. The importance of quality and customer care is continually stressed to employees, partly because the company is exposed to high levels of competition but also because of the need for Hiclas to differentiate itself from other food retailers. The idea that staff should help to ensure that 'shopping is a pleasant experience' is made apparent during the induction period and subsequently reinforced through training programmes and messages on noticeboards and in the company newspaper. One of the company objectives states that Hiclas aims 'to offer our staff outstanding opportunities in terms of personal career development and in remuneration relative to other companies in the same market, practising always a concern for the welfare of every individual'.

A unitarist philosophy is evident in much of the audio-visual material produced by the company, with regular references to being 'vital members of the team', and to the ethos of all working together for the good of the company as a whole. For example, one of the company's induction videos encourages staff to 'buy into' the benefits offered by the company; if staff work hard, look smart and maintain strict hygiene and service standards, it is suggested that Hiclas will be able to ensure that customers receive quality products and treatment, as well as value for money. This will then result in secure employment for staff, profit sharing, good promotion prospects and job satisfaction. In addition, the fact that staff can see relatively open lines of promotion – at least to the level of junior management – serves to reinforce the feeling that working together can represent a way forward for staff and the company alike.

On the other hand, this benign image of 'team-working' and co-operation masks the tight controls that are exerted within the company, especially in the managerial hierarchy. There are strict formulae for the amount of labour that can be employed in any one period, although store managers are allowed some flexibility between full- and part-time employees according to their local needs. Regional managers make spot visits to each of the stores on a regular but unscheduled basis, principally to check on store layouts, queue lengths and general performance. These visits can be a cause of some consternation for managers, as their aim is to 'keep them on their toes', always aware of the need for high-quality service. Disciplinary standards are precisely laid down by the company rule-book, and there are specific instructions about standards of cleanliness and dress. Indeed, the desire to project a high-quality image is central to much of the activity at the store. Finally, video cameras are trained constantly on the sales area in an effort to deter pilferage by customers and to ensure that there is a record of events if the need arises for prosecution; at the same time, although this is not its purpose, the video cameras also act as an instrument of surveillance over staff who are aware that these recordings could be used against them as well as customers.

Hiclas has separate but identical agreements with two trade unions, TGWU and USDAW, which allows for individuals to be represented at the workplace. The agreements came into force in the late 1970s, and it appears that the reason for recognizing two unions (as opposed to one, which many of the competitors do) owed much to existing pockets of union membership in different parts of the country. Collective bargaining is not catered for in the agreements, and recognition is limited to situations where one of the unions can provide evidence of substantial membership within a store. The term 'substantial' is not defined, but it is low; at one of the stores where detailed research was undertaken, USDAW had local recognition despite having only about 25 members (less than 10 per cent of those employed). Check-off (automatic deduction of union subscriptions) is also granted if union density reaches 35 per cent in a store. Once one of the unions has been granted recognition at a store, the other is barred from further activity there. Workplace union organization is weak, with little more than 6 per cent of all eligible employees actually in the unions; there are about the same number in each. The unions generally face difficulty in persuading sufficient people to become representatives, and those who do often lack experience of unionism and of working at Hiclas stores.

Although there is no provision for collective bargaining, it was agreed in the early 1980s that a JCC (joint consultative committee) structure could be set up between Hiclas and the appropriate union(s) at area level if union membership exceeds a certain threshold level − currently 500 members in the area − which is equivalent to about 10 per cent of all eligible employees. Management was keen to initiate the JCC machinery because a number of similar problems kept on recurring in various branches at the same time, and it was felt that these were better resolved at area rather than unit level. The JCC structure provides union officials with the opportunity to meet with a senior personnel manager from headquarters as well as several line managers within the region. The committees meet up to three times per annum at a neutral venue − usually a hotel − and the JCC is preceded by meeting between the full-time officials and representatives from the branches in the area. The issues that are typically dealt with at the JCCs include health and safety, terms and conditions of employment, union reactions to company pay reviews, policies on time-off for trade-union affairs and various general items (such as security in stores or information about new openings).

Pay at Hiclas is determined by management rather than being the subject of collective bargaining, and the system has recently been reorganized through the introduction of a new job-evaluation scheme. The previous system was felt to be too subjective and open to abuse by managers favouring specific individuals, a situation compounded by the growth of the company since the previous system had been introduced. Changes in technology had also rendered some of the previous gradings (for example, in the warehouse) inappropriate. Moreover, senior management was concerned that the existing system was potentially discriminatory, in that manual jobs (such as those typically undertaken by men in the warehouse) attracted higher rates of pay than those that involved contact with customers (such as those typically done by women on the checkouts). The new system has five grades: the top grade includes craft skills (such as senior butchers/bakers) and the bottom grade covers cleaners and trolley assistants/packers. Checkout staff (the largest group in a store) are in the fourth grade. Pay levels are good for the industry, and top-grade butchers and bakers can earn a basic rate of nearly £9,000 per annum; checkout staff can earn about £6,500 for a 39-hour week.

Labour turnover at Hiclas is high at over 40 per cent per annum, and in some stores, especially in the South East of England, rates are often at 200 per cent or more. In the Northern stores, given higher levels of unemployment, rates tend to be much lower and, at the two stores that formed the focus for this study, it was about 20 per cent. The lowest turnover rates tended to be among the middle-aged women part-timers with childcare commitments, whereas higher rates were found for the younger women. These figures are much higher than in manufacturing, but they are not untypical for the retail industry as a whole. These 'crude' figures also mask the fact that some of the turnover is a result of seasonal and temporary employment, as well as the fact that many of the leavers go within the first month of arriving.

Nevertheless, Hiclas has made a number of efforts to reduce this high labour-turnover figure, and so reduce the costs associated with recurrent recruitment exercises. Much greater effort has been put into the whole selection and induction process, and in some stores where it is difficult to retain staff special attempts have been made to attract older people (the so-called 'grey' workers in their 50s and 60s) to apply for jobs. Getting sufficient applicants has not been a problem in the Northern stores, although ensuring that these people are satisfactory has been more difficult; now, store managers and their deputies complete a short, informal interview with potential applicants before the selection process is started in the hope that this will screen out weaker candidates. The selection process still relies heavily on interviews as opposed to the more sophisticated techniques that have become common in some manufacturing organizations for blue-collar employees.

Once recruited, all staff go through a formal induction programme undertaken within the store by a team of trainers. All new recruits receive literature on health and safety matters, the company history, rules and regulations, and details of service-related benefits. This is contained in a handbook that outlines all the key points of the employment package, as well as providing answers to the more typical questions asked by new employees. New starters also receive written information about the customer service campaign, and a series of brochures detailing the required standards of dress and hygiene. This is then supplemented by a set of videos presented by the trainers, and new staff are given the opportunity to ask further questions about working for Hiclas. All these messages are constantly reinforced throughout the individual's employment with the company.

Hiclas also operates a profit-sharing scheme for staff with more than two years' consecutive service, irrespective of the number of hours worked. This means that approximately one third of those employed are members of the share scheme, and payouts for these staff can represent more than an additional month's salary each year. People who leave employment prior to the qualification date are not entitled to any profit-share payment. Staff can opt to take the profit payout either in cash or as shares, and a large proportion choose to take it in the form of shares; indeed, many see working for Hiclas in highly positive terms and, given the increase in share price over the last decade, their loyalty has been rewarded by extra financial gains. As with wages, profit-share allocations are determined by management alone.

In recent years, Hiclas has also attempted to increase employee involvement within the company, mostly through improved communications both of a written and a verbal nature. Unlike many other large organizations, Hiclas has not chosen to introduce a formal communications policy, such as team briefing, preferring to rely on informal channels and face-to-face contact between managers and their staff on an *ad hoc* basis. This is justified by some senior management because of the nature of the product market environment: that is, continuous pressure from customers that requires immediate attention, allied to an employment policy that maintains strict controls on the total number of hours worked in any one store. Accordingly, Hiclas management is unwilling to provide extra payments for the purpose of communicating information to staff in addition to their normal working hours. At the same time, some of their competitors have chosen to implement more formal systems for cascading information to staff, so it could be argued that the product market is not totally deterministic. Although many of the managers who were interviewed in the research felt the informal system worked well and that staff were adequately informed about company and store developments, a significant proportion of employees felt they were not always kept in the picture. Indeed, at one of the stores – where the general manager was more elusive – a majority regarded the grapevine as a more effective source of information. At another store, the 'open' approach adopted by the general manager helped to create a climate in which managers did keep staff better informed. As with any informal system, however, much depends upon the character of the individual managers as well as the ethos of the department and the store. This potential communications breakdown is now beginning to concern some senior managers at regional level and within the corporate personnel department.

Although there is no formal machinery for regular face-to-face information-passing between managers and staff, Hiclas is well renowned for the quality and comprehensiveness of its written communications. At each store there is a system of noticeboards that assumes a key place within the framework of employee relations. Not only are these placed prominently within the stores but they are also regularly updated and well managed – unlike most noticeboards! All employees walk past the board several times each day, on their way to and from the staff restaurant, and new items are highlighted, either on the board itself or on the door into the restaurant. A questionnaire survey of staff undertaken in two units indicated that the noticeboard was the most valued source of information in the store.

The company also prides itself on the quality of its house journal, a newspaper that has been published ten times per annum since the late 1940s. Over that period, it has won a string of awards from various bodies. The paper is edited by a small team of staff at headquarters, who work within the public relations department of the company, and who have a sizeable budget for its development and publication. The journal operates according to a set of written objectives that are broadly concerned with 'furthering good employee relations', 'improving the process of change' and 'conveying information accurately and effectively'. The journal was revamped towards the end of the 1980s, and now has the 'feel' of a Sunday-newspaper colour supplement. It is 28 pages long, and contains the usual mix of information about business items and social activities, although there is rather less of the former than is typical in house journals. All new store openings are featured in the newspaper, along with information about important events; for example, there is an annual report focusing on the company results; there have been a number of feature articles on environmental affairs; and there was a profile of a company that had recently been acquired by Hiclas. Although the decision to change the format of the paper was instigated by management, a team of independent researchers was commissioned to conduct a survey of employee opinion about the type of changes that should be made to the journal. This study comprised a series of interviews with staff from a number of stores, and the recommendations of the team were accepted for the redesign of the journal.

Like the rest of its competitors, Hiclas has developed a range of mechanisms to encourage staff to maintain high-level customer service, most of which are centred around video campaigns and training sessions. For the most part, the videos are shown by a staff trainer — not a line manager — and staff are drawn from different parts of the store as appropriate. There is no attempt to use these sessions as a vehicle for team-building, and it is rare for line managers to attend these meetings. The messages conveyed in these sessions tend to be simple and straightforward, varying in the degree to which they take a prescriptive line about the 'one best way' to serve customers. The image of the customer as all-powerful is central to all the programmes and, once again, the phraseology employed reflects unitarist assumptions. For example,

> Customer care is the Number One skill all Hiclas employees must have. Our future success will depend upon how well you apply this skill.

> Remember it is not what you are doing that is the most important thing, it is what the customer *perceives* you are doing.

> Make sure that you always say good morning etc, please, thank you, use the customer's name if known, always apologize if something is wrong or there is a delay, take customers to a display, always show concern.

Some of the more experienced staff in the stores found these customer-care videos extremely simplistic, and actually became annoyed by them. They resented the way in which the message was put across, as well as the patronizing and condescending tone of the whole presentation. As one of the longer-serving staff commented, 'we have always practised customer care, although we didn't call it that; we don't need management to tell us how to do it'. In addition, the image conveyed by the stores in which the films were made also caused some ill-feeling, not to say incredulity; in these, the actors who were playing staff worked at a very leisurely pace, and had time to laugh and joke with the actors who were playing customers. 'Wouldn't mind a job there!' was the common response of staff in the two stores I investigated. These experienced staff also queried the value of making these expensive videos. On the other hand, senior management saw these devices as necessary in order to maintain the emphasis on high-quality customer service.

## Problems and Opportunities

Before moving on to highlight a number of problems currently confronting management and unions at Hiclas, it is worth reiterating that the company remains very successful not only in terms of market share and profitability but also with respect to its employee relations policies and practices. Accordingly, the case study questions will focus on modifications rather than a complete overhaul.

Hiclas has done much to change from its traditional image of an autocratic management style and to replace this with a vision that encourages a more open approach to people management. All the staff who were interviewed during the research programme noted that management had become more approachable and participative in its attitudes over the last few years. Typical responses were as follows:

> The store manager is on the shopfloor a lot, and he always passes the time of day, asks you how you are, takes an interest in what you are doing.

> When I first came here ten years ago, managers were very frosty and formal; now, they are much more approachable, and the deputy store manager really gets involved with what we are doing.

> All the senior managers from the store came to the last social evening, and they let their hair down just like the rest of us.

At the same time, there remains a strong ethos of centralized control, the need for staff to follow instructions, and the threat of constant surveillance and the use of disciplinary action to those who transgress the rules. Perhaps the tensions and contradictions are best illustrated by the concept of the customer-care programme, which specifies conformance to precise working patterns as well as encouraging genuine (rather than forced) expressions of interest in customers.

The second issue of concern to the company (and more particularly the trade unions) is the future position of unionism within Hiclas. Recognizing two different unions for the same grade of staff is somewhat unusual for this sector, especially since neither has more than a handful of members. Moreover, the majority of staff who are union members show little interest in union affairs and, since store managers maintain a fairly neutral stance in relation to the unions, this is hardly likely to change. At store level, the unions do not appear to act as a brake upon management activity, so the question of union derecognition or avoidance is not one that arouses much interest as an issue to be confronted. Some factions within management regard the unions as unnecessary, and would like to see membership fall yet further, whereas others (notably in personnel) favour a strengthening of the JCC structure. Yet others see no need for this structure at all, arguing for a more informal approach within each individual store. These are issues both for senior management and the two trade unions, as well as for staff who currently see little value in union membership.

Third, there are questions about the direction that should be taken to develop direct employee involvement and communications within Hiclas. Some changes have taken place in the last few years: the house journal has been revamped; the job-evaluation panel comprised a cross-section of employees (men and women), including union members and junior managers; and the annual report to employees has been altered to make it more accessible to staff. But there are other practices that could be reformed. For example, there are doubts about the effectiveness of communications between managers and their staff, and some consideration is being given to implementing a formal, structured programme of team-briefing. In addition, there is currently no mechanism for staff to put forward their ideas for improvements at work. Moreover, given the way in which training is undertaken within the stores, there is little or no opportunity for line managers to engage in any explicit team-building exercises while at work.

Finally, despite a number of recent changes, labour turnover remains at a high level compared with other large organizations in manufacturing or the public sector. Perhaps more could be done to reduce this still further, by improving the selection procedure or the benefits package (for example, the basis on which staff gain entry to the profit-sharing scheme). Alternatively, it may well be that labour turnover levels are unlikely to drop much further.

## Case Study Tasks

Below are a number of questions that relate to the case study you have just read and that should provide a starting point for re-examining the Hiclas case. These are not meant to be exhaustive, however. In addressing the questions, pay particular attention to the practical and financial implications of any ideas you suggest for improving employee relations at Hiclas. At all times, think carefully about the theoretical frameworks within which your actions can be located.

1.  How would you aim to reduce labour turnover at Hiclas? What changes, if any, do you think should be made to the selection procedures, the induction package and the profit-sharing arrangements? Associated with this is the question of 'the flexible firm'; does this have anything to offer in this case, especially with regard to segmentation within the labour force?
2.  What are the arguments for and against the introduction of a formal system of team-briefing at Hiclas? Would you change the current system? Why?
3.  If you were the personnel director, what actions would you take to reform policies on union recognition and joint consultation? Why? (Note that you may decide that the current arrangements are satisfactory.)
4.  If you were general secretary of either USDAW or the TGWU, what would you do to increase union membership within Hiclas? In particular, how would you make the union appear more attractive to women who work part time, given the patriarchal policies of Hiclas management?
5.  What would you suggest, if anything, to improve the training programmes run at Hiclas, especially those on customer care? Should line managers play a greater part in these sessions so as to build up team spirit?
6.  Identify the principal tensions and contradictions in the way in which

Hiclas manages its employee relations. Is it possible for any employer to maintain control over labour costs while simultaneously attempting to treat employees as valued resources in the way implied by some of the human resource management literature?

7. How does the description of employee relations at Hiclas compare with your own knowledge of supermarkets, especially those from the low-cost/ no-frills segment of the market? What factors do you think would account for any differences in management style between these types of organization?

## Essential Reading

Marchington, M. and Harrison, E. (1991) Customers, competitors and choice; employee relations in food retailing, *Industrial Relations Journal*, Vol. 22, no. 4, pp. 286–99.

Ogbonna, E. and Wilkinson, B. (1990) Corporate strategy and corporate culture; the view from the check-out, *Personnel Review*, Vol. 19, no. 4, pp. 9–15.

Sparks, L. (1987) Employment in retailing; trends and issues, in G. Johnson (ed.) *Business Strategy in Retailing*, Wiley, Chichester.

Storey, J. (ed.) (1989) *New Perspectives on Human Resource Management*, Routledge, London.

## Further Reading

Atkinson, J. (1989) Four stages of adjustment to the demographic downturn, *Personnel Management*, Vol. 21, no. 8, pp. 20–4.

Keenoy, T. (1990) Human resource management; a case of the wolf in sheep's clothing?, *Personnel Review*, Vol. 19, no. 2, pp. 3–9.

Marchington, M. and Parker, P. (1990) *Changing Patterns of Employee Relations*, Harvester-Wheatsheaf, Hemel Hempstead.

Ogbonna, E. and Wilkinson, B. (1988) Corporate strategy and corporate culture; the management of change, *Personnel Review*, Vol. 17, no. 6, pp. 10–14.

Purcell, J. (1987) Mapping management styles in employee relations, *Journal of Management Studies*, Vol. 24, no. 5, pp. 534–48.

# CASE 13

## Evaluating Teleworking in an Educational Establishment

### Jean F. Hartley and Mike Fitter

## Introduction

The small group of teaching and computing staff of the Department of Management at the University of Minterne are in yet another staff meeting. They meet regularly these days to develop and implement a radically new method of teaching students, involving communication by computers (computer conferencing). Although conferencing is being used in a number of commercial applications, its use in education so far is exploratory. The group has obtained some funding for the development and evaluation of the innovation and are considering how to use the money most effectively both to assess and improve the system.

At the same time, in a room in the same building, the students are meeting. Although they are all distance-learning students, spread across the breadth of the country, they are having one of their occasional face-to-face meetings, which occurs during the once-termly residential teaching weekends. The students are meeting now because they have heard a rumour that the department is going to introduce assessment based on the use of computers and they are not at all happy with this prospect. Views about the use of computers are very mixed in any case and there is an added concern that students should not be disadvantaged by assessment based on this unproven technology.

## Background

### Teleworking and Computer Conferencing

Teleworking describes work activity where employees (or students) are connected to their organization and carry out tasks through computer communication although physically located elsewhere (Stanworth and Stanworth, 1991; Mueller, 1992). Teleworking requires access to communications technology and systems — for example, computer conferencing and electronic mail. Computer-mediated communication is a general term covering computer conferencing, electronic mail, bulletin boards and remote databases where computers and telecommunications networks are used to exchange information between participants. Universities have been pioneers in the use of computer conferencing for teaching distance students because the technology enables students to be in regular contact with each other and with staff and thus to communicate both academically and socially. Countries with a high level of geographically dispersed students, such as Canada and Denmark, were quick to develop and exploit the potential of computer conferencing for student learning. Companies with dispersed workforces and in regions of high labour costs have been increasingly experimenting with teleworking, though only part of that work may involve computer conferencing.

Computer conferencing is a system of communication that takes place between a *group* of people. The participants are linked through connections made via their personal computer to a mainframe computer which holds the conferencing software. If the participants are remote from the mainframe they can be connected through a modem (linked to the telephone line). Thus any participant with access to a telephone can use the conference (they have to be a user registered with the conference). The computer-conferencing software (which organizes, stores and displays the messages between members of the group) is held on the mainframe computer. Conference participants can read stored messages or add new ones at any time.

Interactions can occur without all having to be present for a discussion at the same time in the same place. Each time a participant logs on to the conference they receive information about new messages waiting to be read. Conferencing combines the speed of the fax message with the advantages of purposive structured discussion between a group of people. Of course, it also has disadvantages, especially as a new medium people are learning to use effectively. As a written medium, it lacks the spontaneity and social information of face-to-face interactions or even of video and audio conferencing. However, it can be useful in circumstances where participants would not have easy access to face-to-face interaction (as in part-time distance education or with dispersed workforces) or where participants are unlikely to be available at the same time (such as sales staff).

There are a number of conferencing software programmes, with slight variations in their messaging structure. At the University of Minterne, the software structures the conferencing as follows. Participants can be members of one or more conferences (for example, a tutorial group, a student group for general discussion, etc). A conference is an area in which discussion can take place. A message in that conference is open to anyone who is a member of that conference. Each conference is made up of a number of topics. Topics provide a means of collecting together messages on a particular subject. The structure of the conference is given in Figure 13.1 and some examples of messaging are given in the Appendix to this case study.

## The University of Minterne

The Department of Management is small, comprising twenty academic staff who teach across a range of business subjects, including organizational be-

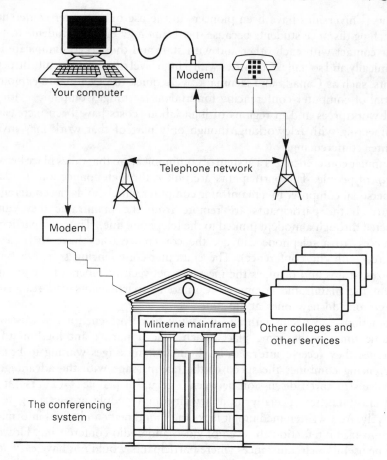

**Figure 13.1** Schematic representation of student connection routes into the Minterne conferencing system

haviour. It is the organizational behaviour staff who were instrumental in developing computer conferencing in order both to reach students unable to study on a face-to-face basis (and thereby to increase student numbers) and also to increase the department's research capacity in the area of teleworking (thereby increasing research and consultancy work in commercial organizations). The staff obtained a grant from an external agency to develop and evaluate the innovations in conferencing. Of this, £15,000 is available for the evaluation project.

The students in the department are all mature students studying part time for their MBAs (over a two-year period). With an average age of 37, and in middle and senior management positions, most of them are self-funded or funded by their employer. As a group, they are confident and assertive about their educational needs and their career plans and they have strong (though varied) views about the value and significance of computer conferencing for their course. They have been told by the staff of the department that computer conferencing can be used to achieve several ends: it can be used for instruction and discussion about the subject-matter of the course itself — essentially having electronic tutorials; it can also be used among the students as a means of social support — to encourage one another, to exchange informal ideas and to act rather like a coffee-bar would in a conventional course. The staff believe the social-support aspect of conferencing may be particularly important given that the students are both part time and scattered across the country. There may be other functions in an educational course that conferencing could serve for students (or staff and students) but the newness of the medium means these have not been explored yet.

Students taking the two-year part-time MBA are taught by three methods. They are given written material covering the course syllabus and that they are expected to work through term by term in a paced way. The written material covers the main theories, research and policy outcomes in a particular area and also refers students to key texts and other reading (e.g. journal articles). The second component of the course is the once-termly residential weekend, which all students are expected to attend. These cover not only conventional lectures and seminars but also practical exercises, case studies and so forth. These two components are such as might be found on many conventional distance-learning courses. The third component is computer conferencing. Thus the course uses both remote and immediate interactions, as is used in some applications of teleworking where employees are both home- and office-based in a particular mix.

Although computer conferencing as a technology can be used flexibly in a variety of ways, the staff at Minterne have decided to use it for teaching and learning as follows. Students are divided into tutor groups, each consisting of 15 members plus a lecturer. There are four tutor groups in each of the two years of the course. Each tutor group constitutes a conference and only members of that tutor group can gain access to the conference (and read and write messages to that conference). Each term the lecturer taking a course with that tutor group gives the students a list of topics that will be discussed during the term, generally focused around a particular question (so far, the analogy with seminar groups in conventional teaching is entirely appropriate). The topics are also given a timetable, for example, that topic 1 will open on a particular date and close two weeks later, during which time students and the lecturer are expected to interact on the topic. Students may input as often as they like (as in conventional seminars, part of the lecturer's role is to encourage the silent ones and moderate the over-enthusiastic contributor!). A student is chosen to summarize the messaging on a topic at the end of the time period, adding the summary to the messages in that topic.

In addition, a couple of topics within the tutor group are open ended in time and may cover any area of social and professional interest. Students tend to use this to offer each other support and to arrange social meetings for those near enough to do that. A great deal of messaging takes place within the social channel. Students also have access to a conference of their own, where all the students in that year group can meet without any staff having access to the conference.

At the time of the discussions that opened this case, computer conferencing had been established for teaching for three months (i.e. just over one term) and both students and staff were still coming to grips with the technology let alone finding out about how to use it for learning, teaching and social support.

## Issues

### Staff Views

In the staff group, the Head of Department, Professor Ford, was outlining some of the circumstances of the decisions to be made: 'As you all know, we have a grant to develop and evaluate the computer conferencing and so we have to decide how to spend this in a way which is most effective. There are some difficult questions here because we have only been using conferencing for the last 12 weeks and so we still have some way to go before we are clear about how it might be used to best advantage on this course.'

'Well, I have to say that I don't think we should be using computer conferencing at all', interrupted Dr Atkinson. 'I have been against this from the very beginning but the more I see of it the less convinced I am about it. How can a lecturer be an effective teacher when you aren't even in direct contact with the students? I know how to run good and stimulating seminars when all the students are present in one room but I find it very frustrating to engage in messaging over a two-week period on a topic – it feels like you never really get going and there aren't the social cues available to check whether students are interested or bored, understanding or lost, excited or puzzled. And how can we communicate to students the culture of Minterne, which is an essential part of university life? I would advocate that we drop the whole experiment now while we've still got time.'

'Whatever the pros and cons of going into this innovation originally, I think we have to press forward now. Indeed, that might be one of the objectives of the evaluation: should we continue or abandon ship? But I think to simply leave it now, on the grounds that some staff don't like this method of teaching, would be premature', answered Professor Ford. 'And don't forget that already our involvement in conferencing has enabled us to increase student numbers dramatically. That, as well as ensuring our continued survival in the current financially constrained climate of education, also has the benefit of putting us in a favourable light in the eyes of the Vice-Chancellor and the Registrar. That, as I probably don't need to remind you, may have all sorts of spin-offs for the resourcing of the department, including resources for research.'

Another lecturer, Ms Hutchings, broke in: 'If we can make conferencing a success, then this will obviously be good for the department in various ways, but what do we understand by success, and do we all understand the same thing by it? For example, I might think conferencing is successful because it reduces my contact hours with students and frees up more time for my research but, on the other hand, Dr Atkinson may be more concerned with the quality of teaching provision for students and the conditions under which they learn most effectively. And what does it mean for the functioning of the department if lecturers can conference from home as well as from the office? Will staff be in the office as much? What will that mean for the ways in which we have traditionally made decisions around here? And then there are the students themselves to consider. Since most are paying for their fees, equipment, software and telephone charges themselves — or getting their employer to — they and the employer want to know that they are getting value for money. They are entitled to ask whether it is all worth it for them. And, indeed, some of them are asking — most vociferously! In fact, they are meeting right now and I know that some of them are disgruntled or even hostile about using it.'

'Yes', said Dr Sutcliffe, 'the evidence of the last four weeks is that there has been a decline in use by students. There are fewer contributions to the tutorial conferences and even in the amount it is being used for general chat. This is a worrying trend which, if it continued, could spell disaster for the project. It appears some of the students are voting with their feet — or rather their keyboards! On the other hand, I know that some of them are quite keen. This raises questions for the evaluation as to whether we should be looking at the differences between students — for example, in their motivation and attitudes towards using conferencing. We are demanding that all students engage in conferencing regardless of ability, personal circumstances or motivation. Yet I know that, in commercial applications, the innovation seems to have worked best where employees (or at least professionals) are able to choose whether to telework or be office based. What are the effects of our compulsory use? Or, there again, we could examine the different ways in which the students are actually using conferencing — at the moment we don't seem to know much about that.'

Dr Fogg then spoke: 'We are one of the first universities to use conferencing in this country and the opportunities for high-quality research are enormous. We could write this development work up in a number of journal articles. To do this properly, I suggest that we set up a proper scientific study to investigate the contribution of conferencing to student learning. If we established a control group of matched students who do not use conferencing then we could really evaluate conferencing. We could correlate conferencing use with exam perform-ance, staff assessments, course-work and so on. So we should start the evaluation with next year's intake and only let half of them do conferencing until the evaluation is completed.'

Mr Hardiman added: 'I agree, but I would go further than that. I think we have data at our finger-tips right now that we could be using in student assessment. The mainframe computer can log how many times a student is using conferencing and the length of their contribution. I think part of the evaluation should be looking at how we can improve the monitoring of student-activity levels and performance. The evaluation can look at how we might improve the management information system contained in the software so that we can move as soon as possible to making conferencing a compulsory part of the formal assessment procedure. Then we can keep a track of students' performance so much better — especially those who are under-performing. The opportunities in new technology for the discrete monitoring of performance are enormous — let's take advantage of that.'

Dr Mundil disagreed: 'I think there is a danger that we get too focused in this evaluation on the specific details of our own scheme. But what interests me is how similar or different is it to the commercial applications. What will we be able to say from this evaluation, which is in an educational setting, to issues about communication, control and culture in both manufacturing and service organizations which are using remote-based working? After all, we are meant to know about organizational behaviour — surely we can generalize to other settings from the experiences we have here?'

Robert Fix, the department's computer programmer who is responsible both for improving the technical aspects of conferencing and for providing technical and practical support for students, spoke up: 'I want to see the evaluation examining how students — and yourselves as academic staff, of course — are actually using the system and how it can be improved. I don't want to see an evaluation which tells me in, say, eighteen months' time, that the conferencing doesn't work very well. I want to have practical, immediate outcomes to the evaluation so that I can use the information in my current work in programming, in advising students and in running training courses for all those using conferencing. Can I remind everyone this is a development as well as an evaluation project?'

'Unfortunately,' said Professor Ford, 'we are running out of time for this discussion and we need to press on to make a decision about what kind of evaluation we are going to undertake. As you all know, we do have some rudimentary information about the equipment students have and we did collect some information about student attitudes to computers before they started the course. The evaluation is not restricted to that but may wish to build on some of that information. I would like to propose that we all go away and design an evaluation for the computer conferencing and then meet again, this time with the students to decide on the key features we wish to include in this particular evaluation.'

## Student Views

As it is a residential weekend, which is part of the course, the full group of students is present: 120 in total. Concern is being expressed about the rumour that the students contribution to conferencing is going to be assessed as a formal part of the course requirements. One student had heard (but it was not clear from what source) that 20 per cent of marks were going to be allocated to 'contributions to conferencing'.

'It's outrageous,' said Pete Davies, 'we have to stop the staff implementing this. They mustn't assess work we do until they can demonstrate that the system is effective as a learning aid. Otherwise it could discriminate against some students, for example those who have had difficulty logging on to the system. I have been alright: I work in personnel for a software company so I have had experts on tap to help me to connect my computer to the Minterne computer but others are not so lucky. Jane Gregg here is self-employed so has to do it all herself and she has also had a number of technical hitches, including a poor line from the telephone company.'

'Even if I was properly connected,' said Jane, 'I am not so sure how much I would learn. Personally, I would much prefer to come into Minterne on an evening basis and have real lectures and seminars.'

'It's all very well for you,' chipped in Andrew James, 'I live in Glasgow and there is no way I could come into the university on a regular basis — I can't afford to fly down here just for a tutorial! If computer conferencing did not exist, then I simply would not be able to do this MBA — or perhaps any because my other constraint is my job. Working as an NHS general manager means that I need the flexibility of the distance learning to be able to have any hope at all of doing a course while doing this job.'

'My sentiments exactly,' said Susan Smith. 'I have a young baby, and a full-time job, so I couldn't possibly do this course if it meant travelling to Minterne every week for classes.'

'I feel really curious about the strengths and weaknesses of this technology,' said Tony Field. 'I believe it could be used in other organizations as well as in higher education. I have been talking with my boss about trialling the system for my organization but I want to know more about how it works here first. You see, I work for a large multinational which is in the middle of trying to change its culture. I work in personnel and we are encouraging the development of more autonomy within the divisions. But we need some co-ordination between the divisions over some aspects of pay and procedures. We can arrange to have monthly meetings of the personnel managers, of course, but they are time-consuming and can only get through a certain amount of business. I would like to see closer informal co-ordination taking place. This may be especially important as we try to change the culture of my company. Computer conferencing would enable the personnel managers in the various divisions to maintain contact on a regular basis and exchange ideas both informally and formally.'

'That sounds very interesting,' said Mark Kerr. 'I am sure there are a number of commercial applications that our involvement here could help us with. For example, my company, although currently occupied with the recession, is also thinking hard about how to attract and retain professional women over the next decade. Encouraging teleworking might help them to combine career and family, or minimize the need for relocation (which would be useful for our male staff, too). If we could establish how communication and careers were enhanced or diminished by using remote working this would be very helpful to us. If conferencing can be used for learning, then why not for "meetings", for report writing, for data analysis and so on. The more detailed the evaluation about individual differences in use and satisfaction, and about the organizational implications, the better for me.'

'But what about the assessment?' Pete Davies returned to the original point of concern. 'Of course, we would like to see how conferencing can be used in other situations but right now we are faced with the possibility of being assessed on our performance on an unproven technology and that surely is inherently problematic.'

As the discussion continued it emerged that the student body were opposed to any assessment of student performance through conferencing because the system was too little understood to allow this in a way that would be fair and equitable. However, the student group wanted to be represented in the discussions about the evaluation, for which they knew a grant had been awarded. They wanted their views to be taken into account in the evaluation design and to have full access to the findings.

## The Task

The task for the users of this case study is to design in outline an evaluation study for assessing the effectiveness of computer conferencing. Assume the grant is sufficient to employ a half-time research worker over a year and that any further work will be undertaken by the academic and computing staff of the department.

It is important that the evaluation meets the needs of the stakeholders as far as possible and therefore a solely technical evaluation is unlikely to be sufficient or acceptable. Computer conferencing is a tool that has been chosen to meet educational objectives and the development and evaluation work are taking place in the context where students may be affected in their learning if the development and evaluation work is inappropriate.

### Steps in the Exercise

It is recommended that the exercise follows the steps as outlined below:

1. *Getting prepared*   Participants should read the information provided above and that provided in the Appendix to the case. They should also read the Essential Reading listed at the end of the study, ideally well prior to the exercise itself. The participants should also clarify any questions of *fact* about the conferencing system and the evaluation.
2. *The participants design the evaluation and answer the associated questions* Depending on the time available, between 40 minutes and two hours can be allocated to this stage. By the end the participants should be clear about what they think the evaluation is to achieve, what its focus should be and how it might collect data for the evaluation. The groups should consider both the overt and covert aims of the evaluation (Legge, 1984) and the extent to which it is likely the stakeholder groups have similar or divergent aims.

   If the group of participants is large, then smaller discussion groups may be formed. A variation might be to give the separate groups different stakeholder briefs. In this case, the groups could present their plans for evaluation to a small committee of Professor Ford and her deputy at the

end of the discussion period. Professor Ford and the deputy chair of the department are empowered as the grant-holders, responsible to the funding body, to make the final decisions about the evaluation.
3. *The participants discuss the questions concerning teleworking (see below)*
   There should be about 30 minutes to one hour for examining the other questions given in the case study. General questions about new technology and organizational change, about evaluation methodologies and about teleworking, can be raised and discussed here.

## Questions

1. Design an evaluation of computer conferencing at the University of Minterne. The evaluation plan should cover the aims of the evaluation, the important variables to be included or considered and the evaluation methods and schedule.
2. Assess the strengths and weaknesses of the evaluation design you have developed. How might you assess the generalizability of this study to other organizational applications of computer conferencing?
3. Identify the main concerns for

   (a) staff;
   (b) students; and
   (c) other relevant stakeholder groups.

4. Propose a structure and procedure for establishing and managing the evaluation study.
5. Considering the application of teleworking in a wider context, what light does the case study throw on

   (a) work organization;
   (b) the management of change; and
   (c) decision-making, control and power?

## Essential Reading

Blackler, F. and Oborne, D. (eds.) (1987) *Information Technology and People: Designing for the Future*, British Psychological Society Publications, Leicester. (See especially the following chapters: Chapter 2, F. Blackler and C. Brown, Management, organization and the new technologies; Chapter 5, B. Christie and M. Gardiner, Office systems; Chapter 6, M. Fitter, The development and use of information technology in health care (sections on stakeholders and the multi-perspective approach); and Chapter 11, J. Long, Information technology and home-based services: improving the usability of tele-shopping.)

## Additional Reading

Hiltz, S. R. and Turoff, M. (1978) *The Network Nation*, Addison-Wesley, Reading, Mass.

Legge, K. (1984) *Evaluating Planned Organizational Change*, Academic Press, London.

Mason, R. D. and Kaye, A. R. (1989) *Mindweave: Communication, Computers and Distance Education*, Pergamon Press, Oxford.

Mueller, W. (1992) Flexible working and new technology, in J. F. Hartley and G. M. Stephenson (eds.) *Employment Relations: The Psychology of Influence and Control at Work*, Blackwell, Oxford.

Stanworth, J. and Stanworth, C. (1991) *Teleworking*, IPM, London.

## Appendix: *An Example of Computer Conferencing: Messages within a Topic*

(*Note*: the messages are reproduced here as written — including the odd minor spelling mistake, which is acceptable within the culture of conferencing.)

---

Group 4/culture #6 pwdavi, 13-Nov-91 13:16

From: Pete Davies
There is/are comment(s) on this message

TITLE: culture
If structure is the way in which an organization formally seeks to achieve its aims, then culture is another variable which both formally and informally affects what actually happens. The structure of an organization shows what is supposed to be happening, whereas the culture gives a guide to what is actually happening.

It seems to be fashionable because it plays a large part in the success ( or otherwise) of an organization. There are a lot of publications which rely on anecdotal evidence or personal theories of the authors , rather than systematic research. This sounds similar to publications on organizational structure 100 years ago.

I havent read all the messages on this topic yet but if no-one else volunteers I'd be happy to summarise.
     Pete Davies

---

Group 4/culture #7, jvryma, 15-Nov-91 12:29

From: Joan Ryman
This is a comment to message 6

I think your comments on culture were very interesting, Pete, especially the second point. I want to add one further point: that some orgs appear to use the idea of culture to justify or give validity to their decision-making processes eg their mission statements.
     Joan Ryman

Group 4/culture #8 jfhutc 15-Nov-91 14:03

From: Hilary Hutchings
This is a comment to message 6

Thanks fo r offering to summarise the culture topic, Pete. I will take you up on
that. We still need someone to summarise the topic on Mintzberg on week ending
Dec 6 − any offers? You also mention the need for systematic research in this area −
what would need to be done ie can you set a research agenda? I address this to the
whole group − don't leave all this to Pete!
     Hilary Hutchings

Group 4/culture #9 hfmaxw 15-Nov-91

From: Hugh Maxwell
There is/are comment(s) on this message

culture: what is it?
Schein: basic assumptoions and beliefs about a number of issues, viz
−where the org is in the envir eg beliefs about the NHS, its value etc
−nature and reality of truth eg what's evidence, on whose say-so, are things done
& when & why eg medical because of expertise, business plans, authority of chief
executive, government minister etc
−human nature and how to motivate, reward and control people
−what human activity ids valued, eg cures, quality of cost to NHS
−nature of human relationships − again, what's valued

I didn't understand the article by Allaire and Firsiroytu − it seemed very complicated − did anyone else get to understand it? It seemed to view org culture as more
about myths and values and ideology − ie softer stuff but I can't get to grips with
that as easily as Schein.they talk of 3 influences: >host society >history >environ-
ment but I felt these could be taken to mean almost anything post hoc.

Theoretically though it seems some of the ideas are clear (I found Schein good
here) and there seems to be growing evidence that cultural differences may be
meaningfully related to structure/performance. I s this just cross cultural evidence
though (eg Japan vs America) or is there evidence on differences in culture between
orgs in one country being related to either structure, performance or other outcomes?
Hilary − do you know a good reference on this? Hope all this was legible/
understandable!
     Hugh Maxwell

Group 5/culture #10, sastan, 17-Nov-91 22:53

From: Susan Stanton
This is a comment to message 9
There is/are comment(s) on this message

I've found all the contributions above very interesting and informative. I thought
that rather than go through some of the academic definitions of culture I would tell

you all about my experiences of org culture as a consultant (if its not interesting then let me know!!) sometimes we got called in to deal with resistance to change. In most cases the problem lay in the lack of acknowledgement, by senior management of the existance of a culture or group of sub-cultures within the organization. Most management teams planning a change process focussed entireley on its effects on structure and ignored culture. Unfortunatley, this often meant that managers designed change on the basis of what should be happening (structure) rather thatn what was happening (culture). I think culture is in many ways what orgs are (culture as the root metaphor as it says in our textbook). Structure is the idealised version or management version of reality. So I think that culture certainly won't be a passing fad and researchers will need to focus on it more. The problem is that culture is a much more nebulous concept and structure is so much easier to explore.

Does this make sense to anyone?
On a differnt note – has anyone got a photocopy of Marshall and Maclean they can lend me – my library hasn't got it. Send me an electronic mail message if you have.

# PART IV

Towards an
Enterprise Culture?

# CASE 14

# The Case of Aborted New-Company Formation: Organizational Failure or Emergent Potentiality?

## Gemma M. Cox

## Setting

Since the early 1980s, the notion of public enterprise in Britain has been dramatically reshaped by its political caretakers. With a shift from public service industry to large-scale privatization, there has been growth in the perception of competitive opportunities within the private sector, and in the emphasis placed on accountability for action carried out in the public sector. In government research organizations, managers are encouraged to move their divisions from cost-centre status to operational profit centres, by employing their research knowledge in consultancy and contract research activities. However, this trend has resulted in impractical constraints for some R & D groups. As they move from basic to applied research, they find the structure of the research organization can withhold the greater capital input required for innovation. The development of an innovation to a standard product is, in many cases, legally as well as practically impossible within the codes of operation that define the activity of the research organization.

One option for a research group that has become impractically constrained is to leave the organization and to create a new company in which it can develop and produce the intellectual expertise or tangible product that has become the group's fundamental activity. This case study examines one such attempt at new-company formation, and considers the factors that prevented the goal from being achieved as initially intended.

## Background to the Problem

In 1987, the managers of the Applied Expertise Centre (AEC) at one of Britain's public research laboratories reached an agreement with a City venture capitalist for financial backing to launch as an independent company – the Applied Expertise Company (also AEC). AEC's scientists had developed a number of techniques and one-off products for contract research clients in heavy industry, which they believed had more general applications and could therefore form the core business for a small, high-technology firm. These techniques could not be further developed within the research laboratory, as the centre was required to generate an operating profit on the basis of contract R & D activity, leaving limited resources for other development work.

Since AEC's formation in 1970 as a research and business centre, it had carried out consultancy and contract R & D work for a wide range of industrial customers with specific research needs. Although from its inception the centre generated an income, it originally received central government financing for its research work. However, the demands on its financial performance grew with time. While initially a partial contribution was sufficient, requirements grew for it to become first self-supporting and then surplus generating.

In 1984, faced with the cessation of government funding and the need to exploit its activity profitably, AEC entered into a collaboration with New Ventures Limited (NVL), the technology-transfer subsidiary of a large City finance house. Under the agreement, NVL had the right of first refusal to fund AEC projects. When NVL took up this option on a project, it provided research funding and then licensed the rights for development to a 'host' company in return for a negotiated royalty, a portion of which would return to AEC.

Initial plans for company formation arose from a number of difficulties encountered in this project-funding and licensing scheme. On the one hand, NVL was entertaining a new focus in its investment programme. It had project arrangements with a number of groups like the AEC, but now wanted to move away from long-term R & D investment – the funding of ideas – to projects it termed nearer the market – the marketing of saleable products. From AEC's perspective, the licensing arrangements were far from ideal, as there were very few businesses with the expertise to take on their projects through technology transfer. AEC now possessed a portfolio of techniques developed for previous clients, some of which had received initial funding from NVL. For both parties, the decision to form a dedicated company in which AEC staff could themselves develop and market their innovations seemed to be a more suitable way forward.

## The Problem

From 1987, AEC's managers worked progressively towards new company formation. A business plan was formulated, the parent research organization was consulted and a new business relationship with NVL was developed and formalized through regular progress meetings. However, the initial date set for company formation, autumn 1988, wasn't met. New deadlines were set for winter 1988, spring and summer 1989, and finally spring 1990. Each successive date set passed without fruition. The diversity of obstacles encountered included securing of finance for pre-production development work, regulatory issues, staffing requirements and production difficulties. As the final date set for formation passed in the spring of 1990, the centre managers conceded they were unable to meet their initial goals for new-company formation. The initial goals, and the various issues that became obstacles to their achievement, are detailed in the following sections.

## Goals and Objectives

In 1987, NVL's interest in backing the proposed new company lay in the belief that projects being undertaken by AEC scientists were commercially viable and close to the production stage. The agreement reached was that NVL would fund the company to be set up, and would staff it with former AEC employees who had worked on the original project research. This would ease the former technology-transfer difficulties, as staff who had transferred from AEC would be involved at the production stage. The new company would also be in a position to cut costs and reduce the significantly large overheads AEC adsorbed from central functions while a part of the research laboratory.

Initially, the company would concentrate on the production of two core products. From NVL's perspective, the new venture offered a better-than-average opportunity. The management and staff of AEC had practical commercial experience of selling instruments and services to demanding contract research customers, as well as possessing their expert knowledge. The formation of a company offered the opportunity to generate income from making and selling, as well as the profit from royalty payments.

## Product Issues

The new company was envisaged, in 1987, to emerge as a two-product venture. One of the potential products was to be tested at a local industrial site, and had been perceived from the outset as eminently exploitable commercially within the electricity-supply industry. AEC had on its staff one of the world's foremost authorities in the technology the innovation employed, and confidence was high that it would attract a large number of orders. Although developments had superseded AEC's progress in that at least one American company already had a similar machine in operation, the information that could potentially be produced by the centre's model was considered to be superior to any other developer's instrumentation.

Two years later, AEC had yet to place a prototype at the local site, had lost another British tender to the American competitors and found the privatization of the electricity-supply industry a serious obstacle to maintaining a working relationship with potential users within the industry. Although company formation was imminent, the centre had no orders for a product that had not yet been developed to prototype stage.

The second product was in an earlier stage of development and, between 1987 and 1989, several problems had been encountered in the incorporation of the innovation into a system of use to an end customer. One of the problems facing this second project was a funding decision made by NVL.

NVL had provided seed capital for it – sufficient funds to get the project off the ground. Following the initial injection, little additional funding was available to carry the project through the development stages. Low funding slowed the pace of development, which in turn affected the centre's capacity to attract customers – it had no end-product to show potential users, and it was again lagging behind producers of a similar technological application.

However, in late 1989, AEC tendered for a government contract to develop the system. When it became clear that the centre stood a good chance of being awarded the contract, NVL agreed to fund the design through the development stage to the point where it could become a viable company product, making AEC eligible for the contract. It was agreed that, given the achievement of the government contract, the new company would commence with a focus on that product, and could then gradually adjust its focus to operate as a two-product company with a longer-term outlook.

## NVL–AEC Relations

The relationship between AEC employees and NVL personnel was affected by internal reorganization at NVL, which resulted in staff and policy changes. In 1984, when AEC first entered into consultations with NVL, the technology-transfer company worked with the assumption that high-technology investments generated high rewards. After successive periods in which NVL was reminded of the high-risk element of new-technology investments, it became less willing to inject funds into projects, after the initial investment, unless there was evidence of a short-term return. This made the centre scientists as well as managers more aware of their relationship with NVL, as their own projects were affected. The change in NVL personnel, which came about in 1987–8, was accompanied by a change in policy requiring evidence of project performance.

However, an interesting political development within NVL during this period was a tendency towards 'project championing'. NVL personnel were eager to present their interests as high-performance ventures to the board. Centre scientists voiced concern over the commercial value that was being attributed to their two projects by business people who were, they said, 'hyping our "products"' without an appreciation of the technology.

The contrast between NVL's inflated projections of financial performance, and the scientists' perceptions of the worth of products the new company would eventually sell, was reflected in an incident that occurred in the autumn of 1989. The second project was moving along slowly in anticipation of the government contract. NVL established a value for the equipment its developers felt hardly reflected its true value. As one of the scientists commented, 'They've invested £—— in the intellectual property, and they want a system that they can sell for five times that'. While NVL was eager to press ahead to the next stage with the project, the scientists were more conscious of what development work there remained to be done. While the parties did learn from each other, differences in opinion and perspective affected their ability to communicate effectively on developmental progress and plans for the company.

## Staffing Issues

Formation of a new company would mean a change from dedicated R & D work to the production, marketing and sale of a limited range of products. Management had to consider who, and how many, would be needed to staff the venture. With an initial focus on products that had been developed at AEC, there was no short-term emphasis on R & D work within the company. Though the centre's scientists were already experienced promoters of their own work to contract clients, management expressed concern whether the 'culture' and 'motivational factors' for research scientists who carried out the work primarily for 'intellectual satisfaction' could be accommodated in a make-and-sell environment.

AEC scientists also expressed reservations, but there was not a homogeneity of response. Opinions ranged from concerns for the insecurity of industrial employment, and the challenges of making a late career transition, to interest in the financial attractions of the change and enthusiasm for involvement in the tangible output of intellectual effort.

AEC management had personal career-development interests in new-company formation, as they perceived heightened opportunities for the expansion of their roles. Within the government laboratory, they were constrained by the dictates of a bureaucratic, role-ordered organizational structure that allowed few opportunities for independent action. For example, they were unable to recruit new staff directly to their group, and staff could be transferred from the centre to another group without their involvement in the decision. The move would be a liberating one for them.

## Organizational Issues

In 1987, one of the most appealing arguments for leaving the research laboratory was the freedom to operate without the restrictions imposed by the larger organization. However, during the period 1987−9 the research laboratory, itself responding to government pressure, began to encourage greater commercial awareness among its employees. AEC management perceived an opportunity: 'It's going to be cosmetically important for them to be seen to be promoting a new way of doing things − there's a certain self-interest from their point of view. There's no obvious benefit . . . other than esteem and political recognition for being entrepreneurial.'

Management considered the options for maintaining links that could be beneficial to the fledgling operation. One was close physical proximity, which could facilitate access to on-site resources. There was also the option of a legal−financial link, for example including the parent as a minority shareholder in the new company. At its best, such a link could, they thought, create a truly effective mechanism for exploiting technological innovation:

> You have all the advantages of the small operation, very professional, etc., tapping into the resources of [the parent] with its high-quality reputation . . . if you combine the virtues of both you're going to get your order on the grounds that we're a small commercially minded

entrepreneurial organization but we're going to use what [the parent] has behind us to assure you the customer that things will be done better, with no drop in standards, and for less.

## Financial Issues

Between 1987 and 1989, projects slowed because of a paucity of funds as described in the previous sections, and changes in direction were made in response to fund availability. NVL's risk-averse response to its earlier losses on high-technology investments led it to support AEC's new company, as an assured-product, near-the-market venture, but also to withhold funds after an initial injection of capital. AEC management soon came to realize that a new legal identity would not necessarily solve the financial insecurities faced as a contract R & D group. None the less, in explaining why company formation was a sound option, financial opportunity remained a prime factor.

The initial company-formation decision was made in recognition of the fact that, within the research laboratory, there was no readily available source of investment capital for product development, even when there was a good market opportunity. Despite the funding problems faced between 1987 and 1989, the desire to obtain the best possible return from its products was cited as a significant factor in the departure decision:

> If you are in a business like ours where you are developing hardware, most of the money is in the making and selling of it ... in standard form to as many customers as you can. ... The main reason for getting into manufacturing and selling is simply to get into the activity where most of the money is made — the strictly financial return reason.
>
> (AEC manager)

In planning the financial role of the new company, AEC managers and NVL contrasted their projected tight financial control with that of the parent organization. They stressed the move from a low financial-accountability environment to one that would reward performance-oriented operation:

> The company will operate as a real profit or loss centre, and have its own real accounts, not some Mickey Mouse bits of paper that nobody believes and in any case are fiddled by people like me.
>
> (AEC manager)

> The financial structure will be different ... the company will make profits.
>
> (AEC manager)

> The business would have to be like any other. It would have to have its business and marketing plans to justify its financing.
>
> (NVL)

> We should be in a good position, if all goes well, in five years to be receiving good, positive cash flows.
>
> (NVL)

## Questions

1. What are the primary obstacles to the formation of the new AEC? Are these typical of those generally faced in the formation of small, high-technology companies?
2. How do the interests of the key players in the process — managers, scientists and funders — impact on the formation of the new company?
3. Are the financial difficulties due to poor management or characteristic of the cost of funding innovation?
4. Does the new company need the expertise of the centre's scientists for successful operation?
5. Would you describe AEC as likely to meet with success or failure in the formation of the new company?

## Essential Reading

Katz, H. J. and Gartner, W. B. (1988) Properties of Emerging Organizations, *Academy of Management Review*, Vol. 13, no. 3, pp. 429–41.

Birley, S. (1986) The role of new firms: births, deaths and job generation, *Strategic Management Journal*, Vol. 7, pp. 361–76.

Oakey, R., Rothwell, R. and Cooper, S. (1988) *The Management of Innovation in High-Technology Small Firms* London, Frances Pinter.

Meyer, M. W. and Zucker, L. G. (1990) Forever failing firms, *Chief Executive*, Vol. 60, pp. 68–70.

## Additional Reading

Daniels, A. K. (1975) Professionalism in formal organizations, in J. B. McKinley (ed.), *Processing People: Cases in Organizational Behaviour*, London, Holt, Rinehart and Winston, pp. 303–38.

Ganwin, D. A. (1983) Spin-offs and the new firm formation process, *California Management Review*, Vol. 25, no. 2, pp. 3–20.

Meyer, M. W. and Zucker, L. G. (1989) *Permanently Failing Organisations*, London, Sage.

# CASE 15

## Decision-Making and Accounting: Resource Allocation in the National Health Service

### Janine Nahapiet

### Organizational Setting

This case is about resource allocation in a region of the National Health Service (NHS). It describes the experience of the region as it approached the implementation of a new national policy designed to achieve a fairer geographical distribution of financial resources across the service.

The case is set in the late 1970s, at which time the NHS had what was widely recognized as a complex structure. At the top, the centralized functions of the service were provided by the Deparment of Health and Social Security (DHSS). Below department level, the service was organized into a three-tiered structure comprising regions, areas and districts (see Figure 15.1). Each of these tiers represented a geographical entity, charged with a particular set of duties and responsibilities, which are described below:

1. *Regional health authorities (RHAs)* Fourteen of these were established as statutory bodies accountable to the Secretary of State. Their main responsibilities were planning and the allocation of financial resources to the levels below them. They were also responsible for some medical activities, through the appointment of senior medical staff and the provision of specialist services. The authority chairperson and members were all part-time and were appointed by the Secretary of State after consultations with relevant organizations. Most regions had between 18 and 24 members, representing interested parties, including the main health professionals, the trade unions, the universities and local authorities. Although not formally designated as such, several members were regarded as representing several sectional interests, including those of the area health authorities. Each RHA was supported by a team of full-time officers and their staffs. Although each officer had specific responsibilities, as the regional team of officers (RTO) they had collective responsibility for framing plans and proposing allocations under a system of 'consensus management', i.e. there was no formally designated head of the team (DHSS, 1972).

2. *Area health authorities (AHAs)* Each RHA comprised a number of AHAs,

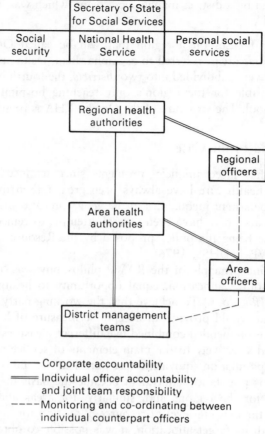

Figure 15.1   The structure of the National Health Service, 1972

also statutory bodies directly accountable to the Secretary of State. AHAs carried full operational responsibilities for the service, and undertook much detailed planning as well as employing most of the NHS staff. They were also responsible for any teaching hospitals within their boundaries. Although most areas were further subdivided into districts, there were some that were not so divided. As with the regions, AHA members were part-time appointees, selected by either the RHA or by local authorities and staff and professional groupings. The chairperson was appointed by the Secretary of State. Each AHA was supported by an area team of officers and their associated staffs. They also operated under 'consensus management' and, although they had professional links to their regional counterparts, they did not report directly to them.

3.  *Health districts*   Health districts managed the operation of the service at local level, comprising the smallest units for which substantially the full range of general health services could be provided. Each health district was

managed by a district management team, which was jointly responsible to the AHA.

This case focuses on a region that will be called Omega. Omega RHA comprised four areas, referred to as Alpha, Beta, Delta and Gamma. Three of these areas were subdivided into two districts, the fourth being a single district area responsible for the region's only teaching hospital and its prestigious medical school. The structure of the Omega RHA is presented in Figure 15.2.

## Background to the Case

The NHS has faced financial problems since its inception. The resources sought for health care have always been greater than the supply, and there have been persistent inequalities in the geographical distribution of resources. Over the years, there have been several attempts to remedy such inequalities, one of these being the policy proposed by the Resource Allocation Working Party (RAWP – DHSS, 1976).

The guiding principle of the RAWP philosophy was 'to secure eventually, through resource allocation, equal opportunity to health care for people at equal risk' (*ibid.* p. 6) To achieve this, the working party sought to develop a formula that would provide an acceptable measure of health care need. The formula it recommended combined five different measures of need, which were then applied selectively to the main elements of service provision in order to produce a 'population equivalent' (see note 1 at the end of the case for further details.) This population equivalent became the basis for establishing 'target' allocations for the regions and, similarly, for areas and districts. Thus, by comparing the existing level of resource allocation for any region (or area or district) with its target allocation, it was possible to obtain an assessment of current levels of under- or over-resourcing.

The publication of the RAWP report stimulated a vigorous debate, attracting criticism of both its methods and its likely impact. Its supporters, however, argued that the accounting formula met three important requirements. First, it provided a way of quantifying an objective it had been difficult to pursue in the absence of an agreed formula. As was stated in one of the Omega discussion

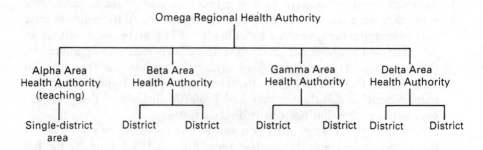

**Figure 15.2** The structure of Omega RHA

documents, 'how can we rob Peter to pay Paul without an agreed formula?' Second, it would enable a change in the process and methods of allocation, encouraging the pursuit of deliberate planning and a move away from the prevailing pattern of incrementalism. Third, it was thought to offer an objective, equitable and efficient way of resolving the difficulties in agreeing priorities in times of limited resource availability.

Following publication of the report, the Secretary of State for Health and Social Services indicated that its recommendations would be used as the basis for future allocations to the RHAs and that he expected the regions to do likewise.

Within the Omega region, the report was quickly viewed by both officers and members as something to be taken seriously. First, it was associated with the goal of equalization − a goal representing the principle of 'fair shares', which had long been espoused within the region. Second, since Omega was one of five regions assessed as being over-resourced in relation to their RAWP targets, it seemed likely there would be little growth money available and there might even be a cut in their existing level of funding. RAWP would thus adversely and imminently affect the financial position of the region. Third, although all the region's four areas were above their national targets, when assessed on a regional basis the resource positions of the four areas differed, with Beta being significantly below target. Unhappy with its funding level, RAWP had been used very successfully as part of a campaign by the Beta area to draw attention to its need for extra resources, a campaign that led to much public criticism of the RHA for failing to meet this need.

This recognition of the potential significance of RAWP was accompanied by considerable confusion and some concern. The vast majority were confused because everyone found the formula extremely complex and the derivation of targets almost impossible to follow. This included most of the treasurers and their staff − the officers most heavily involved in preparing papers and proposals on resource allocations for their authorities. They thus had to work very hard simply to understand what RAWP was about. At the same time, the few who were more familiar with the statistics and methodology of RAWP continued to express concern over the appropriateness of several elements of the formula, reservations that mirrored those being expressed nationally.

Following months of formal and informal discussions across the region, the RTO (comprising the treasurer, administrator, medical officer, nursing officer and architect) concluded that the RHA should endorse the principle of equalization with a view to making allocations that would move areas towards their RAWP target. The RHA did this in the autumn of 1977.

## The Problem

NHS resources are allocated on an annual basis under the two main categories of capital and revenue. The financial year runs from April to March and it is the revenue allocation that is the main focus here.

Once the allocation for the DHSS has been established by government, this is then subdivided into the departmental budget and the regional allocations, the latter becoming the responsibility of RHAs for further distribution to areas and districts. At the same time as the authorities announce their one-year allocations, they are also expected to confirm resource assumptions for a further three years in order to assist the planning process. Each stage of this allocation should take account of current policies and priorities, these being communicated in guidelines issued by the department to the health authorities.

For 1978−9, the guidelines from the department drew the attention of RHAs to several factors to be taken into account in making their revenue allocations. Four were of particular relevance to the Omega RHA:

1. *Provisions for medical teaching*  Additional resources would be needed for teaching hospitals in order to cover the increased costs associated with national expansion of medical schools. The Omega region's medical school, located in Alpha area, was one of the major national schools and was fully committed to expansion.

2. *Commissioning of capital schemes*  In order to regenerate the ageing capital stock of the NHS, the government introduced a scheme in the 1960s whereby it undertook to provide the revenue required to run those new capital schemes it had approved. This provision of the revenue consequences of capital schemes, generally known as RCCS, was withdrawn in the 1970s, although some of the buildings, including major hospitals, that had been planned under the scheme had yet to be completed. During 1977 there had been growing public concern over the failure to open new hospitals and mounting criticism of the government and health authorities. Regions were thus asked to inform the DHSS how they proposed to find the funding for new capital projects. Within the Omega region, all four areas needed additional revenue to support capital schemes due to open shortly, although the greatest demand was in Alpha. For Omega, the two main funding possibilities identified were a subvention from capital to revenue and the sale of land.

3. *Geographical redistribution of revenue resources*  The first full year in which RAWP came into effect was the financial year 1978−9. Although it had originally been anticipated that application of the formula would lead to a redistribution of resources from 'over-provided' to 'under-provided' regions, in the event it was only applied to additional or 'growth' money. The guidelines from the Secretary of State to regions indicated that he expected to see significant redistribution of revenue resources within regions achieved in 1978−9. When applied on a regional basis, the RAWP formula showed that Alpha area was above target, Beta was below target, with Delta and Gamma areas more or less on target.

4. *Spending within cash limits policy*  This limited the amount of over- or underspending within a year to plus or minus 1 per cent of revenue. Beyond this, any excess revenue resulting from underspending had to be returned to the DHSS and any excess overspending was to be deducted

from the following year's allocation. The Omega region was an overspending region, with significant overspending in Beta and Delta areas.

In addition to these policy issues, the Omega RHA was also facing financial pressures because of increasing demand for services arising from population growth throughout the region, but especially in Beta and Delta areas. Moreover, each one of the areas could make a case for additional resources, in line with the government's health-care planning guidelines that used a different formula for assessing need (see note 2 at the end of the case for further details). The criteria and their impact on the financial position of the region are summarized in Figure 15.3.

By the start of 1978, the revenue resource outlook had improved. The overspending forecast had dropped considerably and there were indications that all regions would receive at least some growth money in the 1978–9 allocation. In the light of this improved outlook and in line with its earlier policy decisions, at its February meeting the authority asked the RTO to bring forward proposals on resource allocations to areas, together with three-year resource assumptions, requesting that they should explore all the options in order to establish the best balance possible to achieve

   (i)    a faster move to equalisation
   (ii)   equalising without taking away from any Area; and
   (iii)  to provide some help to Areas to bring into use major new capital projects.

Both officers and members left this meeting spurred on by the Regional Treasurer's observation that 'in theory, it should be easier this year than ever before to carry out this preparatory work in that the Authority has already approved policies and decided on ... the main courses of action for 1978/79'.

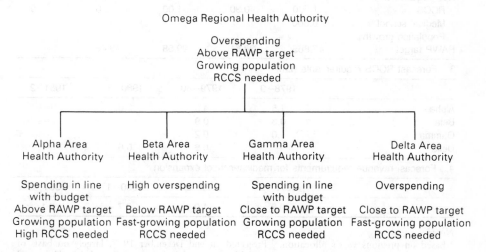

**Figure 15.3**  Financial position of the Omega RHA and its constituent AHAs

Taken in context, this statement was significant because both officers and members regarded the previous year's allocation process as having been very difficult, culminating in Beta's criticism of the authority, which was widely publicized in the local media. It was agreed that this time around every effort should be made to avoid such criticism.

Two days after the RHA meeting, the five members of the RTO met to identify options that would achieve the members' policy requirements on equalization and the opening of capital schemes. In doing so, they had to consider recommendations concerning the allocation for 1978–9 and resource assumptions for the following three years. The resources they had available to them included, in simple terms, an amount equivalent to the previous year's allocation (with allowances for inflation, etc.) and growth money equivalent to 0.7 per cent of the total allocation. Further details are given in Table 15.1

In exploring the options to meet the criteria they had been set, the officers realized for the first time that, in the context of this particular region, the funding of capital schemes and equalization were mutually incompatible, at least in the short term. As reference to Figure 16.3 demonstrates, the area

**Table 15.1**  Key revenue data for the Omega region

**1.  Revenue available: 1978–9**

| | |
|---|---|
| Expected regional allocation | £180 million |
| Additional 'growth money', announced in January | £3.6 million |

**2.  Basic assumptions and requirements (£m)**

| | Alpha | Beta | Gamma | Delta | ORHA |
|---|---|---|---|---|---|
| Allocation* | 43.000 | 34.00 | 51.00 | 30.00 | 22.00 |
| Expenditure[†] | 43.800 | 38.00 | 52.00 | 31.60 | 23.50 |
| New requirements | | | | | |
| RCCS | 1.500 | 0.30 | 1.00 | 0 | 0 |
| Medical school | 0.800 | | | | |
| Population growth‡ | | | | | |
| RAWP target | 47.865 | 38.61 | 29.58 | 43.48 | |

**3.  Forecast RCCS requirements (£m)**

| | 1978–9 | 1979–80 | 1980–1 | 1981–2 |
|---|---|---|---|---|
| Alpha | 1.5 | 4.5 | 2.0 | — |
| Beta | 0.3 | 0.9 | — | — |
| Gamma | 1.0 | 0.2 | — | — |
| Delta | — | 0.6 | 0.6 | — |

**4.  Forecast revenue requirements for medical-school expansion**

| 1978–9 | 1979–80 | 1980–1 | 1981–2 |
|---|---|---|---|
| 0.8 | 1.0 | 0.7 | 0.1 |

*Notes*
* Based on previous year's allocation. [†] Projected, at end December 1977, largely on basis of historical accounts. ‡ No agreed figures available; Beta and Delta most affected, but Alpha and Gamma also growing; this growth will eventually show in the RAWP target since the formula contains population measures.

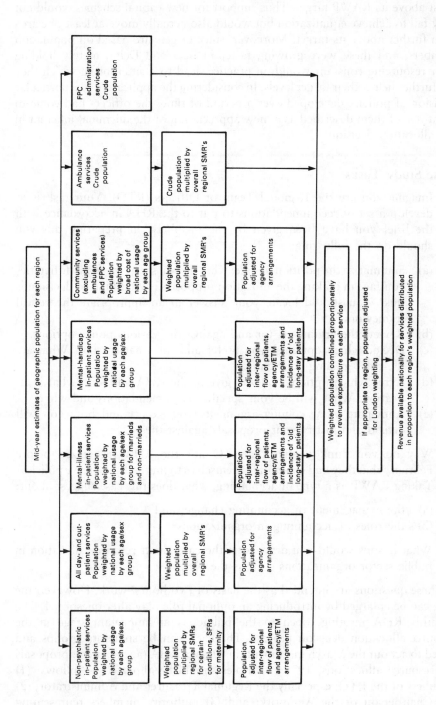

**Figure 15.4** The build-up of a revenue target

requiring most funds for capital schemes was Alpha but it was Alpha that was most above its RAWP target. Thus support for new capital schemes would not only fail to achieve equalization but would also actually move at least one area even further above its target. Moreover, since targets are based on population numbers, and these were growing faster in Beta and Delta, merely holding their resourcing constant would, in practice, lead to a situation in which they fell further below their target levels. In considering the application to a particular decision of policies developed over a period of time, the officers had come to what one of them described as a 'new appreciation of the dilemma' inherent in the allocation decision.

## Case Study Tasks

1. Imagine you are the Regional Team of Officers (RTO). Your task is to develop a set of recommendations to put to the RHA in accordance with the brief you have been given by the members. In preparing this you should do the following:

   (a)  Summarize the position to date: what do you see as the main difficulties you face in making the allocation proposals? What kind of decision is this? You should locate your answer in an appropriate theoretical framework.
   (b)  Review the arguments for and against the various policy options.
   (c)  Decide which option(s) you prefer and for what reasons. What are the rules guiding your choice?
   (d)  Agree which options you will give to the RHA and with what justification. What will be your specific recommendations and why?
   (e)  Anticipate what counter-arguments you expect and how you will defend and justify your proposals against these.

2. Why do you think neither the RTO nor the RHA recognized before February that they had committed themselves to mutually exclusive policies?

3. Taking RAWP as a type of accounting, what does this case suggest about:

   (a)  the management of accounting change; and
   (b)  the roles of accounting in organizations?

4. What lessons would you draw from the case about resource allocation in public sector organizations such as the NHS?

   These questions are intended as the basis of two hours' work. However, the case can be enlarged by introducing an optional role play after question 1. The monthly RHA meeting, open to the public, is an important stage in the resource-allocation decision process. The class can be split into groups and asked to act out the March meeting of the Omega RHA (agenda item: proposals for resource allocations, 1978–9). Roles should be allocated as follows: (1) members of the RTO, especially the Regional Treasurer and Administrator; (2) the Chairperson of the Authority; and (3) authority members representing important and separate constituencies, including the areas and the medical school. This requires up to a further half day to allow for adequate preparation beforehand and debrief afterwards.

## Notes

1. In the RAWP formula, need was assessed in relation to the population size, the age/sex distribution of the population, population mortality rates (used as a proxy for morbidity), cross-boundary flows of in-patients and medical and dental education. The service elements to which these factors were applied were: non-psychiatric in-patient services; all day- and out-patient services; mental-illness in-patient services; mental-handicap in-patient services; community services; ambulance services; and family-practitioner administrative services. Figure 15.4 shows the build-up of a revenue target.

2. Health-care planning guidelines were derived from the NHS planning system, which was launched the same year as the RAWP report was published. The planning process attempted to identify appropriate service levels for a range of health care services, only subsequently considering the resources required to fund these levels. While RAWP was primarily concerned with the allocation of resources, planning was concerned with their deployment. Working from the DHSS, RAWP represented a top-down approach to health care provision in contrast to the bottom-up approach of the planning system. While they drew on some common information, many of their databases were different.

## Essential Reading

Cooper, D. J., Hayes, D. and Wolf, F. (1981) Accounting in organized anarchies: understanding and designing accounting systems in ambiguous situations, *Accounting, Organizations and Society*, Vol. 6, no. 3, pp. 175–91.

Maynard, A. and Ludbrook, A. (1980) Budget allocation in the National Health Service, *Journal of Social Policy*, Vol. 9, no. 3, pp. 289–312.

Pfeffer, J. (1977) Power and resource allocation in organizations, in B. M. Staw and G. R. Salancik (eds.) *New Directions in Organizational Behavior*, St Clair Press, Chicago, Ill.

Seed, A.H. (1970) The rational abuse of accounting information, *Management Accounting*, January, pp. 9–11.

## Additional Reading

Beech, R., Bevan, G. and Mays, N. (1990) Spatial equity in the NHS: the death and re-birth of RAWP in health care UK 1990, *Policy Journals*, Newbury, pp. 44–61.

Boland, R. J. and Pondy, L. R. (1983) Accounting in organizations: a union of natural and rational perspectives, *Accounting, Organizations and Society*, Vol. 8, no. 2/3, pp. 223–34.

Burchell, S., Clubb, C., Hopwood, A., Hughes, J. and Nahapiet, J. (1980) The roles of accounting in organizations and society, *Accounting, Organizations and Society*, Vol. 5, no. 1, pp. 5–27.

DHSS (1972) *Management Arrangements for the Reorganized National Health Service*, HMSO, London.

DHSS (1976) *Sharing Resources for Health in England: Report of the Resource Allocation Working Party*, HMSO, London.

Hall, R. H. and Quinn, R. E. (eds.) (1983) *Organizational Theory and Public Policy*, Sage, Beverly Hills, Calif.

Klein, R. (1983) *The Politics of the National Health Service*, Longman, Harlow.

Levitt, R. (1976) *The Reorganized National Health Service*, Croom Helm, London.

March, J. G. (1981) Decision making perspective, in A. H. van de Ven and W. F. Joyce (eds.) *Perspectives on Organization Design and Behavior*, Wiley, New York, NY.

Mintzberg, H. and Waters, J. A. (1985) Of strategies, deliberate and emergent, *Strategic Management Journal*, Vol. 6, pp. 257–72.

Wildavsky, A. (1974) *The Politics of the Budgetary Process*, Little, Brown & Co., Boston, Mass. (2nd Edn).

# CASE 16

## Southglam: Managing Organizational Change in a District Health Authority

### Michael Reed and Peter Anthony

## Background to the Case

In 1983 a committee of inquiry set up by the government to examine the administration and management of the National Health Service (NHS) published its report. The Griffiths Report, as it became known, made a number of general recommendations concerning the reform of existing management structures and organizational processes within the NHS aimed at producing a more efficient and effective delivery of health care services. At the core of this reform strategy lay two proposals intended to implement a 'managerial revolution' within the NHS: first, the introduction of 'general management' at all levels of the NHS – that is, from hospital level up to central-government department level; and, second, the rationalization of functional and advisory management structures whose primary role was to provide a representative mechanism for professional and semi-professional groups. Both of these reforms were based on the assumption that the NHS – at all levels of the organization – had suffered from an administrative culture in which consensus management was the dominant ethos. Consensus management, the Griffiths Report argued, had encouraged a form of decision-making that lacked any kind of managerial direction or control. Instead, the decision-making process over resource allocation and utilization within the NHS was dominated by an administrative culture that valued compromise between competing interests above all else. The NHS wasn't managed, it was administered on the basis of a 'lowest common denominator' form of decision-making in which the maintenance of consensus between different group interests was the over-riding priority.

The introduction of general management and the rationalization of functional and professional structures was intended to move the NHS towards a streamlined organizational system in which effective managerial direction and control would be realized. General management entailed the introduction of line managers with overall executive authority for decision-making at all levels of the NHS. They would provide a mechanism of command and control over organizational performance, which had previously been dispersed among the clinical, administrative, nursing, para-medical and support groups that delivered health care services. Part of the remit of general managers would be to reorganize and simplify existing decision-making structures and procedures in such a way that bureaucratic delay and professional 'veto power' would be minimized − if not totally eradicated. This would entail the subordination of professional interests to the overall priorities general managers established for the organization as a whole, rather than the narrower concerns of particular groups.

Health authorities in England and Wales moved relatively quickly to implement the reforms the Griffiths Report had recommended. The recommendations indicated that the impact of the reforms would be felt most immediately and dramatically at district health-authority level − that is, at the level of authorities responsible for the provision of a wide range of general and specialized health care services within a defined geographical area. Most districts consisted of a number of 'units' − groupings of hospitals or patient services brought together under the aegis of a unit general manager (UGM) who would be responsible for the overall performance of his or her unit to a district general manager (DGM). The introduction of general management at unit and district levels, the Griffiths Report contended, would lead to much higher managerial *control* over resource allocation and utilization than had been the case under previous arrangements. In particular, it would strengthen managerial monitoring of and control over the costs of health care services *at the point of delivery*. General managers would have the authority and the control mechanisms necessary to monitor and modify operational costs, particularly those incurred by doctors in their provision of various treatment regimes. In this context, the instigation of various types of control mechanisms by general managers (such as clinical budgets, management by objectives, performance appraisal systems and more advanced information technologies providing more reliable data about patterns of resource utilization by professional groups) was seen as being critical for the success of the Griffiths 'revolution'. Figure 16.1 provides a simplified organizational chart of a typical district health authority (DHA) in the post-Griffiths era.

## Organizational Background

Southglam is a DHA serving, primarily, an urban catchment area consisting of a population of approximately 300,000 people. While the authority has some 'peripheral' units located in semi-rural areas, the major focus for its activity is a large city population with very distinctive disparities in terms of housing, employment, income, education and social/welfare facilities. It has a very large and prestigious − as well as costly − teaching hospital, which treats large numbers of patients from other district authorities. At the time that the Griffiths reforms were introduced, the authority was under severe pressure to reduce its relatively high levels of expenditure on both 'core' and 'support' services. Many of the latter (such as haematological services) were used extensively by neighbouring authorities, but without appropriate levels of financial recompense. In this respect, the organizational changes introduced under the auspices of the Griffiths Report were implemented during a period of extreme

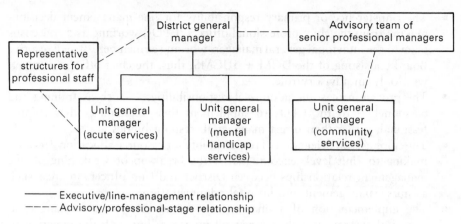

Figure 16.1   A simplified post-Griffiths district health authority

financial stringency and gave rise to additional pressure on all the various interest groups involved in the change process. In short, senior management within the authority were determined to be less generous in the services they provided to neighbouring authorities at a time when a reassertion of managerial control over escalating costs was the major policy priority. The implementation of Griffiths-type reorganization occurred at a time when the authority was already under considerable pressure to contain its costs and to introduce control systems that would match its expenditure to more stringent budgetary requirements.

## The DGM's Strategy

The health authority agreed a policy statement with its DGM that provided the wider rationale within which his implementation of the Griffiths proposals could be justified. It argued that

> The main thrust of these changes must be to identify individual managers for each unit and function, each of whom has clear *personal responsibility* and *accountability*. This will establish, clearly, one point of contact for each part of the service, thereby easing communication ... At every level of the authority there should be no doubt about the responsibility of the *individual manager* to provide leadership and motivate staff; to be responsible for a constant search for major change and cost improvements; to ensure that decisions affecting more than one function are taken quickly and effectively, and that the necessary action follows.

The appointment of general managers at unit level and the devolution of more decision-making responsibility to these managers became a major part of the organizational change process this statement initiated and legitimated. Their position was strengthened by a significant reduction in the influence professional groups exerted over managerial decision-making. This was achieved through a number of additional organizational changes the DGM initiated:

- The transference of primary responsibility for line management decision-making from the chief professional officers (CPOs) working as a consensus team to the individual general managers working as members of an Executive Board consisting of the DGM + 5UGMS; thus, the chief officers were left with only an advisory role.
- The provision of some additional responsibilities – such as training and personnel – to the CPOs to supplement their remaining advisory/professional, rather than direct managerial, responsibilities.
- The emphasis on delegation of responsibility for resource allocation decision-making to Unit level, encouraged by the break-up or weakening of line management relationships between District and Unit officers in areas such as nurse management and hospital administration.
- The implementation of a 'management by objectives' performance and appraisal system, initially for general managers but with the intention of widening its scope to officers.
- A much more formalized distinction, not to say separation, between 'professional' and 'managerial' roles: thus the Authority's 'Revised Management Arrangements' policy document stated that 'general managers are the managers of the service and all officers are managerially accountable to them'.
- The introduction of more flexible structures at Unit level so that different units would have differing organizational arrangements depending on the services they provided and the tasks required to carry them out.

These changes in formal structures were supplemented by a reorientation of managerial thinking and action towards a more 'corporate approach' into which professional groups (and particularly clinicians) were to be incorporated, if in a subordinate role, within 'mainstream' managerial decision-making. This process was carried through by a number of training and development programmes. It was clearly recognized that it would take considerable time to work its way through the authority and would require a dramatic change in sectionally based occupational attitudes and cultures towards a more 'collective', organizationally focused approach. However, the DGM also introduced several structural and technical innovations to help along this process of attitudinal restructuring/cultural transformation:

- A substantial weakening of consensus-based decision-making focused on multi-disciplinary teams 'led' by an administrator and the simultaneous strengthening of line or general management structures at unit and district levels.
- The introduction of management budgets for general managers and chief professional officers in order to foster enhanced 'cost consciousness' and, eventually, more effective operational control over costs.
- The more extensive use of information technology – particularly at unit level – to secure more detailed and accurate budgetary and management information; the latter, it was anticipated, would forge a clearer connection between medical activity, its cost and managerial control systems geared to the realization of increased levels of operational efficiency and effectiveness.

As already indicated, these changes were introduced incrementally over a period of two to three years. The formal restructuring was implemented relatively quickly – except in the case of one unit where the appointment of a general manager and the new structures in which that individual would function were delayed due to recruitment and selection difficulties – and the other, more process-oriented changes over a longer period of time. But the overall impact of this package of organizational restructuring was to produce a 'cadre' of general managers responsible for direct decision-making in key operational and resource allocation areas. Professional officers, at both unit and district levels, found themselves in formal administrative and advisory support roles that were far more restrictive than anything they had experienced under consensus management. They still had formal responsibilities for ensuring acceptable standards of patient care within their respective professional domains, but the wider organizational context and policy framework in which patient care services were provided became increasingly remote and beyond their influence. The authority was moving towards a situation in which general managers were exercising a much tighter grip on the decision-making processes and procedures through which organizational change was planned and implemented.

## The Response

Each of the three major 'specialist' groups working within these radically transformed organizational arrangements – clinicians, nurses and administrators – responded in varying ways to the new structures of managerial decision-making and control. However, they were all aware, to some degree, of the scale of the changes that were in the process of being implemented and their potential, longer-term impact on protected 'occupational territories'. Each of them reacted in rather different ways to the radically altered organizational setting in which they now operated.

## *The Clinicians*

On the whole, clinicians were most hostile to the changes that were being introduced. They saw management as a very inexact science, which was in danger of intruding into clinical decision-making in an extremely heavy-handed and unproductive fashion. While prepared to accept managerial prerogative on relatively 'low-level' decisions (such as resource allocation to small-scale information-technology initiatives) they staunchly resisted the proposition that management budgets could ever, or should ever, play a significant role in clinical decision-making. Their response can be characterized as entailing a mixture of ignorance, bewilderment and downright hostility. Very few indicated any positive interest in becoming involved, indirectly or directly, in management decision-making structures. Doubts about the efficacy of management seemed to be firmly entrenched within their professional consciousness and occupational socialization. In essence, many believed that medicine and management were incompatible; medicine could not be managed because the patient is the doctor's sole responsibility and that responsibility could not be compromised by financial or organizational constraints. Management is necessarily a restriction upon clinical judgement and a potential threat to clinicians' professional autonomy. Thus they perceived a fundamental conflict between the post-Griffiths organizational reforms that were being implemented within the authority, and their understanding of the central task of the health service and their role within it. They believed they controlled, and must continue to control, the delivery of the service. The occupational changes the DGM and his UGMs were implementing were a direct threat to that professionally based control continuing. Consequently these changes were to be resisted: through a variety of avoidance tactics, delay, pressure and subversion.

These resistance strategies, and the tactical ploys through which they were undertaken, took a number of different forms. Some doctors simply attempted to avoid the organizational restructuring the DGM was implementing and reverted to their belief in and commitment to professional clinical autonomy in a much more fundamental way. As one senior clinician put it

> The general manager is never going to manage the service in the way that business managers run factories or stores. He will always have to wait for the professionals to have their say before anything can happen. The basis for health care provision is the 'doctor—patient' relationship and nothing will change that. General managers may be able to make 'small' decisions about minor expenditure, but they won't make a great deal of difference. The Griffiths proposals were cooked up on the wind. We'll still have to make everything happen.

Other clinicians within the authority took a less sanguine view of general management and the process of organizational rationalization it had initiated. Opposition, rather than avoidance, was required in order to ensure that general managers were eventually forced back into the more limited co-ordinating and consensus-preserving role once performed by hospital administrators. Thus a consultant in the acute unit offered the view that

> Clinicians are in the supervisory role and that's how things should stay. Standards of patient care are the first responsibility of the doctor. You can only have one captain of the ship and that captain has to be the doctor. Medical decision-making has to be based on the professional authority of the doctor. Nothing or nobody can take that away. The management of patient care has to remain in the hands of the professionals and they have to protect patients against the cost-cutting mentality of the manager.

In its most extreme form, this oppositional stance legitimated withdrawal from the wider representative and administrative structures in which clinicians had always been involved — to a degree. The encroachment of control by managers should be positively resisted by a reassertion and revitalization of independent and autonomous professionalism. Doctors were the last bastion of professional autonomy within the NHS and their resistance, which had already been undermined to some extent, needed to be stiffened by a resurgence in medical power and authority. As a registrar maintains 'You have to fight management every foot of the way and make sure that they stay out of our domain. They have no real knowledge of or sympathy with the problems which we face'.

While there were clearly some tactical differences between clinicians over the specific form that 'resistance' should take, they were broadly united in their opposition to the introduction of general management and its associated organizational innovations. In particular, they were deeply suspicious of, not to say openly hostile to, the claim of general management to speak on behalf of the organization as a whole, rather than some sectional interest group within it. Clinicians saw themselves as the 'guardians of the general good' of the organization and interpreted the rise of general management as entailing the introduction of an alien culture and practices clothed in the rhetoric of collective well-being and scientifically based rationalization. That the extension of managerial authority and control also entailed significant encroachments on their professional autonomy — particularly in terms of the external constraints it necessarily imposed on clinical freedom and medical discretion — was simply incidental to their 'principled' opposition to further extensions of unrestrained managerial prerogative. At least, this was how the situation looked from their point of view!

## The Nurses

Broadly speaking, the nurses were somewhat more ambivalent about the growing power of general management and the process of organizational restructuring it had initiated. They welcomed a degree of managerial responsibility and accountability being vested in the authority of one person — that is, the general manager — as an antidote to the bureaucratic obfuscation and delay, which characterized so much of health service decision-making. At the same time they were much more sceptical about the capacity of general managers to manage nursing manpower in an effective and efficient manner. The latter simply lacked sufficient knowledge of and sympathy for the complexities of nursing care and the constant pressures nurses worked under, particularly at a time when money was so short and there was so much emphasis on cutting the basic costs of patient care 'to the bone'! As one ward sister argued

> I can see some sense in general management. My anxieties are whether we're going to make the same mistakes again ... The changes general managers are making haven't been clearly thought out; there does not seem to be any overall plan or strategy. What worries me most is that they think they can manage us without any real understanding of the day-to-day problems we face and the flexibility which we need to do our jobs properly.

In this respect, nurses were highly critical of the imposition of crude cost-cutting regimes and the substantial weakening of nurse-management structures the transition to general management entailed. They saw themselves as losing out in the restructuring process in the sense that responsibility and accountability for the management of nurse manpower had been transferred from nursing professionals to line managers. Their professional autonomy and standing had been badly damaged by the introduction of general management structures that cut through some of the confusion and delay associated with consensus management decision-making, but simultaneously emasculated the nurse's role to one of subordinate adviser:

> By taking us out of mainstream management decision-making concerned with the use of nursing manpower, general managers in this authority have put us in a position where we're 'outside looking in'. It signals to everyone else that nurses and their professional managers are now in a subordinate position to general managers. While general managers talk about the need to consult nurses and to bring them fully into decisions which involve them, the reality is that we're being locked out of that process. More and more we are finding ourselves dictated to by budgets and other financial controls which general managers impose from 'on high' in the hope that they will be able to get a grip of the major cost factor in patient care − us!
>
> (A nurse officer)

Thus, nurses at all levels of the nursing hierarchy seemed resigned to the imposition of a restructuring process within the authority that would leave them in a much weaker position than was the case pre-Griffiths and the general management 'revolution' it had initiated. There was little sign of any concerted resistance on their part, apart from a deep-rooted scepticism over the capacity of general managers to realize the detailed control over operational costs through more sophisticated information systems and budgetary mechanisms that were remote from the point of patient care delivery. While general managers mouthed the rhetoric of 'hands-on' management practice in true Japanese style, the reality (given the inherent complexity of and divisions within healthcare work organization) was likely to be very different. In particular, nurses felt that general managers would very quickly become detached from the 'hurly-burly' of everyday hospital life and would find themselves ensnared in the bureaucratic routines and Byzantine centralized structures so typical of health service administration.

## The Administrators

Administrators had much to gain and, somewhat paradoxically, much to lose with the introduction of general management in Southglam. Individually, they stood to gain quite substantially in terms of their perceived status as 'embryonic' general managers − ready to metamorphose themselves from administrative ugly ducklings into managerial swans once the Griffiths revolution had begun to take hold within the authority. Collectively, those left behind in the scramble for general management positions − by definition, the majority − were likely to find themselves in a situation where their decision-making authority and organizational status would be severely reduced.

In pre-Griffiths times, the administrator stood at the hub of a web or network of organizational exchanges and relationships within which they performed a crucial co-ordinating and crisis management role. The administrator was like a constantly revolving 'distributor cap' who picked up problems from any point within the organization and put them down again where they could be solved. It was the administrator who was responsible for co-ordinating consensus-based multidisciplinary teams and for edging them towards some sort of a decision where continued procrastination seemed to threaten. In all these respects, the administrator was the 'general manager in waiting' in the sense that he or she was the key player in negotiating a viable pattern of working relationships between the various occupational and professional specialisms that had to be brought together to deliver patient care of a consistent standard and quality.

In the post-Griffiths era the position of administrators was likely to be very different. They were likely to be reduced to the level of providing low-level routine administrative support to managerial and professional groups, which negotiated 'organizational order' between themselves − that is, without the intermediary role previously performed by the administrator. Once administrators had lost their critical co-ordinating, negotiating and directing functions to a new breed of general managers who now had executive powers or line authority for decision-making undreamt of by the administrators, then they would be swept away to the organizational margins.

Consequently, administrators had much to fear from the implementation of general management structures and control mechanisms in Southglam. As one hospital administrator speculated

> We are being asked to move from the culture of consensus management and the culture of a group of equals to a culture of the boss over everyone. We've never really had this before and it's going to require the introduction of all sorts of structures and practices which are 'foreign' to our previous set-up ... These will drastically simplify the chain of command and consultation within a corporate management structure. They will attempt to break down professional barriers and strengthen line management. This will mean a bleak future for administrators; a lot of their previous functions, like planning and budgetary control, will simply disappear. There is a great deal of uncertainty and apprehensiveness as to the future for administrators within this authority. They are likely to come out on the bottom of the pile because they haven't got the prestige and status of the professional disciplines. The administrator will end up as a 'chief clerk' for the general manager.

However, as an interest group, administrators seemed largely powerless to do very much about the impending transformation that Griffiths-style general management entailed. The authority would still need most of them to administer the new structures and systems the general managers were introducing, but they would inevitably find themselves with far less discretion and involvement than was the case under the 'ancient regime' of centralized administrative planning and decentralized operational control. The benign conservatism of consensus management, in which they had performed such a critical role, had been superseded by an era of much more proactive managerial direction and control in which the centre of organizational gravity was rapidly moving away from them and towards general managers. This shift towards such a proactive and directive, even 'Taylorite', form of management within the authority would leave administrators in the unenviable position of losing a strategic organizational role without finding an alternative base or rationale for their once-proud status as the NHS's arch 'fixers'.

## Organizational Outcomes

The implementation of Griffiths-style reforms within Southglam generated an organizational climate in which anxiety, distrust and opposition, coupled with a degree of retreat or withdrawal on the part of some individuals, were the prevailing responses from key professional/occupational groups caught up in the change process that the move to general management had initiated.

The DGM and his supporting UGMs seemed confident and powerful enough to push through the structural and operational changes they regarded as absolutely essential to the achievement of effective managerial control over *organizational* performance. Indeed, they were emerging as the new managerial coalition within the authority, which was determined to realize the broad objectives the Griffiths Report had laid down in relation to more effective command over and control of health care *delivery*. They were attempting to achieve this through a combination of formal restructuring, technical innovation, cultural manipulation and political incorporation, which would, in the fullness of time, radically transform the normative foundations of work organization within the authority. By streamlining formal structures so that professional input into decision-making was reduced to a subordinate or advisory role, and by implementing a more sophisticated battery of budgetary and information systems, general managers hoped to bring professional task performance and resource utilization under their effective control. These innovations were to be supported by a range of training and developmental programmes that, over time, would convince recalcitrant professional staff that 'there is no alternative' to the permanent revolution that the Griffiths Report had instigated.

However, three years after the implementation of this package of organizational and administrative changes, the DGM was forced to admit that progress had been much slower than he had anticipated. In particular, the cultural changes to which he and his group of UGMs had aspired – in terms of the inculcation of a set of attitudes, beliefs and values more sympathetic to managerially led restructuring – was much more piecemeal and ephemeral in its impact. In addition, the tensions and conflicts between different professionally and occupationally based interest groups had intensified to the extent that they were more fragmented, not to say polarized, into different 'camps' than had been the case under the pre-Griffiths arrangements. While the formal structures and administrative processes of the authority had been indelibly transformed, the underlying 'status quo' values and prejudices that shaped day-to-day organizational behaviour seemed to be still firmly in place.

## Case Study Tasks

This case study can be analyzed from a number of different, but complementary, perspectives. First, one can focus on the change strategy implemented by the DGM in terms of providing a critique of its underlying assumptions/rationale. This may then lead on to a consideration of alternative ways of attempting to realize similar strategic objectives but through rather different organizational means. In this latter context, a more focused appreciation of the cultural, rather than structural, preconditions for successful organizational reform would seem to be in order. Has the DGM become so obsessed with formal organizational change that he has totally neglected the cultural preconditions of successful restructuring and the much more 'participative' mode of implementation the latter requires?

A second way of tackling this case study would be to formulate a diagnosis of 'what's going on' from the point of view of the various 'stakeholders' involved in the situation (managers, doctors, administrators, nurses, etc.), and to assess organizational outcomes from their perspective. Here, the varying 'readings' of different, but interdependent, occupational and professional groups, and their implications for individual and/or collective action, is likely to emerge as the central issue. Analyzing the case from this angle – that is, from the perspective of those on the 'receiving end' of organizational restructuring and attempted cultural transformation initiated by general managers – is likely to make a compromise solution seem much more practical and attractive.

Finally, the case may be approached from a more 'macro-level' perspective in which the impact of government initiated reforms on organization-level developments and outcomes becomes the primary concern. In this context, issues focusing on the relative balance between 'external constraint' and 'organizational choice' (particularly for general managers) assume greater significance. How much 'room for manoeuvre' is there available to general managers in their search for an organizational structure and cultural framework, which will deliver both effective control and meaningful commitment? To what extent are general managers being forced to act as the direct agents of policies determined at a higher level of organizational governance, which will inevitably undermine their position as potential catalysts for cultural transformation?

The questions and role-playing exercise outlined below provide different, but interrelated, ways into the diagnostic perspectives and organizational issues raised above:

1. What are the major assumptions underpining the DGM's strategy for implementing and managing organizational change within Southglam?
2. How would you characterize and explain the views and responses of the three central groups involved in the change process initiated by the DGM?
3. To what extent can the limited success of the DGM's change strategy be explained in terms of underlying political and/or cultural factors he has failed to anticipate?
4. What alternative change strategy would you follow if you were in the DGM's shoes? How would you justify your alternative?

5. How consistent are the assumptions and directives of the Griffiths Report (as revealed through this case study) with the 'Eight Lessons from America's Best Run Companies', as embodied in Peters and Waterman's (1982) *In Search of Excellence*? To what extent are Peters and Waterman's eight lessons applicable to a public sector service organization under pressure from central government to generate more 'value for money' from their operations?

## Role Play Exercise

As part of the programme of organizational rationalization and cost-cutting implemented by the DGM in Southglam, a number of ward closures — mainly centred on geriatric and mental handicap services — are to take place. You are to imagine yourself in one of three roles: the UGM who has to implement these closures; a consultant who is directly responsible for the provision of medical care services on the geriatric wards; and a nurse manager responsible for the provision of nursing services on the wards due for closure.

As the UGM, you have to implement these ward closures to stay within your budget and to conform to the authority-wide policies that are being introduced concerning the de-institutionalization of mental handicap/health services and the greatly extended use of private agencies in the provision of geriatric care.

As one of the most senior consultants for geriatric care within the hospital/authority, you find yourself in a situation where the 'Cinderella' status of your specialism is becoming more pronounced everyday. Consequently, with this latest round of ward closures, you find yourself in a situation where you feel that you have to defend what is left of your specialism before it is completely destroyed. You also find yourself in a situation where the standards and extensiveness of patient care generally offered by private sector agencies is substantially inferior to what you regard as professionally and morally acceptable.

As a nurse manager you find yourself operating in an environment in which the pressure for operational efficiency and effectiveness is having a negative effect on the standards of patient care you have previously taken for granted. While not unmindful of the resource pressures under which general managers and clinicians are functioning, you feel that neither of them are really sensitive to the problems of old people who are physically and mentally ill, and the special kind of attention they require.

This role-play exercise asks you to perform one of the three central roles available in this situation and to 'perform the script' offered you — without forgetting the wider organizational and institutional context (and constraints) in which you function. You must keep in mind the problem of how you need to balance a concern for your own interests and values with the constraints arising out of the organizational arena in which your interests and values have to be articulated and mobilized. How is the UGM to implement the required number and type of ward closures to remain within budget, while at the same time avoiding alienating the staff to the extent that they withdraw the level of commitment and co-operation required for everyday operation? How does the geriatric consultant defend the need for wards to remain open without compromising her position as a professional who is appreciative of the broader resource constraints within which an efficiently run health service has to function? How can the nurse manager support the case for more intensive and sensitive treatment of old people, who are often physically and mentally ill, and avoid being seen as a defender of narrow professional interests?

Considered in these terms, each of these roles needs to be thought about and performed in the light of an assessment of the complex interaction between the role demands inherent within particular organizational positions and the pressures emanating from the broader institutional setting in which the roles are performed.

## Essential Reading

Anthony, P. D. (1990) The paradox of management culture or 'He who leads is lost', *Personnel Review*, Vol. 19, no. 4, pp. 3−8.

Peters, T. J. and Waterman, R. H. (1982) *In Search of Excellence: Lessons from America's Best-Run Companies*, Harper and Row, New York, NY.

Schein, E. H. (1985) *Organizational Culture and Leadership*, Jossey-Bass, San Francisco, Calif.

Strong, P. and Robinson, J. (1990) *The NHS under New Management*, Open University Press, Milton Keynes.

## Additional Reading

Coombs, R. and Green, K. (1989) Work organization and product change in the service sector: the case of the UK National Health Service, in S. Wood (ed.) *The Transformation of Work: Skill, Flexibility and the Labour Process*, Unwin Hyman, London, pp. 279−94.

Cousins, C. (1987) *Controlling Social Welfare: A Sociology of Welfare State Work and Organization*, Wheatsheaf, Brighton.

Cousins, C. (1988) The restructuring of welfare work, *Work, Employment and Society*, Vol. 2, no. 2, pp. 210−28.

Cox, D. (1991) Health service management: a sociological view, in J. Gabe, M. Bury and M. Calnan (eds.) *The Sociology of the Health Service*, Routledge, London.

Fox, A. (1974) *Beyond Contract: Work, Power and Trust Relations*, Faber & Faber, London.

Mintzberg, H. (1983) *Structures in Fives: Designing Effective Organizations*, Prentice-Hall, Englewood Cliffs, NJ.

NHS Management Inquiry (1983) *The Griffiths Report*, DHSS/HMSO, London.

Pettigrew, A. (1973) *The Politics of Organizational Decision-Making*, Tavistock, London.

Pfeffer, J. (1981) *Power in Organizations*, Pitman, London.

Pollitt, C. (1990) *Managerialism and the Public Services*, Blackwell, Oxford.

# CASE 17

# The 'Perfect' Professional

## Susan Walsh

## The Setting

Andrew is the district head of a clinical department that provides a service within the National Health Service (NHS). Andrew has overall responsibility for thirty members of staff. The staff are divided into five different specialisms each led by a specialism head. There is roughly an equal number of men and women in the department. Apart from one woman, men occupy all the head of specialism posts. Clinical specialisms are in the child, adult (under 65), older adults (over 65), learning disability and forensic areas.

The managerial structure of the hospital is such that Andrew is managed (alongside four other different departments) by an associate unit general manager. The current individual occupying that role is antagonistic to the department and does not believe the service provided is sufficiently important to merit its current uptake in resources. The departmental service is not medical in nature and, as a result, is perceived as specialized and peripheral.

The history of the department is one in which, though there are head of specialism posts, staff have been managed in a very loose fashion and have been able to function independently of any clear management structure. As a result there has been room for staff to follow up their own clinical and research interests. However, the current pressures being placed on the department have led to a shift in emphasis away from a flexible clinical remit to one aimed at reducing the waiting-list. With an unsympathetic external management, the department's safety may be ensured only if it can be perceived to be reducing an ever-increasing waiting-list. This change in political emphasis has had a consequent impact upon the staff, with a fall in morale and an increase in absenteeism mirroring the increase in their workloads. It has also changed the amount of control staff feel they have to determine the direction and range of their own jobs.

The service provided by the department has been wide ranging and includes work with distressed and disabled clients, family work, education and training of other NHS personnel and facilitating organizational change in institutions. The department also provides resources for a number of professional training courses and has a commitment to service development and research. A number of the members of the department have used their dual experience in research and clinical practice to establish an advisory group for their own and other professions looking at the issue of quality assurance within the NHS. Allied to this role of trying to assure quality of service delivery, senior staff also offer a supervision service to both junior members of the department and other professional groups. The process of supervision provides staff with an opportunity to discuss any clinical difficulties. The definition of 'clinical difficulties' tends to be wide ranging and covers anything from advice on new areas for service development to informal assessment of clinical practice. The particular content of supervision is determined by the individual needs of the supervisee.

The department is a very busy and lively place. Staff rush in, check their pigeon-hole, arrange a meeting and rush away again because three quarters of them are contracted to provide a service within the community as well as within the department itself (which is located within a general hospital site). At most, two members of staff will provide a service to one community, and they do so alongside a range of different professionals. The term 'community' covers both the city areas as well as isolated rural communities. Those staff who are contracted to provide a service to the rural communities often spend a great deal of time driving from place to place, and generally work on their own. Because of the variability in the structure of each individual's job, the department provides a place where staff make contact with each other.

We join Andrew at what is usually a low-key, apathetic, departmental meeting. Andrew chairs that meeting and has just finished describing the impact of changes and cutbacks in departmental funding. It is already clear to staff that such changes are having an impact, at a number of different levels, upon their professional lives. There is increased pressure on staff to reduce waiting-lists, coupled with tighter managerial control and assessment of the efficiency of the department, and an increased necessity for staff to justify their commitment to other forms of work other than waiting-list work. Increasingly, other professional skills in the areas of training, research and development and organizational intervention are viewed as peripheral to the main task, which is narrowly defined as client-focused work. Staff are antagonistic to these changes while feeling powerless to prevent them. The departmental meeting has been sulky and angry. Staff are feeling undervalued.

## How the Problem Develops

The point at which we join this group of staff is when Andrew is about to close the meeting and has asked if anyone has any other pressing issues they would like to mention. Barbara (a new member of staff and a specialism head) raises the question of how demoralized she feels the department is, and she wonders whether there was anything they can do as a department to combat this. 'We work long hours, and it's hard to meet for support and supervision with other staff members. With current high workloads you have to book an appointment three months in advance to meet with anyone to discuss work issues.' Barbara went on to say that planning future work, the development of services and assuring quality of service delivery suffers because you end up working in isolation. There was little chance for feedback to generate new initiatives and to swop ideas.

The staff group responds with a shocked silence. Yes, they had moaned to their friends in the department about how awful they felt about work but no one had reached the point of wanting to make it a public issue. Staff had just increased their individual workloads (while trying to maintain their own interests and other forms of work commitments), and worked in an increasingly isolated but frenzied manner. Barbara's comment for the first time raises this issue as something that might touch them all.

Initially, Andrew tries to deal with Barbara's comments by gently suggesting that, though he appreciates her views, he feels her sense of isolation and lack of support are due to the fact that she is a fairly new member of staff and, of course, it takes a long time to feel you belong in a new team. This comment goes down fairly badly and, rather than closing the discussion, it injects it with new life. People begin to get angry. Other members of staff respond to his comments by stating that they, too, feel unsupported and demoralized, and that it wasn't how long you had worked in the department that necessarily predicted how you felt − rather it was working in the department *per se*!

Andrew is stunned. He has always viewed his department as if it were a large family. Yes, they have had their disagreements in the past, and they were all having a hard time at the moment but, like most families, you ended up resolving your differences. He was head of that family and had always believed his employees felt positively about the department: 'My door is always open to anyone with personal difficulties. In the face of cutbacks and an increased need for efficiency and productivity, it is important that people feel that they can come to me so that together we can iron out their little difficulties as quickly as possible.'

Moira, a long-serving member of staff, responds by saying she thinks he has missed the point: 'Andrew, the issue is not so much staff needing to come to ask you to solve their problems. Rather, it is about legitimizing on a departmental level the need for mutual support. The consequence of this might be to ameliorate the stressful nature of the job, but an equally realistic outcome may be that we maintain thinking time in our diaries so that services can be generated effectively in the current political climate.'

Moira went on to say that she was fed up with last-minute, knee-jerk responses to service planning. Furthermore, she was concerned (both at a personal and a political level) about the increasing work demands that were being absorbed by everyone. At the political level she described a potential irony that would be the result of the department 'successfully' eroding the waiting-list. For example, Moira said she could imagine management's response to a request for increased resources: '"Why do you need more resources when you don't have a waiting-list?" But the reason why we don't have a waiting-list is because we are working ridiculously long hours. Our strategy of trying to keep up masks the costs of doing that without additional resources. Just constantly responding to the demands upon us, without even stopping to assess their validity, and without establishing whether we, as a department, can create a different way of responding to organizational pressures, rather than just relying on individuals to mop up the demands, seems a disastrous strategy.'

Primarily, Moira felt that for staff to absorb continually an increasing workload was not only damaging to them but also potentially damaging for clients and institutions because they got less and less in the way of a good-quality service. At this point there had been much nodding from the less verbal members of staff.

Andrew responded by saying, 'No, you have misunderstood me, Moira. Of course I would be positive about any support initiative. I just need to know what people want. I didn't realize that people weren't coping with their jobs. If people need to take sick leave then they must take it.'

There is a menacing lull in the conversation. Brian, a quietly spoken, withdrawn individual breaks the silence. He describes how isolated he is. He is a worker delivering a service to an outlying rural district. He works alone, covering a huge area, and there is no possibility of any other worker being appointed because of the shortage of funds. As a consequence, he is running around not knowing whether he is doing a good job anymore. He also affirms he is so busy he doesn't even have time to think clearly let alone meet with anyone to establish whether he is thinking clearly. There is another lull after Brian has finished speaking.

'Is Brian's description of his job familiar to anyone else?' asked Andrew. There is lots of agreement. 'As head of department I think it's unprofessional to allow ourselves to get so isolated and overworked, and that it is the responsibility of each individual member of staff to plan work more effectively. The way to do this is obviously to ensure that everyone books some time-out for themselves in their diaries so that this sort of thing does not happen. I can't see that there is any great problem about booking time-out.'

'Well, I think one of the difficulties is that there is quite a stigma attached to making time for ourselves. You end up feeling guilty if you are able to find that kind of space in your working day. It means you are not doing enough work, or you are shirking,' stated Cathy, a younger member of staff. 'I mean, I've been in post now for eight months. You would have thought, as a junior member of staff, I would feel able to say I don't know, or be able to go to the more senior members of this department and ask directly for their advice. But I don't feel that. And I don't think that I am the only one either. The stupid thing is that, although we all moan about the pressure we are under, we just don't say no to anything. I think we are all getting competitive and macho about how much of a workload we can carry before we burn out. I feel guilty if I leave before seven o'clock each night. I think the way to prevent individuals feeling bad about having needs of their own is for the department to publicly validate some kind of refuelling time, and then we wouldn't get into these competitive games with each other.'

'Perhaps one way of making this support time legitimate at a departmental level is that it should be written in to our job contracts. In that way everyone would be forced to make time for this. If members of staff fail to take the space then they would be being unprofessional and so he/she would have to meet with me and justify their failure,' stated Andrew. He then goes on to explore how he could enforce this arrangement and what the penalties for failure to comply might be.

Moira again states he is missing the point ('Why was the woman so difficult?'). She reiterates the need for a departmental initiative that legitimizes support time: 'Do you really think, Andrew, that members of staff are going to use such time effectively if they think you are monitoring their performance whilst they do it, or are thinking that there is something wrong with them for not doing it? Effective support can only take place when the individual can say that they didn't know, or that a piece of work they did last week was substandard, and feel okay about discussing the quality of our professional service. Do you not think that organizing some kind of policing of that process would totally sabotage it?'

'Perhaps a stumbling block is that we don't know what we mean by support time. Perhaps we could usefully spend some time defining what we mean by support,' chips in Jack.

'Well, what I mean by support is exactly as Moira described it, somewhere I can say I don't know or I failed and feel safe enough to explore why I didn't deliver a good-enough service either to clients or organizations. It requires trust if you are going to be that open,' states Helen. She continues: 'You can't always receive good support from, say, your head of department because you would be feeling as if he is monitoring your performance. I'm not saying that as a younger member of staff my performance as a practitioner should not be evaluated by my manager. However, certain forms of support would be most effective from and with our peers. Also this time should be a regular commitment, not done solely when work is in crisis. It should be in our diaries taking equal precedence alongside all the bloody meetings.' Again there is a great deal of fervent mumbling and nodding from other members of staff.

'What I think we need to make clear,' continues Helen, 'is to think about support systems working at a number of different levels. At one level I would tentatively argue for some form of individual appraisal system. However, that alone is not enough because, if it is done badly, it could easily fit in with this macho culture we have all got ourselves caught up in. You know, having to take on even more work in order to get through our appraisal. At a different level we need almost to create a counter-culture which provides a regular forum for peer-group support. Just off the top of my head my fantasy of this is that it would be an arena that would allow us to ask for guidance and direction about our work interests and roles minus the appraisal element. And what about the whole issue of quantity versus quality in the work we do? If I could just stop for a moment to assess the work that I do I might feel empowered to actually say "no" to something. We are all carrying very large workloads, and I should imagine none of us can afford to take on anymore. We could all do with cutting back. But my saying "no" to something, and thereby taking care of myself, and ensuring the quality of the work I do, probably has knock-on effects for somebody else in this room, because they will feel they have to pick up that piece of work. So my survival strategy will lead me to being resented. So it becomes almost too costly to look after yourself.'

'Are you saying, Helen, that we should be looking at the ways in which this department actually prevents good professional practice?' inquires Andrew.

'Yes, I think I am. But we have to look at this issue within the current context of the NHS. For example, how ongoing political demands are undermining the work we do, and devaluing the work we do. We have tried to keep up, at some costs to ourselves and to the quality of the work we do. I think we need to make two decisions. First, can we keep going like this and what are the political costs if we don't. Second, if we feel we should change our response to these demands how should we organize it?'

'To take up your first point, of course I am concerned that members of staff should be working in a person-friendly environment. However, I am at the same time concerned about the potential cost of these developments. How can I justify to my managers that my department is spending a quarter of their time supporting one another? I mean, quite honestly, it does not look good, does it? In quite an explicit way we are talking about a direct trade-off with our waiting-list work,' says Andrew.

'Well, if that's the case then we've got to protect this initiative. There must be some available data proving the link between efficient output and caring attitudes towards staff. Surely that would be an effective response to managerial criticism?' comments Barbara.

'Well, I think we are overstating the case.' This time it is Richard, who joins in, who is another long-standing member of staff and head of one of the specialisms. 'Obviously, some individuals are having personal difficulties but, surely, the best people to talk to are our wives and friends. I have always found my wife very supportive. Alternatively, if people are unable to talk to their partners in this way then they can, of course, come and talk to me in confidence.' People glare silently at Richard.

The meeting draws to an end. Andrew states he has been shocked by the strength of feeling and clearly something has to be done by him about staff self-care in his department: 'Would anyone like to take responsibility for finding out what people want/need, and then we can arrange a new meeting to establish good practice guidelines. What about you, Barbara? It was your intelligent and perceptive comment which brought this issue to the fore. I'll meet with you in a week when you can discuss with me some of your strategies for finding out what people want, and how you will implement this system of staff care.' The meeting is brought to a hurried close.

## Case Study Tasks

1.  For this group of staff, what are the functions of support at work?

2. Can you identify the blocks to support (at the personal, professional and organizational levels)?
3. What tactics or solutions did Andrew use to prevent any organizational change?
4. In what ways can Andrew manage the contradictory pressures of the demands for increased care of staff with the need for extra productivity by managers?
5. Describe the role gender played in the case study.

## Essential Reading

Cockburn, C. (1988) The gendering of jobs: workplace relations and the reproduction of sex segregation, in S. Walby (ed.) *Gender Segregation at Work*, Open University Press, Milton Keynes.

Fisher, J. D., Nadler, A. and Whitcher-Alagna, S. (1982) Recipient reactions to aid, *Psychological Bulletin*, Vol. 91, no. 1, pp. 27–54.

Freidson, E. (1973) Professions and the occupational principle, in E. Freidson (ed.) *The Professions and their Prospects*, Sage, London.

Georgiades, N. J. and Phillimore, L. (1975) The myth of the hero-innovator and alternative strategies for organizational change, in C. C. Kiernan and F. D. Woodford (eds.) *Behaviour Modification with the Severely Retarded*, Associated Scientific Publications, Amsterdam.

Marshall, J. (1984) *Women Managers: Travellers in a Male World*, Wiley, Chichester.

Menzies, I. E. P. (1977) *The Functioning of Social Systems as a Defence against Anxiety (Tavistock Pamphlet No. 3)*, Tavistock Institute of Human Relations, London.

Morgan, G. (1986) *Images of Organization*, Sage, London.

# CASE 18

# The Introduction of a Performance Appraisal System

## Barbara Townley

### General Background: Performance in the Public Sector

Government policies in the 1980s have been concerned to introduce a greater economic discipline into all areas of the public sector. Pressure on resources has led to demands for economies and increased questioning of efficiency and competence. Acting as a substitute for profitability measures in the private sector, performance measures and indicators have been introduced into the public sector as indices of productivity and efficiency, designed to assist effective management.

Measuring performance in the public sector has, however, proved contentious. The complexity of public sector objectives, reflecting the need to respond to differing publics and the importance of political consensus, has been identified as leading to a weakness in clarifying accountability and measurement structures. For example, is the primary purpose of education to supply employers' needs for a suitably trained and skilled labour force; to provide people with the opportunity to develop their talents to the best of their ability; or to socialize individuals into those mores that will maximize their prospects for advancement socially and economically? Is value for money to be measured in terms of 'outputs' reflected in employment rates, numbers of students graduating per year or levels of qualifications attained? Is the function of the health service and the criteria to be used in guiding the commitment of its resources the provision of least-cost service, or health-awareness programmes and preventative medicine, or care for the chronically sick, or clinical medicine? Is its principal responsibility to the individual patient, the 'community' or the tax-payer? Are those most able to evaluate the provision of services in education and in health its direct consumers, students and patients, or do both areas involve the application of specialized knowledge such that their administration and organization should be left to the professionals who provide the service?

Measuring individual performance is a particularly problematic issue. This is especially the case for those who provide intangible services or where there are broad areas of individual discretion. In the case of professional staff, where performance consists of staff using their training and professional judgement (for example, a social worker's judgement as to how to handle client cases or a physician's clinical judgement in treating patients), measuring quality of public service delivery is especially difficult.

The following is an example of some of these issues as seen in the introduction of performance appraisal into universities.

## The University Context

Since 1981 when universities suffered cuts in funding ranging from 5 to 40 per cent there has been a plethora of reports on their improved management and value for money. The most notable of these was the Committee of Vice-Chancellors and Principals (CVCP) report into the efficiency of universities (1985), more commonly known as the Jarratt Report, after its chair. Its remit was 'to examine whether management structures and systems are effective in ensuring that decisions are fully informed, that optimum value is obtained in the use of resources, that policy objectives are clear and that accountabilities are clear and monitored' (*ibid.* p. 6).

The tone of the report was heavily imbued with the language of private sector commercial organizations. The view that emerged was that of the university as corporate entity, the provider of 'services' to the consumer and, as such, requiring new styles of management and organization, corporate planning and corporate management methods. Several 'impediments' were identified as hindering this development. The organizational structure of the university with its separation of powers between council and senate was a system of decision-making that was 'not familiar to senior managers in industry or even in local authorities and civil service departments' (*ibid.* p. 8). (University councils are governing bodies having responsibility for financial and employment matters, on which there is external representation; senates are an internal decision-making body with responsibility for academic matters. The relationship between the two varies. Councils may have executive authority or may be required to act only with the advice of the senate.) Traditions of self-government and participation were also identified as 'powerful constraints' inhibiting the 'optimal deployment of resources'. The managerial and administrative process was seen as being further complicated by the professional loyalties of academics. The majority of academics are, in Gouldner's (1957) terms, 'cosmopolitans', that is, their primary loyalty and main reference point is to their academic discipline and its members, rather than their specific university. As the CVCP report (1985, p. 5) lamented, 'staff often regard their status as physicists, surgeons, lawyers or technicians at least as important as their membership of a university'. Thus, as is common in professional organizations, professional loyalties and principles of self-government were all identified as giving rise to divided loyalties and conflicts of interest (Freidson, 1984; Raelin, 1986).

Jarratt's recommendations reported in favour of a more explicit managerial strata. Vice-chancellors were no longer the head of an institution being held in trust for the public — 'chairmen seeking consensus' or 'scholars first ... acting as a chair of senate carrying out its will' — rather, they were to adopt the role of chief executive officer. Deans, as heads of academic faculties, were to have more formal powers rather than relying on influence and persuasion and to operate within a direct management reporting system. Heads of department were also to function more as line managers. As a result, 'managerial' capabilities were to be privileged with academic leadership being delegated to others. In addition to a formal managerial hierarchy the introduction of formal planning and accounting procedures were also recommended – among them the appraisal of university staff.

## Appraisal in Universities: Collegiate vs. Managerial Assumptions

As about 70 per cent of university finance is spent on salaries, it was inevitable that individual accountability would be a prominent consideration. Jarratt (CVCP, 1985, p. 28) commented that 'universities are unusual in that little formal attempt is made on a regular basis to appraise academic staff with a view to their personal development and to succession planning within the institution'. The report noted that formal review generally took place at confirmation of appointment, salary bar and promotion, commenting 'this is a somewhat intermittent approach, commonly without any formal feedback' (*ibid.*). It concluded that a formal review procedure would benefit both staff and the university, and recommended that an annual review be introduced. Jarratt identified three objectives of performance appraisal: a recognition of the contribution made by individuals; assistance for individuals to develop their full potential; and allowing the university to make the most effective use of its academic staff. It recommended that reviews be conducted on a hierarchical basis, starting with senior people being reviewed by the head of the organization, and that there should be central co-ordination of staff reporting processes.

Although it is possible to idealize universities, presenting them as a guild model of collegial decision-making, by comparison with business organizations they are relatively non-hierarchical, making wide reference to the principles of self-government and consensual democracy. The faculties of the university effectively 'operate the enterprise', exercising both professional judgement and managerial authority. Although a department member is required to work under the direction of a head of department, both individuals essentially meet on equal terms in the discussion of policy decisions on curriculum and the nature of syllabuses. The development of specialist knowledge within subject areas sustains a tradition of *primus inter pares*. Within broad limits the individual has the right to determine the nature of their work in terms of the subject and nature of research, the content and style of teaching and the way their time is organized. Individual autonomy and discretion has been sustained by employment patterns that allow a high degree of individual freedom, seen as essential for the production of high-quality work. Tenure of employment subject to good behaviour was a feature of this system.

The highly discretionary and evaluative nature of academic work, and the relative lack of easily identifiable and quantifiable outputs, entails a large subjective component in work organization and provision, and limits the imposition of standards of work performance. The autonomy deriving from professional knowledge, which is a feature of a number of public sector organizations, influences the extent to which work organization is experienced as being hierarchical or not, the nature of internal reporting structures that evolve and the type of management structures that emerge. There is neither the command structure nor the reporting system associated with the private sector; hence the problems that emerge in trying to introduce an explicit managerial role or tier, as seen, for example, in the introduction of greater administrative controls over doctors in the National Health Service. Traditions of election in universities (for example, of chairs of departments) further reinforces a culture that places a strong emphasis on normative authority. Principles of hierarchy and control are rendered problematic as potentially conflicting rationalities – especially over professional judgement and control over work – emerge. It is these features of some public sector organizations that lead Ackroyd, Hughes and Soothill (1989) to conclude that professional autonomy leaves public sector management with little that is distinctly managerial to do, given that a great deal of self-management is already in place by virtue of the nature of work.

In making its recommendations, Jarratt essentially brought into conflict several issues: a managerial versus a self-governing ethos; formal versus normative authority; and hierarchy versus collegiality. In essence the collegiate or collaborative model of self-government, autonomy and self-regulation came into conflict with managerialist assumptions that decisions and control are relayed from the top of the organizational hierarchy. Jarratt (1985) was seen as privileging a particular concept of organization and a particular concept of management.

## Putting Appraisal into Practice

In line with Jarratt's recommendations, performance appraisal was agreed to as a prerequisite of a pay agreement, in which a 24-per-cent pay increase over three years was negotiated. The guiding principles of such a scheme were to be agreed at national level between the CVCP and the Association of University Teachers (AUT).

The changing context of the 1980s, however, was reflected in the views taken on the issue of performance appraisal. The time-scale of the 1981 cuts had meant that savings could only be made through shedding staff, largely through voluntary redundancies rather than natural wastage. The cost of implementing the cuts through voluntary and early retirement schemes was high. Voluntary schemes had left universities little discretion over which staff left, with the result that many were later re-hired on a contract basis. The experience of trying to decide the criteria as to who should go, whether this was to be done through reference to academic merit, last-in, first-out procedures, etc., had raised a number of issues associated with assessment and appraisal. In some cases the decision had been handled by heads of departments having to decide if colleagues should receive a letter informing them that their services were essential to the university, or one that informed them they would be allowed to leave should they wish to do so. As a result of these experiences, there was some support for devising procedures that provided management with improved quality of information about staff performance. As one vice-chancellor commented, 'it's important to make the unions think of people as a resource and not as a scholar. Appraisal is an important part of the planning process and the allocation of resources'. The CVCP, therefore, was in favour of a system of appraisal, a position further reinforced by the government indicating that future funding would be dependent on such a system being in place.

Within the AUT, there was support for the idea that appraisal as a system of getting people to think about their jobs was a good idea. As one negotiator commented, 'it would force some heads of departments to talk to members of staff and force members to think about what they are doing anyway'. The AUT stressed the view that the efficient operation of an organization could be enhanced through the professional self-development of its staff, but was firmly against a judgemental system – 'the idea is to correct the problem, not shame the individual'. Their national position therefore was to enter negotiations for a developmental system. However, within the AUT there was also a strong feeling that the wider context of the impact of funding cuts, promotion block-ages, the relative decline in pay and the perceived devaluation of the profession were more important factors affecting academic and organizational performance. There was concern that public sector initiatives were prompted as a mechanism for increased budgetary control rather than as a genuine concern for measure-ment of performance in a professional service. For some, appraisal was viewed as a system to 'weed out the dead wood', and that involvement in negotiating any appraisal system would therefore involve the AUT in selling an essentially disciplinary mechanism to its members.

These conflicting interpretations were brought to bear on the negotiations of the national guidelines on appraisal and influenced a number of different issues: the purpose and function of appraisal; its relationship with organiz-ational hierarchy; the choice of appraiser; the appraiser's role; appraisal's links with promotion and disciplinary procedure; and views on confidentiality of the appraisal material and the degree of quantification and standardization of reports.

The CVCP and the AUT commenced discussions and the guidelines that emerged included agreed procedures on the following:

- The objectives of the scheme – to help individual members of staff develop their careers; to improve staff performance; to identify changes in the organization that would enable individuals to improve their performance; to identify and develop potential for promotion; to improve the efficiency with which the institution is managed.
- The procedure to be followed – to apply to all staff; be compatible with equal opportunities policies; operate on an annual or biennial basis; appraisal was to be 'a joint professional task shared between appraiser and appraisee with the latter being involved at all stages'.

- Who was to appraise — appraisers were to have the confidence of their appraisees and be experienced and responsible members of staff; heads of department were to have 'a significant role to play in the appraisal of staff', although others were not excluded.
- What was to be appraised — no specific format was agreed but was to involve an appraisal of present work duties.
- The content of records — an agreed record of the discussion and any agreed follow-up action.
- Issues of confidentiality — the records were to be kept by the appraiser, appraisee and head of department.
- Relationship between appraisal and promotion and discipline — an agreed summary of the appraisal document could go to promotions committee.
- Time period for retention of records — to be agreed locally.
- Training and development provisions — no mention in the guidelines.
- Co-ordination of the scheme — no mention in the guidelines.
- Arrangements for monitoring and evaluation — no mention in the guidelines.

Although national guidelines were agreed between the CVCP and the AUT, the non-binding nature of the agreement gave individual universities a broad leeway as to what type of system to introduce. As individual institutions began their negotiations, the Secretary of State for Education announced that promised finance for universities would be contingent on commitment to the introduction of greater flexibility into pay structures and a noticeable move towards an element of 'performance pay'.

## Case Study Tasks

The university has established a committee in order to respond to the national initiative, of which you are members. Your task is to review the proposals of the CVCP/AUT, establish your response and devise an appraisal system for your university. A secretary should note some of the issues raised during negotiations and how these were resolved. The following are some positions of team members.

### Management

The team is composed of representatives from administration and academics. It includes the following.

A senior academic who has been at the university for a long period of time and is well respected by colleagues for integrity and fairness. This person is committed to traditional academic principles, and is deeply concerned with what is happening to the education system generally and universities in particular. In her view the problem of universities is the attraction and retention of high-quality staff who are committed to the pursuit of knowledge and its dissemination through teaching and research. She is concerned that career structures in departments, lack of opportunity for advancement and the failure to attract young scholars into research, bode ill for universities in the future. Known to be well respected by the vice-chancellor, she will be influential in steering any scheme that is recommended through senate.

Once harbouring dreams of becoming an academic, the registrar is mindful of the financial circumstances of the university and is anxious that any scheme falls within the province of those that would be acceptable to the Department of Education and Science in order to secure future funding.

A representative of the business school, who is anxious to build up the school's reputation and increase links with industry, seeing the latter as a possible source of future finance. This person is concerned to introduce more management information systems into the administration of the school in order to run it on more efficient lines. Fully in favour of the Jarratt recommendations, this person views the procedures and decision-making processes of universities as anachronistic. This representative is in favour of a move to explicit performance guidelines in which publications in 'top journals' and the results of student evaluation of teaching are to be used to justify annual salary increments. In this person's view, 'it is useful to have a system where there is the setting of objectives – a management by objectives system for everyone. It may be that if there's a deficit analysis over a period of time you have to do something about it'.

A senior academic from a small department in the arts faculty, which has had increasing difficulty in securing resources. This person's main concern is that 'it is important to recognize low morale in the arts. There are problems of introducing appraisals in a cuts' situation. It would be wrong if it were seen as wielding the axe'. Privately sceptical of the academic credibility of some of the courses offered by some departments in order to secure finance, this person is concerned that national debate concerning the purposes of education is being pre-empted by financial constraints of universities. This person is also generally opposed to the increased centralization of decision-making, which seems to be taking place in the university.

A departmental chair who has had experience of a 'problem' member of the department who is not thought to be pulling their weight: 'What do you do with people who don't respond? Take the case of someone mid-50s who teaches to a minimal level, has never written or done research, and there are no new books on the shelves since the mid-70s.' Also in the department are a number of particularly good PhD students soon to be looking for employment. It is thought that appraisal might be an opportunity to resolve some of these issues.

## Union

Your team comprises a number of different people, all of whom have been active in the union for a number of years.

A representative of academically related staff, conscious that some of your membership is frustrated at the lack of opportunity for advancement, and feeling that senior management is 'out of touch' through a lack of communication with lower levels. There is also concern that some academically related staff have borne the brunt of financial cuts and that failure to fill positions has led to increased workload. There is therefore some support for appraisal in that it is thought that this will provide the opportunity for senior management to become aware of difficulties staff face. As one employee expressed it, 'it's the opportunity to get the head of department to oneself for two hours'.

A science faculty representative. This person works in a department where the department head unilaterally introduced an appraisal system a few years previously. This system is not particularly liked by the staff in the department and a university system is seen as offering the opportunity to remedy some of its defects. As one colleague commented, 'it's the opportunity for those who take on responsibility and those who are good teachers to get the recognition they deserve'.

A social-science faculty representative. This person is firmly opposed to the introduction of performance appraisal systems, arguing that the real issues in universities are those of low morale and low salaries: 'Appraisal in this context is like unilateral management by objectives and the criteria are money and papers.' This person is concerned that, if appraisal is introduced, it should not be a 'top-down' scheme but should involve some assessment of the performance of those in senior positions in the university: 'If there is going to be appraisal, why not appraise within grades? What about someone who was appointed professor ages ago when the going was soft – why not appraise their perform-ance?' There is also concern that any scheme that is introduced should have the support of the members of the university and should be voted on in a formal ballot.

An arts-faculty representative. This representative has had experience of a number of personal cases where there has been conflict between academics and department chairs over whether individuals should be recommended for promotion. In some cases there have been accusations of restrictions on academic freedom as individuals have felt under pressure to change their particular research interests. In this person's view, 'there can be no authority without responsibility. An open, formal appraisal system is a means of ensuring that those in authority act responsibly.'

A representative of the law faculty whose concern is that any appraisal scheme should reflect 'due process' and should not be in contravention of any relevant legislation. As she expressed it, 'if there is formal assessment then there must be machinery safeguarding the rights and interests of members of staff. You have to ensure the rights of individual members of staff.'

## Questions

1. Do you wish to follow the national CVCP/AUT guidelines for an appraisal system, or do you wish to devise your own system? What are the advantages and disadvantages of adopting the national guidelines as opposed to adopt-ing your own?
2. The members of your team are not well versed in appraisal. What are the

sources you use to inform yourselves of how appraisals operate? How relevant are they?

3. What are your objectives in establishing an appraisal system?
4. What are the main problems encountered in devising one?
5. Examining the elements of an appraisal system listed above, what system and what format/documentation would you recommend to senate for approval to be adopted in the university?
6. In order to examine the issues raised in the appraisal case in a more direct way, you might consider role playing the following scenarios in an appraisal interview:

   (a) An appraiser who has had experience of industry and has developed a distinctly managerialist approach to the role, appraises an academic who is strongly committed to a collegiate view of university life.

   (b) A young academic who has written a number of publications and conference papers based on work done for a PhD, is appraised by a head of department who entered academic life during the rapid expansion of universities in the 1960s. The latter has no higher degree, a relatively light publication record but a great deal of experience in university administration. The young academic considers the department head as 'dead wood' and out of touch with debates in the subject area.

   (c) A department chair, and appraiser, has personally received several complaints about the teaching style and lack of preparation of the colleague she is appraising. Other members of the department are concerned about the light administrative load the appraisee seems to have. The appraisee, however, has one of the best publication records of the department. As the appraiser was heard to remark: 'What do you do with a gifted researcher with an international research reputation, who is not young, whose teaching is, shall we say, eccentric?'

   (d) The appraisee has had primary responsibility for the development and introduction of a Women's Studies Programme. She has recently been passed over for promotion in favour of a more recently appointed male colleague and feels her work is undervalued.

## Essential Reading

Ackroyd, S., Hughes, J. and Soothill, K. (1989) Public sector services and their management, *Journal of Management Studies*, Vol. 26, pp. 603–19.

Fletcher, C. and Williams, R. (1985) *Performance Appraisal and Career Development*, Hutchinson, London.

Freidson, E. (1984) The changing nature of professional control, *Annual Review of Sociology*, Vol. 10, pp. 1–24.

Jarratt Report (1985) Report of the Steering Committee for Efficiency Studies in Universities, CVCP, chaired by Sir Alex Jarratt, HMSO, London.

Pym, D. (1973) The politics and rituals of appraisal, *Occupational Psychology*, Vol. 47, pp. 231–5.

Randell, G. (1989) Employee appraisal, in K. Sisson (ed.) *Personnel Management in Britain*, Blackwell, Oxford.

## Additional Reading

Carley, M. (1988) Beyond performance measurement in a professional public service, *Public Money and Management*, Winter, pp. 23–7.

Gouldner, A. (1957) Cosmopolitans and locals: towards an analysis of latent social roles, *Administrative Science Quarterly*, Vol. 2, pp. 281–306.

Raelin, J. (1986) *The Clash of Cultures, Managers and Professionals*, Harvard Business School Press, Boston, Mass.

Stewart, J. and Ranson, S. (1988) Management in the public domain, *Public Money and Management*, Spring/Summer, pp. 13–19.

# CASE 19

## Ownership and Management: The Case of Fulham Football Club

### Nick Woodward

## Organizational Setting

Fulham Football Club is a member of the Football League, an organization of the senior professional clubs in England and Wales. The league is divided into four divisions, and during a season (August to May) each club plays every other club in its division, at home and away, with three points awarded for a win and one point for a draw. These points are aggregated to form a league table, with top clubs promoted to the next division, and bottom clubs relegated. The top clubs in the First Division qualify to play in the European Cup, and the next places qualify to play in the UEFA cup. Both these cups bring together teams from relevant participating European countries.

Currently, home clubs retain all gate receipts, and gates tend to increase as a club moves up divisions. However, the higher the division, the higher the wages, and the higher the transfer fees to attract good players.

Most clubs maintain at least three teams – a first team, playing in the league, and a reserve team and a junior team (apprentices) playing in a variety of local leagues. The number of full-time professional players on a club's books averages between 20 and 30. Players are members of the Professional Footballers' Association.

## The Case: Introduction

In February 1987, David Bulstrode, then Chairman of Fulham Football Club, announced plans to merge Fulham with Queens Park Rangers (QPR), with the new club playing at Loftus Road, the home of QPR. Both clubs were owned by SB Properties, a subsidiary of Marler Estates plc, and the merger would release Craven Cottage, Fulham's ground by the Thames, for residential development subject to planning permission, providing a potential gain to SB Properties. Marler Estates also owned Stamford Bridge, the home of Chelsea Football Club.

The announcement was widely reported in the national press ('Fulham Park Strangers'), which also reported vituperative reaction. The local Labour MP expressed concern that 'the future of clubs and football grounds should become a plaything for people whose principal objective is property speculation'. The Chairman of the Professional Footballers' Association was reported as saying that 'Football is not just bricks and mortar. I'm not prepared to stand aside while the whole history of a club like Fulham is about to be wiped out overnight'. The Secretary of the Football League indicated that the merger might not be sanctioned; the local council, Hammersmith, affirmed the policy of maintaining three football clubs in the borough, and that any planning application for development of the Fulham ground (as opposed to perimeter development) would be refused; and local London football supporters, in concert with Fulham fans, formed an action group. Some months later, the Department of the Environment under a Conservative government listed Fulham's Stevenage Road stand and Craven Cottage as Grade II buildings.

Legally, SB Properties were owners of both clubs, and were entitled to dispose of their assets as their commercial judgement — essentially concerned with the asset values of their shares — judged appropriate. But after this announcement, the Chairman of the club ceased to attend Fulham matches, and his office staff effectively sent him to Coventry. Few officials or supporters in the football community saw SB Properties as in any sense the owner of a football club, but rather as the owner of freehold land with valuable development potential — on which professional football was an inconvenient and loss-making operation.

## Football

Football, like many sports, evokes passion — a passion that extends to those who write about it: 'There is more eccentricity in deliberately disregarding it than in devoting a life to it. It has more significance in the national character than theatre has ... The way we play the game, organise it and reward it reflects the kind of community we are,' wrote Arthur Hopcraft in 1968 (p. 9).

Football in its modern form emerged in the public schools in the 1840s, encouraged by such headmasters as Thomas Arnold, of Rugby School. In the years following, it was played mainly by ex-public schoolboys, leading to the formation in 1863 of the Football Association by 'a convocation of gentlemen, drawn mainly from commerce, finance and the professions' (Wagg, 1984, p. 3). It then spread among the working classes, encouraged principally by clergymen concerned to promote healthy exercise and 'muscular Christianity' (Dixon, 1976, Ch. 24), in the context of Victorian urban conditions. Many famous clubs started as church teams — including Fulham St Andrews — while many others were founded as works' teams, sponsored by employers. As the game acquired popularity as a spectator sport, charges for admission were levied, leading to official admission of professionalism in 1885, and to the formation of limited companies to manage clubs' affairs.

Violence both on and off the field was widely reported in late Victorian times — though the term 'hooligan' was originally applied to gangs of youths rampaging on a late-Victorian bank holiday, fighting each other, attacking foreigners and police (Pearson, 1983). The more successful teams often took the name of their locality (Thames Iron Works became West Ham United, for instance), and 'the growth of working class interest ... soon revealed two further fundamental concerns among the majority of supporters: the strong desire for victory and the fierce resentment of authority' (Wagg, 1984, p. 15). The desire for victory has spread with football throughout the world, while elements of the resentment of authority have survived, particularly on the terraces, into the late twentieth century: 'Ultimately the problem is that in football ... the power to control the institution does not rest with those on whose behalf it has been created' (Critcher, 1979, p. 184).

In brief, the marketing view of supporters as passive consumers, looking for entertainment and comfort, does not match the reality of many dedicated supporters (fanatics) spending much of their spare time attending home games, travelling to away games, arguing, discussing and dreaming about their team. Both sense of identity, of tradition (going back through families) and membership of a strong social network are derived from this support. And this support generates a real sense of ownership.

So contemporary football clubs exhibit a variety of anomalies. Players are described as professionals, yet are bought and sold and fined for disciplinary offences both on and off the field; and yet loyalty and dedication are demanded from their mercenary warriors by managers and supporters. Supporters, though united in the desire for victory, are separated physically by price and fencing – ranging from those who stand on packed terraces, often exposed to the elements, to those who sit in comfort in the stands. Supporters of all ages are often treated as potential hooligans by stewards and police, yet the marketing rhetoric treats them as consumers, to be entertained and cosseted, while commercial sponsors are provided with enclosed hospitality suites, complete with TVs, food and drink. Clubs are described as commercial businesses, yet directors subsidize them without prospect of financial return and, if results are unfavourable, endure vituperation from supporters. Each supporter holds passionate, particular views on players, managers, team selection and territory, ensuring that discussion of play and players is fraught with passion and potential conflict for, as with politics, what is owned is in common ownership.

## Fulham: Some Background Information

Fulham started life in 1879–80 as an amateur side linked to a local church. The ground at Craven Cottage (the club's ninth home) was acquired in 1896 on a long lease from the Church Commissioners – a derelict piece of ground adjacent to the Thames, on the site of a cottage built by Baron Craven in 1780. By 1898 the site was ready for football, entry to the Southern League was gained and the club turned professional, being incorporated as a limited company in 1903. A new stand (and a new Craven Cottage), designed by Archibald Leitch, was opened in 1905, and entry to the Football League gained in 1907.

The majority of the succeeding seasons (48 out of a possible 74, excluding war years) have been spent in the Second Division, with 12 in the First

Division. During this period many famous names have played for the club at various stages of their careers, including George Best, Rodney Marsh, Allan Clarke, Bobby Moore, Malcolm Macdonald, Bobby Robson, Alan Mullery, George Cohen (Fulham's representative in England's 1966 World Cup side) and Johnny Haynes, who spent his career with Fulham, winning 56 caps for England between 1956 and 1962. The club reached the Cup Final in 1975, losing 2–0 to West Ham at Wembley. The club has shared in the general decline in attendances, with gates currently averaging about 5,000 in the new Second Division.

'Many professional football clubs owe their original development, subsequent growth, and (often) current survival to a rich patron' (Turner and White, 1987, p. 45), and Fulham's history has conformed to this pattern: 'for much of its existence the club has been under the control of one individual or clique, whose dictatorial style has varied only in the benevolence shown to the manager, players and supporters.' (Ibid.) As with many football clubs, over the years there have been various boardroom disputes and upheavals.

More recently, when Eric Miller, a majority shareholder, committed suicide in 1977, one of his associates, Ernie Clay, emerged as Chairman. During his nine-year period in office, Fulham were relegated to the Third Division, promoted in 1982 and relegated again in 1986. With gates declining, a number of players were sold, while the Chairman publicly aired the problems of making ends meet. From 1977 to 1985 current liabilities rose from £0.82 million to £3.383 million (Turner and White, 1987, p. 52). Clay also managed to negotiate the purchase for just under £1 million of the freehold from the Church Commissioners, a deal financed by a Manchester firm, Kilroe Industrial Enterprises. When plans for perimeter development of the ground were turned down by the local council, Clay sought a buyer for the club, eventually selling at a net gain of £4 million to SB Properties, a subsidiary of Marler Estates plc, with Bulstrode acting as chairman of both companies. (SB stands for Stamford Bridge Properties, which was the owner of Stamford Bridge. Seventy per cent of its shares were purchased by Marler Estates from its Chairman, David Mears, in September 1983. The Mears family had built Stamford Bridge in the 1890s, and tried to persuade Fulham to move to their ground. When they were turned down, they started their own club – Chelsea.)

Kilroe, with its interest in the freehold purchase, applied independently for development, retaining the ground and stand, but this application was rejected in February 1987. After this rejection Bulstrode proposed the merger of QPR and Fulham.

## Reaction to the Merger Proposal

The Football League Management Committee refused to sanction the merger and, within a fortnight, Bulstrode indicated that he would be willing to sell the football club while retaining the freehold to the ground. By April 1987, Jimmy Hill, an ex-Fulham player (297 appearances) and TV football commentator with experience of both football management and direction at Coventry City, had put together a consortium of Fulham supporters with sufficient capital to negotiate the purchase of Fulham's footballing activities. SB Properties retained the original Fulham Football Club Ltd, and the new club was formed as Fulham Football Club (1987) Ltd, with a three-year lease on the Cottage. Jimmy Hill became Chairman, with one of the principal subscribers, Bill Muddyman, as Vice-Chairman, and other major subscribers as directors. Bulstrode became Chairman of QPR, and attempted unsuccessfully to buy QPR from SB Properties before his untimely death in September 1988.

Fulham, however, remained at risk. The new club's only assets were their status as a league club, their existing players, the willingness of directors to underwrite financial deficits and the dedication of their supporters – playing on a ground with precarious tenure.

In Spring 1986 a Labour council had been re-elected in Hammersmith, with a public commitment to maintaining three football clubs in the borough, on three sites. As part of this commitment, the council published a planning brief early in 1988 containing guidelines for any future development of Craven Cottage, essentially restricting residential development to the north (Hammersmith) end. During the 1987–8 season, the new club experienced a deficit of some £300,000, financed partly by the sale of some players and partly by a bank overdraft guaranteed by the directors.

In 1988 SB Properties submitted a planning application that allowed for a capacity of 11,000 standing, with 3,400 seats in the old Stevenage Road stand. From the footballing point of view, this would be adequate for a Third Division club, but the Taylor Report (the official inquiry following the Hillsborough disaster), which recommended all-seater stadia for First and Second Division clubs, would have severely restricted capacity for a club with promotion ambitions. Six thousand objections were received to this proposal, and the council took the view that it was unacceptable in the light of their planning brief, and began investigation of the possibility of issuing a compulsory purchase order (CPO) on the ground, in the public interest. They duly rejected the planning application and, in November 1988, voted to issue a CPO. SB Properties appealed to the Secretary of State for the Environment against both this rejection and the CPO.

In the following year the interests of Marler Estates were bought by Cabra Estates plc, who thereby took over both the property assets and the ongoing appeal. Robert Noonan, a director and major shareholder in Marler, left 'with compensation, worth £2.27m plus millions more for his share stake' (*Estates Gazette*, 10 August 1991). Cabra submitted a further application for development of the whole site, with a scheme designed by Quinlan Terry, preserving the listed Cottage and Stevenage Road stand. This also was rejected by Hammersmith Council. During this season (1988–9), Fulham reached the Third Division playoffs, but failed to gain promotion.

## Planning Inquiry

The public inquiry, triggered by SB Properties' appeal, was eventually set for

January 1990. Several thousand letters of support for the CPO and for the preservation of football at Craven Cottage were received by the inspector. Representatives of Fulham Football Club (1987) Ltd were to be major witnesses at the inquiry, which followed the normal procedure of a quasi-legal process, presided over by a professional Department of Environment inspector, with Queen's Counsellors representing principal parties. Ironically, the appellant was Fulham Football Club Ltd — the original company still owned by SB Properties.

However, during the weekend before the inquiry, the Fulham board were contacted by Cabra Estates with a financial offer conditional on the club dropping its opposition at the inquiry. Over this weekend the board, with its legal advisers, concluded a deal involving a series of conditional payments — £2 million to be paid immediately, £3.5 million when the club vacated the ground, £5 million when planning permission was granted, £500,000 if no ground sharing could be arranged and a further £2 million on realization of the site's value by Cabra Estates — making £13 million in all.

This decision, so close to the inquiry, came as a shock to the council representatives and to most supporters, whose letters to the inspector had emphasized the close connection between the ground, the club, its history and traditions. The board's position was that their responsibility was to ensure the future of Fulham Football Club — not just Craven Cottage — and the Cabra deal would enable them to secure the financial and playing position of the club, and provide time to consider alternative options. The threat of the CPO had enabled them to secure this deal. They stated their case at public meetings and in the programme, and many supporters, mindful of the threat to close the club three years earlier, were sympathetic to their decision. Others, however, regarded the deal as a betrayal, feeling the club and ground were inseparable.

During the remainder of this season, and the following season, supporters' spirits (and attendances) were not helped by performance on the field. The club avoided relegation to the Fourth Division by one place for two seasons running, despite the purchase of a number of new players. This performance led to vocal calls for a new chairman and manager — a common occurrence in clubs where supporters' aspirations are dashed by results.

The inspector's report to the Secretary of State for the Environment rec-ommended rejection of Hammersmith Council's CPO, but upheld the council's rejection of planning permission for the proposed developments, Cabra have submitted a further planning application and having agreed to sell Chelsea's Stamford Bridge at 1988 values — at a price of £22.8 million set by an independent valuer. At the time of the Marler deal (early 1990) Cabra shares traded at 110p; in 1991 they traded between 7p and 19p (having tracked the slide in property values), but they were also affected by uncertainty over the future of the Fulham and Chelsea grounds.

Fulham made a good start to the 1991–2 season but, after a poor run of results, the manager left the club by mutual agreement, to be replaced by a new manager, Don MacKay, under whom results have improved. With a lease ending in 1993, the club were actively looking for a ground-sharing arrangement

Figure 19.1 From the Fulham 'Fanzine' *TOOFIF* (There's Only One F In Fulham), No. 17

with Chelsea, against council and local opposition, or an alternative location outside the borough, while supporters dreamt of the opportunity to buy back the freehold at an affordable price – which was unlikely to reflect its development value (see Figure 19.1). At the end of the 1992 season, the Directors confirmed that the club would be staying at Craven Cottage for the 1992–3 season at least.

## Questions

1. Who 'owns' a football club?
2. Does a legal/accounting convention of ownership by shareholders provide a useful model for analysis?
3. What mechanisms might be established to give supporters a say in the running of a football club?

## Supplementary Question

In what sense does management of a football team constitute 'management'?

## References

Critcher, C. (1979) Football since the War, in C. Clarke, C. Critcher and R. Johnson (eds.) *Working Class Culture*, Hutchinson, London.

Dixon, N. (1976) *On the Psychology of Military Incompetence*, Jonathan Cape, London.

Dunning, E. (ed.) (1971) *The Sociology of Sport*, Frank Cass, London, Chs. 5 and 8.

*Estates Gazette* (1991) 10 August. *Company File: Danbury signs up Noonan.*

Hopcraft, A. (1968) *The Football Man: People and Passions in Soccer*, Simon & Schuster, London.

Pearson, G. (1983) *Hooligan: A History of Respectable Years*, Macmillan, London.

Turner, D. and White, A. (1987) *Fulham: A Complete Record 1879–1987*, Breedon Books.

Wagg, S. (1984) *The Football World: A Contemporary Social History*, Harvester, Brighton.

# PART V

Strategy, Structure and
Management Development in
A Competitive Environment

## CASE 20

# Falkner Wilks: Managing Growth in a Professional Firm

## Tim Morris and Helen Lydka

## Background to the Case

As Cliff Falkner finished a long meeting with his senior partners he cast his mind over the implications of winning an important and prestigious contract in the Docklands area of East London. It was by far the largest project in which his company, only started twelve years ago, had ever been involved. Under his leadership, Falkner Wilks had grown to a medium-sized and well-respected quantity surveying practice, but Falkner still felt he could achieve much more, which was why the Docklands project was so important.

Yet, thinking back over the previous few years and the tremendous strides that had already been made, Cliff Falkner knew that growth was not without its problems. Last year, the practice had to recruit 76 surveyors, 50 per cent of whom were new appointments. Salaries had accelerated and he had to provide cars for all his senior staff. The increasing complexities of running a company that was diversifying into related areas and also establishing offices in the provinces and abroad had meant he was having to spend money on the systems and managers to run the business efficiently — no longer could he and his partners cope with all the day-to-day administration as well as going out to win business.

Furthermore, the whole market was going through unprecedented change. Medium-sized firms such as Falkner Wilks were going to find themselves under particular pressure in this environment, lacking the strength to take on the largest firms and yet with higher overheads and less flexibility than the smaller ones. Also, it was uncertain how long their present growth would continue; coping with the inevitable, periodic downturns in the market-place created problems of its own.

Now aged 57, Cliff Falkner had been the driving force behind every important decision at Falkner Wilks and it was his energy and vision that had made the partnership what it was. How could he now ensure it was properly organized to face the turbulent times ahead and yet continue to lead the company in accordance with this original philosophy of a high-quality professional practice that succeeded by being utterly responsive to the needs of its clients?

## Organizational Setting: Origins and Growth of Falkner Wilks

Twelve years ago, Clifford Falkner and Colin Wilks had left the firm of chartered surveyors with which they were both employed to establish a quantity surveying practice of their own. Both were professionally qualified with chartered membership of the Institute of Quantity Surveyors. Their good contacts, technical skills and innovative ideas enabled them quickly to establish a reputable practice.

Wilks had retired some years later but Falkner continued to build and develop the organization. Indeed, Cliff Falkner had been the driving force behind the organization's growth and success. From the start he tried to adopt a more market-orientated approach, believing that the traditional profession lacked commercial awareness. In his view, surveyors were more attracted to doing technically demanding work, regardless of its profitability. They would therefore take on projects they found interesting even if this meant other more profitable work was neglected. Nor were surveyors skilled at managing their teams or particularly motivated by this part of their job: it seemed to be assumed that surveyors could organize themselves and establish their priorities without direction. Cost and time over-runs consequently resulted. Falkner's commercial strategy was to offer high-quality work in which his partners and senior managers were closely involved and to charge premium prices for the service. His strategy had paid off, not least because he did not carry the overhead costs of his larger competitors and therefore his prices did not seem exceptionally high. The firm also had a proven reputation for good-quality work and reliability in terms of completing its various projects on time and to budget.

Falkner believed future success also lay in the ability to utilize information technology to assist not only in the work itself but also in the achievement of cost and labour efficiency. Consequently, Falkner Wilks had invested heavily in a network of computers offering databased methods of construction management and to provide a complete design, management and cost advice service.

Its headquarters were in central London with a network of six regional offices in the UK as well as four in Europe. Falkner Wilks now employed over 200 people, excluding its 21 equity partners, and had considerably expanded its range of professional services to include project management, design management, building surveying and maintenance and interior design, as well as quantity surveying. The organization of the firm is set out in Figure 20.1.

It competed in all areas of the surveying market from small-scale projects (such as private building renovations) to large-scale ones, including the construction of an international airport terminal, prisons, hospitals and major commercial developments. Table 20.1 summarizes the financial performance for the past five years.

## Quantity Surveying

Quantity surveying involves the estimation of the amount and cost of both the

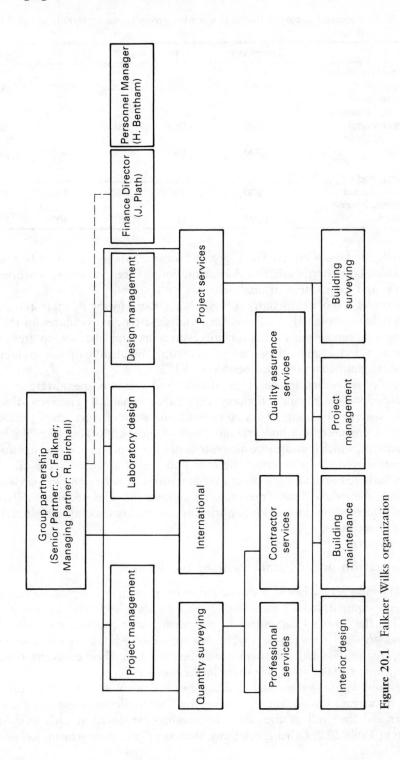

**Figure 20.1** Falkner Wilks organization

**Table 20.1**   Financial history – five-year record – group summary (£000s adjusted for inflation)

|                                         | Current year | −1    | −2    | −3    | −4    |
|-----------------------------------------|--------------|-------|-------|-------|-------|
| Profit and loss account, turnover/fees  | 4,000        | 3,200 | 1,850 | 1,280 | 1,000 |
| Total direct costs (incl. labour and subcontracting) | 2,280 | 1,650 | 800 | 480 | 320 |
| *Sub-total*                             | 1,720        | 1,550 | 1,050 | 800   | 680   |
| Overheads and interest charged          | 930          | 850   | 550   | 310   | 150   |
| Profit before tax and drawings          | 790          | 700   | 500   | 490   | 530   |

materials and labour involved in a specified construction job. It covers building economics, cost-control contract documentation services, valuation of work in progress and preparation of final accounts.

The profession of the quantity surveyor is regulated by the Royal Institute of Chartered Surveyors (RICS). The RICS establish selection procedures for those wishing to become recognized quantity surveyors and also set up training procedures and examinations; upon successful completion of this training, individuals gain chartered membership of RICS.

Quantity surveyors are one type of chartered surveyor specializing in the construction industry and providing expertise in financial, contractual and design aspects of buildings. They co-ordinate the work of contractors (such as architects, engineers and builders) on behalf of clients. Working from the bill of quantities, which indicates the dimensions of a construction and the quantities of materials required to convert the plan into reality, quantity surveyors are closely involved in advising a client over any project changes and in managing the client's interests during the project's completion. This requires skills of contract negotiation, progress monitoring of construction and agreeing interim and final accounts.

## Organization and Management of the Firm

Falkner Wilks had adopted a classic partnership model of organization. Full partners acquired some equity in the firm on their appointment and then shared in the financial success of the partnership on a proportional basis. As the firm grew, salaried partners were also appointed who did not hold equity in the organization but were senior members of staff. Their expectation was subsequently to take an equity share in the business.

For those with a professional qualification, Falkner Wilks provided a career route from trainee to quantity surveyor to team leader/manager to salaried partner and then full partnership. The numbers employed at each level are shown in Table 20.2. Other specialisms, such as project management, followed

**Table 20.2** Falkner Wilks employment − five-year record (nos. of employees)

| | Current year | −1 | −2 | −3 | −4 |
|---|---|---|---|---|---|
| Partners | 21 | 19 | 17 | 15 | 13 |
| Salaried partners and managers | 46 | 32 | 31 | 28 | 24 |
| Surveyors and trainees | 124 | 95 | 85 | 76 | 65 |
| Admin. full−time equivalents | 61 | 56 | 46 | 43 | 39 |

a similar route upwards. No formalized training for this progression operated in the firm and there was a great reliance on on-the-job experience. Promotion relied on working hard and getting noticed by senior partners. Salaried partners normally came up through the ranks except where they were recruited directly for their particular skills or brought additional contacts.

To become an equity partner was the career objective of most of the professionals, and those who were very successful could achieve this in their mid-30s, although the numbers appointed depended on the rate of growth of the firm. Appointing too many would make the firm top heavy with highly paid senior members, and dilute the profit-sharing. On the other hand, it was expected that if professionals demonstrated they were not capable of reaching partnership they would leave, rather than block the promotion channels for more able juniors. One of Cliff Falkner's main headaches was to hold onto his more talented staff by providing career opportunities as he realized the future success of the business was closely tied up with their commitment.

Both equity and salaried partners were expected to bring new clients with them if they joined from another firm and, once employed, to spend much of their time bidding for new work. This meant the partners were extensively involved in trying to sell to potential clients through their networks of contacts as well as dealing with existing clients. Frequently they were away from the office, as about 80 per cent of their time was taken up on client business. Even the salaried partners, who had more operational duties than the equity partners, would spend around 25 per cent of their time in generating new business and about a further 35 per cent liaising with clients. The remainder of their billable time was spent managing the teams of surveyors who carried out the core work of the firm. This selling work was vitally important because, broadly speaking, the direction the company took and its rate of growth was determined by the success or failure of each partner to secure new business. But it was also part of Cliff Falkner's philosophy that no work was ever turned away and he himself continued to play a major role in acquiring new contracts.

Each part of the partnership, such as project management or building design, operated independently under the overall responsibility of a senior equity partner. Other partners were responsible for one or more project teams or for an office (e.g. a regional branch). The teams typically comprised eight or nine people and were managed on a day-to-day basis either by a salaried partner or a manager depending on the size and importance of the job. Manager was the first stage of promotion for professionals after qualification. In this job, the skills of bringing a project to completion on time and within planned costs was learnt. A great deal of technical know-how was necessary to solve the on-the-job problems and advise or check the work of the team members. Sometimes specialist groups would be set up to undertake feasibility studies into particular areas using advice from the various working teams as necessary.

Work was generally divided into either pre-contract or post-contract stages. Pre-contract was the responsibility of the partner who generated the business to bring together a team with the most relevant skills to do the job. Post-contract work would occasionally be reallocated to a regional office if this allowed for a better geographical match. In general the principle was that the partner who had first obtained the work continued to liaise with the client and to take any decisions pertinent to the contract throughout its duration, although the day-to-day management would be delegated to a manager. When the partnership did not possess enough resources internally to cope with the work in progress, agency personnel would be employed.

Although the partners functioned relatively autonomously, Cliff Falkner kept track of all incoming and ongoing work through the monthly partnership meetings. As he also saw all the incoming post he was immediately aware if any problems arose and could contact the partner concerned at once to find out more about the situation, even if it involved one of the offices out of London. Falkner saw this ability to keep tabs on work as crucial to ensuring customer needs were properly looked after, although he tried to avoid interfering with the technical judgement or the business contacts of the partners.

He also liked to take advantage of other opportunities for growth. For example, on his own initiative he managed to persuade a group of quantity surveyors who had been working in the National Health Service but were about to be made redundant to join him on the assurance they could continue to work as a team. By acquiring employees in this way Falkner planned to gain the benefit of key skills as well as the guaranteed work the new employees would bring with them as part of the deal with their former employer. Falkner's partners tended to accept these spur-of-the-moment decisions, which he only revealed to them after the event, with a mixture of resignation and amusement. After all, they usually reasoned, such gambles had paid off in the past and to try to restrict Cliff Falkner's natural instinct for growth would run against the very culture of the firm he had founded.

## The Problem: Managing Growth

Winning the Docklands project had focused Cliff Falkner's mind on some of the critical issues facing the firm. One was how to manage growth efficiently. This was made difficult by the project-based nature of the work, which meant that growth was not incremental but occurred in discrete steps: gearing up for the Docklands project meant promoting two managers to partner and hiring over twenty professional staff as well as administrative back-up, and the company even had to consider the purchase of a new set of offices. Then, maintaining growth to keep those resources fully employed when the project was finished required further sales.

At the same time surveying firms faced more difficult conditions. After a number of good years, a downturn had occurred in the market and things were not expected to improve for the next two or three years. Profit margins were also coming under increasing pressure as larger institutional clients were using their buying power more effectively and non-surveyors were expanding into some of the markets where surveying firms operated, such as project management and design. Additionally, in-house surveyors employed by big construction firms, financial institutions and retailers were all beginning to offer their services to other parties. If Falkner Wilks was to continue to prosper it had to become more efficient and get the best out of its staff.

One of the key moves in trying to manage the growth of the firm and improve efficiency had been to appoint a Managing Partner. Some three years previously, Richard Birchall had been elected to this position unanimously by his fellow partners. He was now aged 38 and had joined Falkner Wilks as a qualified surveyor two years after the firm had started. From the start he had shown a combination of excellent technical skill and the flair for bringing in profitable business and had been rewarded by entry to the partnership at a comparatively early age with wide respect from his peers. As Managing Partner, he was given a broad brief to sort out the internal operations of the group, which the partners recognized were becoming increasingly chaotic. For example, the record of work in progress was frequently not kept up to date because no single person had responsibility for this. Nor was there a central record of the workload of each of the surveyors, and some were clearly working much harder than others.

As a condition of taking up the post of Managing Partner, Richard Birchall brought in a number of support staff to set up and manage systems and departments spanning the whole company. These included the financial controls and planning systems, office management, information systems and personnel. After his appointment, Birchall naturally continued to do what he was good at and enjoyed – bringing in business and working on surveying projects. This inevitably involved him in long periods out of the office seeing clients. He tended to delegate decision-making as far as possible, believing that partners should have the responsibility for running their own areas of the business and making any important decisions, such as hiring of staff and project bidding. This view was popular with the majority of his fellow partners, who basically felt that if Birchall's staff dealt with what they saw as tiresome administrative work this would allow them to concentrate on the interesting and profitable job of dealing with clients' work.

At the same time as Birchall was made Managing Partner, Falkner appointed his secretary, Hazel Bentham, as Personnel Manager. This role was largely administrative, involving the development of proper staff records and job descriptions, distribution and maintenance of standardized employment contracts, handling sickness, pensions and other benefits and dealing with the procedural side of any grievances or disciplinary matters. This again was a popular move as Bentham had been with the firm since its inception and knew most people very well. She was also adept at managing Falkner, who had a pretty short temper when things went wrong, particularly with client work, and was inclined to confront people bluntly with his opinions. The partnership had agreed in principle that the Personnel Manager should take control of hiring and develop a salary structure. In practice, individual partners, including Cliff Falkner, continued to recruit staff, allocate them to teams as they saw fit, make promotion decisions and distribute bonuses on the grounds that they were the owners of the firm and ultimately responsible for its future. Personnel would be informed of their decisions after the event.

More standardized systems of financial control had started to be introduced some five years ago. Until then, partners had been responsible for calculating fees and billing clients so there was no central control over debt collection. A dispute with a large client over charging had prompted the change and then, eighteen months ago, a chartered accountant, Julia Plath, had been hired and made a salaried partner with the title of Finance Director. She set about tightening controls further by extending budgeting and by trying to develop more accurate overhead allocation methods. While most partners were happy to co-operate, a minority resented the idea of having to stick to budgets, particularly in the area of new-client development work, muttering that accountants were taking over the running of a perfectly fine company and that Plath simply did not understand how a surveying firm had to be run.

Indeed, things had started to come to a head since Plath's arrival, and a particularly difficult partners' meeting last month had revealed real divisions within the partnership as to the future. These focused around the issues of the firm's strategy and structure. On the question of developing a more explicit strategy for the partnership, two of the senior partners had argued that the firm should plan longer term, restricting itself to specific market segments where its reputation was best, and it should concentrate on selling an integrated service that cut across the disciplines in the firm to differentiate itself from other surveyors. This was, after all, the way the market was evolving. Generally, there was a great deal of sympathy for this among the partners, but it was recognized that everyone in the firm would have to change the way they worked and that a major reorganization, which cut across professional specialisms, was implied.

Plath voiced her support for this but she added that one serious problem was the refusal of some partners to stick to an internal transfer pricing policy for work done by one department (such as the design management department) for another (such as project management). Under the partnership structure, internal pricing had been customarily fixed between partners and even when a list of internal prices was instituted by Plath, informal negotiating continued. Several partners voiced the opinion that such bureaucracy as transfer pricing actually prevented the company from fully co-ordinating its activities, and pointed to the occasion when an external design organization was employed on one project rather than the partnership's own service because the internal price was double the cost of the external agency.

Plath went on to say that she found it frustrating to be excluded from the equity partners' meetings where decisions with important financial implications, such as promotions to partner, new work and partners' drawings from profits had been discussed. As she put it, she was always amazed that each partner seemed to be able to choose where he or she worked, which projects they took on and how hard they worked. She felt that clearer reporting lines would be very helpful. This observation touched a raw nerve among several of the partners since the monthly partnership meetings had now reached such a size they were somewhat unwieldy and made decision-making problematic.

Birchall and several other senior partners had strongly resented what she said and didn't like the idea of a corporate strategy. Pointing to the fees earned, they saw no need for change and that the essence of the firm was its collection of individual talents. Birchall put it to Plath that 'We are the firm. It is in our interests to make it work without targets and controls. Professional people don't need reporting lines and instruction manuals; they know what is for the best without being told because they have been well trained'.

Falkner's views were more mixed. He had set up the firm to do things his way and he detested bureaucratic systems and controls. If he was to vote for some sort of fixed strategy would this impinge on his entrepreneurial nature and therefore the capacity to take quick decisions when opportunities for growth presented themselves? After all, just recently he had been able to make the snap decision to purchase a provincial surveying firm after only the briefest of consultation with his senior partners. On the other hand, better controls and targets might stimulate some of his partners who were less energetic than the others and who appeared quite happy with the status quo rather than continued growth, or those who liked doing technically interesting work but with little concern for its commercial value. Talking to the Personnel Manager, he was also aware the administrative staff were demoralized because a partner's authority was needed for even the most trivial of decisions, such as the purchase of a new desk.

There was also the question of the future leadership at the back of his mind. Richard Birchall looked like his natural successor but since Julia Plath had been hired Falkner had been increasingly impressed by her management skills, her dedication to the firm and her capacity to think through some of the longer-term issues facing Falkner Wilks. Generally, he was becoming more persuaded by her argument for greater central control and direction, and the need for more attention to managing people. But this would add up to a major change in the direction of his firm, and quite how to implement change without alienating his partners and the other professionals was obviously going to be a very difficult task.

## Case Study Tasks

Imagine you are Cliff Falkner:

1. What are the main problems facing the firm from your point of view?

2. What are the options for the future direction of the firm and what is your preferred plan? Why have you chosen the plan you have selected?
3. What implications does your plan have for the organization and management of the firm, and how do you propose to overcome any difficulties you might foresee?

## Essential Reading

Maister, D. (1982) Balancing the professional service firm, *Sloan Management Review*, Fall, pp. 5–19.

Mintzberg, H. (1983) *Structure in Fives: Designing Effective Organizations*, Prentice-Hall, Englewood Cliffs, NJ (Chap. 10).

Raelin, J. (1986) *The Clash of Cultures: Managers and Professionals*, Harvard Business School Press, Cambridge, Mass.

## Additional Reading

Abbott, A. (1988) *The System of Professionals: An Essay on the Division of Expert Labor*, University of Chicago Press, Chicago, Ill.

Drazin, R. (1990) Professionals and innovation: structural-functional versus radical-structural perspectives, *Journal of Management Studies*, Vol. 27, no. 3, May, pp. 245–63.

Gouldner, A. (1957) Cosmopolitans and locals: toward an analysis of latent social roles, *Administrative Science Quarterly*, Vol. 2, pp. 281–306.

# CASE 21

## The Growing Pains of Harvey (Engineers) Ltd

### *Fiona E. Mills*

## Organizational Setting

Harvey (Engineers) Ltd is the vision of one man, Mr Harvey. Starting as a 'one man band' in 1970, he has been centrally involved in the development of the company to this very day. With the support of his wife, the company reached a record annual turnover of four and a half million pounds in 1990, which approached six and a half million pounds in real terms by the middle of that year. The company currently employs over a hundred personnel. Over the years the company evolved a very simple multi tasking functional structure, headed by Mr Harvey, and reflected in the emerging Senior Management team (see Figure 21.1). This prevailed until around 1987. The 'Lawson Boom' in the construction industry in 1988 onwards, and the surge of business that resulted, threw this slow evolutionary process of emergent organisational design into turmoil. To cope with a rapid expansion of business, new staff were recruited quickly, raising questions about their appropriate place in the existing organisation structure, its continued suitability, and issues of career progression and management development.

Until this time only those employees with long service were considered for positions of responsibility as they had 'grown up with the company' and had therefore gained the trust of Mr Harvey. All had been employed in shopfloor or menial worker positions. The increased demand, however, required the injection of new personnel into newly developed roles as it was realized that, by dividing responsibilities and task areas, a more efficient and effective service to the customer could be achieved. It is the consequences of this change in personnel practice this case study aims to address, as well as the issues that arose when the market pendulum began its regressive swing.

## Background

The company was founded in the south of England in 1970. Having occupied a number of jobs in his life, Mr Harvey saw an opportunity to develop a business in farm building construction. Thus 'Harvey (Engineers)' was born.

At this time the numbers employed were few, relying mainly on family members to help out, as and when necessary. But, the numbers employed by the company grew steadily and, in 1975, two of the current senior management personnel, Mr Dawson and Mr Lishman, were taken on as manual staff. In 1979, through the advice of an external accountant, the company acquired limited status, with the appointment of Mr and Mrs Harvey as the joint stock holders of the enterprise. It was at this time that a further ten employees were introduced to accommodate a market boom in the industry. Although, traditionally, the focus of the company was on steel fabrication, gradually its portfolio began to change with the complementary addition of civil engineering. This was stimulated by the recession that arose in the agricultural building industry in the early 1980s which instigated a shift of focus to a new and yet similar market: that of the industrial building.

Although the shift in market sector was successful a further development evolved from this action; the company switched its main operational focus. The majority of current trade is now acquired through the company's talents in civil engineering rather than through its traditional expertise in steel fabrication work. However, the company in a sense has the best of both worlds, for it can offer both services to the customer; the construction of a building by skilled civil engineers, and the steel fabrication supports for the building under construction. This eliminates the need to subcontract for one or other of these facilities, giving Harvey (Engineers) Ltd a perceived source of competitive advantage in the construction industry.

In order to get a clear picture of the company's operating practices, it is vital that we assess the role of the founder within the organisation, as management practices he has established over time undoubtedly affect the performance of present Senior Management personnel in their daily routines and in their communications with the newly acquired Middle Management employees.

There is no doubt over the extent of Mr Harvey's commitment to the company. He still shows a keen interest in the business and all of its activities, and often comments on the 'millions of duties' he must still perform: 'He's a workaholic. He never stops ... the other night he was here at ten o'clock at night to pick up a truck ... and that was him here at ten o'clock at night!' (Pre-Contracts Manager, Phil Vokes).

Although his level of involvement in the company is high, a desire to pursue other external interests was expressed by Mr Harvey. Before he is prepared to relinquish his current position, however, he has stated the need for reassurance that, in his absence, the organization will continue to operate effectively. The alternative, to sell the company as a going concern, is not an option Mr Harvey is prepared to consider because of strong family involvement and a son who hopes to take ownership at some stage: 'The alternative was to sell out and retire type of thing, but I don't see any point in it. Adam's one of the reasons for that. He's head over heels in the company ... what he decides to do is what the company will decide to do basically' (Mr Harvey).

Such a statement, suggesting the possible withdrawal of Mr Harvey from the company, is strongly contradicted by other accounts. For example, the results of a previous DTI report on the company, completed in 1986, stimulated the following response when Mr Harvey questioned one of the conclusions made: 'basically [it] said that I should retire and get out … said that I should stand down as Managing Director and put in a Managing Director and me go as Chairman. I didn't think it was a good idea … to get an outside man in would absolutely upset everything'.

This view is also substantiated by some of the now senior-management personnel:

> I don't think John [Mr Harvey] will ever retire, personally. I did ask this question at one meeting, 'What was the retirement attitude of the board of the company', and I was told in no uncertain terms by Mrs Harvey, 'You don't have to retire here. Nobody has to retire unless they want to', and she turned to John and she says, 'and you're certainly not retiring!' … John keeps telling me, 'You better get somebody to back up for you.' I just say, 'I'll see you out, you old bugger, don't you worry!'
>
> (Quantity Surveyor, Ken Pearson)

The devastating effect of losing the centre-piece of the organization and other key members without a considered succession strategy, is clearly an issue that is avoided.

Although at the helm of the company's development, Mr Harvey has utilized the skills of other employees. Indeed he differentiates his company from others because of the 'type' of people holding senior management positions: 'None of us are really paperwork minded because we've all come up from the shopfloor and this is probably the difference between us and a lot of other companies because they work with professional men.'

The General Manager, Pete Dawson, has the following account of how he came to work for Mr Harvey:

> How long have I been here? Thirteen or fourteen years I think. I came in to operate the saw in the workshop. I worked for Billing Steads before that. I was made redundant, he went way down, so I was looking for a job. At the time I would take anything, so I got on the saw working for John. It was a temporary job, type thing, see how it went. From there I took charge of his workshop and started organizing things.

The Civil Engineering Manager, Ian Lishman, tells a similar story. Being slightly younger than the General Manager he explains how his career has progressed within the company from the position of steel erector to the senior management post he now occupies. Ian Lishman comments on the change he has experienced in this management role in the last six or seven years: 'For a beginning it was, what can I say, 50 per cent of your time office work and organizing and 50 per cent actually physically labour and work. As it got bigger the gap went, then it was all office work really.' It is these two employees who have supported Mr Harvey for the longest period of time, since 1975.

In 1984 Ken Pearson was employed in the capacity of a buyer, having moved on from the loss of his own 'multi-million pound organization', according to his own attribution. Since his appointment, Ken has gained increasing influence within the company and has become a prominent member of the senior management team in the capacity of quantity surveyor. It is these three employees who represent the functional core of the senior management. The fourth member, Jackie Griffiths, having been with the company since 1980 in a clerical capacity, has been appointed Office Manager. With the external appointment of Phil Vokes, in 1990, to Pre-Contracts Manager, the existing Senior Management structure was complete (see Figure 21.1).

These personnel needed increasing support as the demand for industrial and other buildings grew in the mid-to–late 1980s. A functional structure began to evolve in accordance with the new demands, twelve months prior to the events outlined, in 1989 (see Figure 21.2). All of the appointments to 'middle management', excluding the site agents, came from external appointments. Mr Harvey justifies the appointments as an 'injection of professionals', as these individuals all had relevant higher/further educational or previous broad experience.

The new functional structure, however, gave rise to numerous difficulties, which were expressed by those who participated in the formalized version of what once was an *ad hoc* structure.

## Problems Experienced

With the increase in organisational size, the need to develop 'systems' for various procedures was recognised and acted upon. The effectiveness of these 'systems', designed by Mr Harvey, was questioned, especially by the middle management. A basic lack of trust became apparent as the senior management's roles became increasingly overloaded as their ability and willingness to delegate to more professional (and, hence, potentially threatening) middle management remained minimal.

Problems relating to communications were expressed, especially by the new Plant and Transport Manager, Paul Mortimer. He is responsible for setting up new sites and getting all the necessary equipment and materials to the location ready for work to commence on a given date. In order to do this there is certain information he obviously requires: 'Oh, like everybody thought somebody had told me, and somebody thought Pete [General Manager] would have

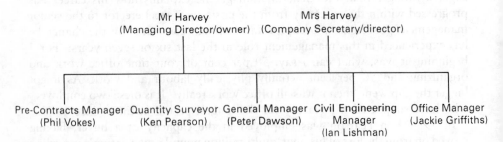

Figure 21.1   Senior management team

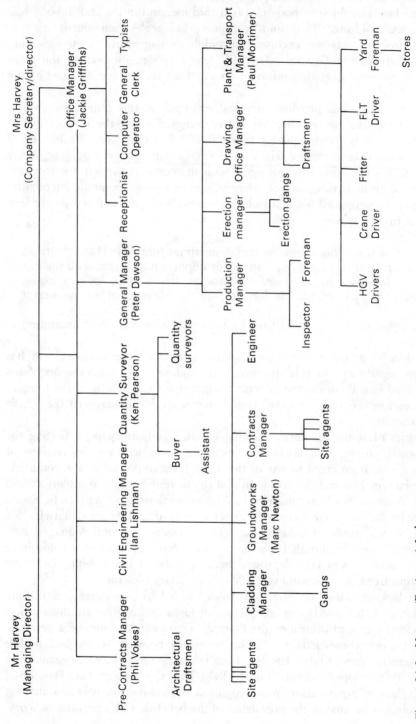

**Figure 21.2** Harvey (Engineers) Ltd

told me, and Pete thought Ian [Civil Engineering Manager] would have told me, and Ian thought somebody else had told me, and in the end nobody had bloody well told me.' (Plant and Transport Manager – Paul Mortimer)

This problem was not exclusive to middle management, as the following comment from the General Manager, Pete Dawson, illustrates: 'the main problem we have is getting information ... Like we're guessing most of the time.'

The postal system provides an ideal example of this point. All mail is delivered to, and opened by, Mr Harvey, regardless of the notification of addressee. This is a technique he utilises in order to keep himself informed of actions within the company. He also receives a copy of every outgoing letter before it is sent. Should he not agree with the contents the letter is stopped. Because of his increasing outside interests, and therefore spasmodic attendance, post may go unopened for relatively long periods of time and replies are sent without his knowledge:

> it's a slow turn-round time as well. Sometimes John [Mr Harvey] sits on stuff for three or four days, waiting for important quotes and all the rest of it. He sees it as addressed to whoever, has a quick look at it and doesn't see the relevance. He doesn't know the relevance of how important it is.
>
> (Plant & Transport Manager, Paul Mortimer)

This slow response is detrimental to the company's performance and has created significant morale problems throughout the organization. Such formalized but ill-considered systems instigated for the benefit of the founder can therefore be seen to have caused immeasurable damage to the whole organization.

In spite of some attempts at formalisation, significant gaps, reflecting the traditional culture, still remain. For example, no official job descriptions or outlines have been given to any of the individuals employed by the company, as Mr Harvey believed this would inhibit the flexibility of the company should people decide to work to rule. This has caused numerous concerns to be voiced by employees but none have been directed towards Mr Harvey himself: 'It's debatable really what the hell I am, quite honestly' (General Manager, Pete Dawson). 'The first month I was here I could have gone away. I could have been in tears. I was very depressed because I didn't know what they were expecting from me' (Groundworks Manager, Marc Newton).

This lack of clarity on given job roles has led to considerable confusion. Individuals either overlap in completion of tasks (hence jobs are done twice) or, as in the case of informing the Plant & Transport Manager of a new site, tasks are not completed at all. The boundary between senior and middle management responsibility has also been left undefined: 'lack of organization again. We're tripping ourselves up badly' (General Manager, Pete Dawson).

This 'lack of organization' was recognized and yet no time was allocated for its resolution because of the prevalence of the belief that 'the pressure of work' made it impossible to find time to resolve the problem. The source of pressure was perceived to emanate from the boom in the industry and was therefore seen to be beyond the organization's control. This feeling of environmental determinism was reflected in the explanation Mr Harvey expressed for his company's massive expansion of sales from just over £1 million in 1988 to sales exceeding £4.5 million in 1990!: 'I can't say that anything caused the expansion other than just natural growth.' As a result of this fatalistic belief in environmental determinism the company operates in a vicious circle of confused, reactive 'seat of the pants' management.

Although the complaints highlighted above are expressed throughout the organization, the newly appointed middle-management tier are experiencing specific problems relating to their personal roles. For example, all letters going out from a functional area have to be signed by the senior management representative. Middle management believe the reasoning behind this 'system' again is lack of trust: 'I write letters and yet I can't sign them. For thirty-odd years I've been writing to everybody from the Prime Minister downwards, but suddenly I'm not allowed to do that any more ... to my mind I should be if I'm accepted into the company and found trustworthy' (Contracts Manager, Dean Halden).

Middle management meetings were originally held to allow such issues to be raised. These were cancelled. The reason given for this, once again, was the 'pressure of work'. Meetings were recently reinstated whereby senior management and middle management join to discuss operational issues alone:

> In the middle management meetings that we had it's been brought up time and time again. 'Look,' you know, 'I'm whatever manager. I'm getting paid this money to do ...', why can't I get on and do it?' You know. Whether it's a lack of trust or whatever ... but if it's a lack of trust, then the guy shouldn't be in the job, you know.
>
> (Plant & Transport Manager, Paul Mortimer)

A good example of the atmosphere between these parties is an incident whereby a member of middle management mentioned they were discontented with the practice of senior management taking the minutes at such meetings. This comment was later followed by Mr Harvey, at a senior management meeting, commenting on how rarely he actually received a copy of this information!

Senior management hold conflicting opinions on the believed inadequacies of the middle-management tier: 'you're employing men but you're not taking the load off. It's still drifting back to the same people' (Civil Engineering Manager, Ian Lishman), which they convey to Mr Harvey: 'In other words, we've now increased the salaries of these people, and increased people as well, but we're getting no more management out of them. All we're getting is followers' (Mr Harvey).

Nevertheless, some senior management were prepared to take responsibility for the occurrence of this situation: 'Yeh, but we're paying him the wage to do it; but, we've bugger all to blame but ourselves because we're not feeding him the information either to work on ... we're not actually telling him to do it either' (Civil Engineering Manager, Ian Lishman).

No recognition of middle management's grievance of wanting more responsibility was expressed, nor any suggestions made as to how these issues could be resolved. Some senior managers were more perceptive of the situation than others, but the majority still tended to follow the belief that they were 'carrying' middle management personnel.

Middle management have their own explanation of the problems they now face, which rests on the fundamental assumption they are 'different' from those people who have been employed by the company in the past:

> I mean a lot of these, don't forget, are local, they've grown up with the firm. They don't know anything outside it. All they know is Harvey (Engineers) Ltd. It's a small firm, it's built up. You know they're just not aware, maybe they are aware I don't know, maybe they're just not interested but the likes of meself, and the others, you know, we've been in our own respective fields ... You can't say they're slow to change, they just don't want to change.
>
>        (Plant and Transport Manager, Paul Mortimer)

Many of middle management have tried taking their grievances directly to Mr Harvey but have been cautioned by him for evading the correct procedure; they must go through the chain of command.

One of the loudest voices of unrest came from the Plant & Transport Manager, Paul Mortimer, who was blatant in his criticism of the company's management policies and yet is still respected throughout the organization due to a macho manner in tune with the culture of both company and industry. He questions the ability of some senior managers to adapt to their newly found 'managerial' role:

> if he's not capable of doing the job, he shouldn't be doing it. That is a clear black-and-white definition ... they're too well established now. I could wipe out this management team quite easily. Put in people with far less experience and they'd do a damn sight better job.

Certain members of the senior management team have also expressed concern with regard to their new administrative and supervisory roles as they feel they are ill-equipped to oversee the specialized areas for which they are now responsible. The General Manager, Pete Dawson, is one such individual who is actually responsible for overseeing Paul Mortimer, the Plant & Transport Manager: 'I suppose I'm General Manager really, but to my mind I shouldn't be. I should be concentrating on the fabrication side, because that's the one that I know best. I'm feeling my way in the others and I would say jobs aren't getting done properly.'

Just as such debates were starting to come to a head throughout the summer of 1990, there was a substantial turnaround in the building industry. A market that was once booming suddenly began to regress as customers began to check their spending and investment in properties. The action taken by the company in response to this unanticipated slump was to silence all voices of discontent.

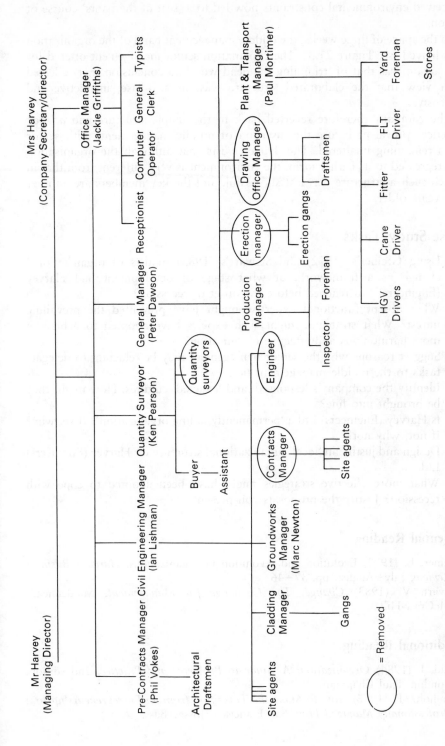

**Figure 21.3** The current situation

Perceived environmental constraints now led to a 'seat of the pants' course of action.

In the space of three weeks, the middle management band of the organization was halved (see Figure 21.3). The explanation senior management offered for this action was that of 'trimming the dead wood', a conclusion that reflected their view that the elaborated structure was, in any case, ineffective and expensive.

The company therefore reverted back to the simple structure and *ad hoc* practices prevalent before the insertion of middle management, with senior roles remaining unaltered. The danger exists that although the organisation has regressed to its earlier form, the environment is very different from that in which such a structure was last successful, and the key members are another five years older.

## Case Study Tasks

1. Using Greiner's (1972) and Stewart's (1983) models of organizational change as a framework, at what stage of development had Harvey (Engineers) Ltd reached before the onset of recession?
2. What absent functional expertise might have prevented the prevailing unrest? What strategies might such experts have adopted to achieve a more harmonious and effective organisation?
3. Suggest reasons why the senior management may be reluctant to delegate tasks to the middle management tier.
4. Identify the company's 'espoused' and 'enacted' cultures. How might they be brought into line?
5. Is Harvey (Engineers) Ltd a 'permanently failing organization'? If so, why? If not, why not?
6. Design and justify an 'ideal' organizational structure for Harvey (Engineers) Ltd.
7. What more effective strategies might have been adopted to cope with recession? Justify the proposals you present.

## Essential Reading

Greiner, L. (1972) Evolution and revolution in organizations, *Harvard Business Review*, July–August, pp. 37–46.
Stewart, V. (1983) *Change. The Challenge for Management*. Maidenhead: McGraw-Hill.

## Additional Reading

Child, J. (1984) *Organization: A Guide to Problems and Practice*. 2nd edition. London: Paul Chapman.
Flamholtz, E. (1986) *How to Make the Transition from an Entrepreneurship to a Professionally Managed Firm*. San Francisco: Jossey Bass.

Garratt, B. (1987) *The Learning Organization*. London: Fontana Collins.
Gibb Dyer, W. (1986) *Cultural Change in Family Firms*. San Francisco: Jossey Bass.
Handy, C. (1985) *Understanding Organizations*. Hammondsworth: Penguin.
Meyer, H. and Zucker, L. (1989) *Permanently Failing Organizations*. Beverly Hills: Sage.

# CASE 22

## Muddle in the Middle:
## Restructuring in Autospares

### Sue Dopson

## Organizational Setting

Autospares is one of the largest motor-spares dealers in the UK. It sells to franchise dealers, large retailers and to the public. It has a national network of 185 branches, divided into 14 regions and supported by a national warehouse. Branches are usually located on trading estates away from town centres.

Autospares experienced two periods of growth by acquisition in the mid-1960s and the early 1970s, followed by a period of chronic loss and poor morale. The parent company decided it had either to expand market share or leave the market altogether. Choosing the former option, it acquired two other motor-spares dealers. This led to the problem of merging three sets of management, three headquarters and three distribution centres. The financial performance was disappointing for a number of years, resurrecting the doubts of the parent company. While the financial performance has still not reached a level considered to be satisfactory, there has been some sign of improvement in the last two years.

Autospares now has a turnover approaching £100 million. A typical successful branch has eight or nine staff, stock of £75,000 and 200 credit accounts representing about £50,000 of debtors at any one time; 70 per cent of the business is done on the telephone.

Managers at branch and regional level (regarded as middle management) have generally always worked within the industry, most since leaving school. In a market serviced by many competitors, Autospares considers there to be four major rivals. The need to survive has been the stimulus for many changes.

## Background to the Case

A new Managing Director was appointed two years ago. His vision for the company is expressed in its mission statement: 'To create decisively the leading chain of factors in the UK ... securing much improved and consistent financial performance'.

The strategy designed to accomplish this mission comprises a number of elements, including

1.  cost leadership, through exploiting the economies of being a large company and utilizing a central warehouse;
2.  differentiation from the competition by investing in training and development and improving information systems;
3.  reducing stocks; and
4.  encouraging branch managers to be more entrepreneurial in developing their businesses according to the demands and opportunities of the local market.

The Managing Director (MD) sees branch managers as 'the critical agents for change' and central to achieving his strategy. He frequently referred to the need to empower this group of managers. A number of major changes have been made in an attempt to support the empowerment of branch managers.

## Regions

As Autospares has sought to rationalize and economize, regional boundaries have been redrawn, leading to a reduction in the number of regional general-manager posts (RGMs) from 20 to 14. The MD sees the centre's role as being to draw up a realistic strategy for the company and to monitor its implementation. He looks to the regions to achieve the strategy, to which end the RGMs are issued with performance targets (the branch managers' targets mirror the RGM's). The RGMs, all of whom have been in post for some three years, are expected to monitor and support all the branch managers in their region.

## The Sales Function

Most branches have one sales representative, but some larger branches have two, and smaller branches may share a rep. The almost exclusive focus of the company on sales in the past meant that branch and sales staff had always worked closely together. The sales representative was accountable to the branch manager and, through him, to the RGM.

After the reorganization of the sales function – initiated and implemented by headquarters alone – sales representatives continued to be accountable to their branch manager, but there was added a 'dotted line' to a new post of area sales manager (ASM). The role of the ASM is to train and monitor the performance of the sales representatives in his area. He is also responsible for pursuing and maintaining major accounts on behalf of the branch network.

An ASM is responsible to a regional sales manager (RSM). The RSM is in turn accountable to headquarters, but he also has a 'dotted line' to the RGM. The relevant parts of the organizational structure are shown in Figure 22.1.

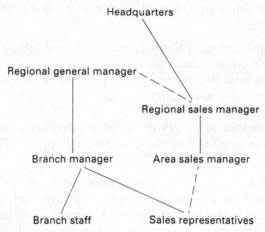

**Figure 22.1** The position of the sales function

## Branch Specialization

Each branch is required to find a specialist market niche within a radius of approximately twenty miles. The move to specialization has to be a compromise between what the local market suggests is an opportunity for growth and the capability of the branch.

## Purchasing and Distribution

As a result of a central decision to rationalize product lines, Autospares now concentrates on six main product groups. A central warehouse acts as the main source of supply for the branch network. Attached to the warehouse is the 'marketing department', which negotiates directly with suppliers. This centralized negotiation system has meant that branches no longer have to deal with suppliers if products are available from the warehouse, so the company has generally been able to secure better terms.

The warehouse offers a weekly delivery service that, it is hoped, will become daily. A second warehouse has been introduced to redistribute stock that will not sell in particular branches.

## Improved Branch Environment

A standard layout for branches has been introduced, which makes for a more attractive and professional-looking work environment.

## Computerization

Computers were introduced relatively recently into the branch network over a period of two years in a programme costing some £3 million. The computer provides branches with information on stock, prices, sales, debtors and profit.

Branches can assess customer spending and offer appropriate discount, thus improving over-the-counter service. Invoices contain correct price information and appear 'more professional'.

Prior to computerization the only daily information available to branch managers was on total sales, and there was no stock control system. Profitability calculations were reported twice a year, two months after stock-taking.

## Performance Targets and Incentives

Formerly, branch managers and their staff were monitored and rewarded on the basis of monthly sales. The bonuses of branch staff are still based on monthly sales but, three years ago, a new system was introduced whereby the branch (and regional) managers were monitored and judged on five targets – sales, costs, profit margins, stock and debtors. There was an incentive scheme based on the difference between actual and budgeted branch contribution over a six-month period, with adjustments according to the results for debtor days and stock-turn.

In the estimation of budgeted contribution, branch managers were issued with central guidance about expected market conditions and corporate aims. They then submitted their bids to their RGM who, once he had agreed it, passed it to headquarters. Having been vetted by RGMs, budget submissions were generally accepted by headquarters without amendment.

Partly as a result of the incentive scheme, branch managers' salaries increased by an average of 35 per cent over three years, considerably above the level of inflation. Branch managers now earn an average of £10,000 basic per year, with the possibility of up to £4,000 in bonus.

The MD was concerned that the multiple targets involved a manager in difficult trade-offs. Discussions were held at board level, and a new scheme has been introduced. Managers are now expected to achieve a return on branch assets (ROBA) of 80 per cent, where

$$\text{ROBA} = \frac{\text{Branch contribution}}{\text{Stock} + \text{Debtors}}$$

One senior manager at headquarters commented, 'We don't mind how they get there as long as they do'. Branch budgets are now set centrally in consultation with the appropriate RGM.

## Training and Development

Formalized training for branch managers was begun a year ago. This is run in-house and consists of well-tried contributions in the areas of managing budgets, teamwork, interviews and sales. Plans for the future include courses on customer care, the image portrayed by branches in the market-place and using the information available on the computer.

A systematic, modular training programme for all branch staff has also recently been introduced. Having previously had discretion over training of his staff, the branch manager is now held responsible for the completion of staff-training modules. There is a target of six-days training per year for each member of staff. They receive certificates for attendance, passing a skills test and completion of a development module. All certificates are endorsed by the MD.

## The Problem: Changing the Role of the Branch Manager

Inevitably the changes listed above meant a change in the scope and nature of the responsibilities of the branch manager, as well as requiring a change in their approach to the job. In the past, branch managers were regarded as successful if they achieved high sales and were able to foster useful networks within the industry. Now they had to find a specialist niche for their branch, orient their activities towards achieving ROBA, manage and develop their staff, understand and use information technology, as well as satisfying more demanding customers.

Recently the MD has been concerned about the willingness of branch managers to accept the changes. He is particularly worried about their adopting a more entrepreneurial management style, the centre-piece of his strategy. His concern has been fuelled by reports from the RGMs that many branch managers continue to keep their stocks high in order to ensure a high sales figure and are concentrating on achieving sales rather than a high ROBA target.

In addition, he has received a number of complaints from branches about 'interference' from headquarters and regions. A number of examples have been given, including: the tendency of the central computer automatically to prevent customers from taking extra credit if they fail to settle an invoice within 60 days; the centre's training initiative; the marketing department's guidelines on which products to buy; and the 'continuing interest' of the RGMs in sales issues.

The MD is also aware of a dip in the motivation of the RGMs. He feels this is due partly to the redrawing of regional boundaries, which means there are fewer posts, but mainly because of the new sales structure that, when it was introduced, provoked a great deal of criticism from RGMs.

## A Closer Look at the Problem

The majority of branch managers accept the need for change in an era of even tougher competition. They like the MD, consider him charismatic, and admit that, unlike previous senior management, he does not 'relax in his ivory tower' but gets his 'hands dirty at the coal face' by making a visit to every branch at least once a year. They are less enamoured with the MD's senior team, who seem not to be as committed to the view that the success of the company depends on the branch manager.

All the senior managers (six) accept that the branch manager of the future should be more performance oriented; however, when pushed, most senior managers admit to being 'horrified' at the prospect of controlling 185 entrepreneurs. Indeed, some feel strongly that the centre ought to take most of the business decisions currently being made at branch level, leaving the branch managers to act as salesmen − a role they have shown they are good at. This group of managers believe the MD has 'his heart in the right place' but they see him as naïve in thinking that a group of poorly educated branch managers, the majority of whom have spent all their working lives in the trade, could take sound decisions to grow branch business. Most regional managers, if privy to senior managers' views, would share them.

The majority are unhappy with the MD's changes, seeing them as devaluing their role and possibly leading to a less profitable organization. The increase in the number of branches each RGM has to oversee has meant less contact with branch staff, leaving them to feel 'out of touch with local issues'. Many RGMs argue that branch staff miss contact with someone who can give them the 'bigger picture'. However, privately RGMs feel uncertain as to what is happening in the 'policy arena'. As one put it, 'I am running a £10 million business for the company, yet I don't really have a say in what is going on at any level.' The RGMs meet with the MD and their area managers (four) twice a year, and are only invited to director-level meetings if required to speak on a particular issue.

RGMs see the sales reorganization as the most negative of all the MD's changes. The majority complain they have responsibility for sales without having responsibility to direct the sales force. Brought up on a diet of sales, these former branch managers see their skills lying in this area. Only two RGMs think they could not do justice to both a monitoring and sales role.

While the MD believes the reactions to the changes among branch staff are negative, in fact there are a variety of reactions. Those branch managers who are enthusiastic about the changes admit to feeling more motivated in their jobs because of

1. the opportunity to earn more money and grow their business;
2. the company's efforts to improve the working environment; and
3. their confidence in the ability of the MD to achieve success.

This group of managers feel their jobs have changed significantly; in particular, they feel they now have more choices in their jobs.

Access to reliable information is seen as a significant and positive change − most branch managers feel they now have sharper tools with which to make decisions. However, some are so busy they cannot find time to invest in interpreting the information; others do not understand the information available, let alone how to use it. Computerization does mean that branch performance is now more visible and can be compared. Some branch managers enjoy this new competitive challenge; others see it as jeopardizing previously good relationships among colleagues.

Most branch managers believe that, in essence, much of their job remains the same: for example, they still have responsibilities for cost, debtors, sales and stock, and they still rely on 'gut feel and experience'. They argue it is the context of the job (the nature of the motor trade and company policy of specialization) more than the job itself that seem to have changed, thus breeding scepticism about the claims of a new entrepreneurial culture.

For some branch managers specialization has meant their jobs have become more focused on stock reduction rather than offering an opportunity to decide their own destiny. Some managers miss the wheeler-dealing with suppliers, and feel they miss out on hearing about new product lines because of the marketing department's guidelines, which are often out of date and contradictory.

Four concerns are shared by all branch managers. First, the performance targets set by the centre. As one branch manager argues,

> The company says the key measurement is ROBA, yet branch managers get a free holiday and a tankard if they achieve high sales. So the signals are there and these other targets get in the way. For example, because sales are down we have now been told to go for pound notes.

The second shared concern is evident in the following quotation, again from a branch manager: 'You are judged on a day-to-day basis and you are only as good as yesterday's results. Past achievements don't count for a lot.'

The third concern is career paths. Branch managers who are acknowledged as top performers and who achieve a healthy bonus feel they cannot move from their branch to another for fear of losing income: 'I do feel once you are a successful branch manager in this company that there is nowhere else to go. The natural progression is into the regional manager post, but there aren't that many. When each regional manager leaves, they just expand the region.'

Finally, managers are concerned about the tendency of headquarters to issue dictates without consultation, for example, remove credit facilities for customers without investigating reasons for non-payment, and the requirements on them to train staff.

The introduction of bonuses, while relished by some, are considered by others to be destructive to customer service: 'The pressure is on me to think about how my decisions affect my bonus rather than how they affect customers.' Some feel the bonus system discourages them in thinking objectively and longer term:

> It is very hard to sit in this chair and think what to do for the best. Do I go for pound notes [sales], or do I concentrate on contribution? Do you think of yourselves or do you think of your staff? If you think of yourselves, you keep up the contribution and ROBA, but my staff get their bonuses on sales.

Another frustrating aspect of the new situation for most branch managers is the interference by the RGMs in sales as well as *ad hoc* visits to the branches to discuss the 'state of play'.

## Case Study Tasks

Imagine you are a consultant brought in by the MD to advise him on the content of the changes he has introduced and the method of their introduction. He has briefed you on his strategy and voiced his concerns that the changes have met with some resistance at regional and branch level. He has a number of questions for you to address:

1. What are the major problems faced by my company? Why have these arisen?
2. What are the strengths of my strategy and how might I build on them?
3. In what ways have middle management jobs (branch manager and regional manager) changed?
4. What are the advantages and disadvantages of the changes for

   (a) branch managers;
   (b) regional general managers; and
   (c) senior managers?

5. What additional changes do I need to make to achieve my vision?
6. What lessons can I draw from the existing situation when managing future change?

## Essential Reading

Dopson, S. and Stewart, R. (1990) What is happening to middle management?, *British Journal of Management*, Vol. 1, pp. 3–16.

Emmanuel, C., Otley, D. and Merchant, M. (1990) *Accounting for Management Control*, Chapman & Hall, London (2nd edn – especially Chapters 1, 5, 7, 9 and 10).

Legge, K. (1984) *Evaluating Planned Organizational Change*, Academic Press, London.

Stewart, R. (1982) *Choices for the Manager: A Guide to Managerial Work and Behaviour*, McGraw-Hill, Maidenhead.

## Additional Reading

Goffee, R. and Scase, R. (1986) Are the rewards worth the effort? Changing managerial values in the 1980s, *Personnel Review*, Vol. 15, pp. 3–6.

Hofstede, G. H. (1978) The poverty of management control philosophy, *Academy of Management Review*, Vol. 3, no. 3, pp. 450–61.

Torrington, D. and Weightman, J. (1987) Middle management work, *Journal of General Management*, Vol. 13, no. 2, Winter, pp. 74–89.

# CASE 23

## Management Development:
## A Tale of Two Companies

## *John Storey*

## Introduction

It is the financial year 1990−1. Two electrical engineering companies, one in Britain and one in Japan, are reassessing the ways in which they 'grow' their management stock.

## Background to the British Case

Smiths is a large, conglomerate-like engineering company headquartered in the British Midlands. In the past its main manufacturing sites were located predominantly within the local region and it enjoyed buoyant growth during the period when it supplied the British motor industry and that industry was itself thriving. During the past decade or so the company has diversified and it is now far less dependent on the British motor industry. Seventy per cent of its sales are now achieved in overseas markets and the company in fact has relocated many of its operations to foreign locations − largely through an active strategy of acquisition. It now has a presence in some 40 countries and has 62,000 employees worldwide.

Its group sales total some £2.2 billion and the group operating profit in 1990 was £175 million. To reflect its newly diversified form, the group is now divisionalized. It has five major divisions and these essentially reflect product groups: − one of them remains, for example, as a motor-components business. The others are computer products, industrial machinery, aerospace and instrumentation.

## Background to the Japanese Case

The Japanese company, Watanabe Industries, has a very similar profile to its British counterpart. The size of its turnover and its profitability are of the same order and it too has diversified rapidly in recent years. Its organizational structure reflects that diversification in that the group is constituted of some 30 major 'businesses' that, like Smiths, are based on 'product families' − but one point of difference is that Watanabe has not divisionalized itself in quite the same way as Smiths. The essential point of contrast is that, although Watanabe operates its component parts very much as distinct 'businesses', it none the less still very much manages itself as a corporate whole — taking full advantage at every turn of being a large company. It seeks to tap economies of scale and to enjoy the synergistic advantages of being a large company composed of varying parts and opportunities; and this is witnessed, not least, in the sphere of management development.

## The Management Development System in Smiths

In many regards, Smiths is well ahead of the game when it comes to training and development — at least within the British context. The company has a long-standing reputation as a 'training company'. It has traditionally invested a good deal in training and, for a long time, has taken more than its share of apprentices — both trade apprentices direct from school and graduate apprentices for its professional and managerial training programmes. In essence the problem with which the current senior managers at Smiths are grappling is that the long-standing system of training and development, which served it well in the post-war period, virtually collapsed in the financial-crisis period of the early 1980s. During that period not only was there a programme of massive redundancies and factory closure but also the training and development infrastructure was largely dismantled.

During the period of turnaround in the mid-1980s the company underwent a significant transformation. There were two main components to this:

1. There was the diversification strategy noted above.
2. This was accompanied by a restructuring of the organization so that the clear emphasis was placed on a host of distinct businesses — or, as they were termed, 'strategic business units' (SBUs). One hundred and fifty of these were identified worldwide — some of them quite small scale with turnover of around £5 million and others being very substantial concerns with turnover of £200 million plus. These SBUs were grouped into the five divisions already described. There was also a strategic shift in that the perceived 'deadweight' of the central bureaucracy (which meant not only staff at the corporate centre but also the procedures and systems) was drastically cut. Responsibility for training and development, as for so much else, was passed to the managing directors of each of the businesses (that is, to SBU level, though the divisional managing directors were also charged with this responsibility for the senior managers throughout their divisions).

By the late 1980s there was a growing concern within the company that, insofar as management training and development was concerned, the 'baby had been thrown out with the bathwater'. In many areas, activity of this kind had all but ceased. A project team was set up and charged with the responsibility of investigating the nature and extent of the problem.

# The Review

This team, whose membership included the group personnel director, the group director of manufacturing, the group commercial director and three other co-opted managers of a lower rank, commissioned a wide-ranging study to see how serious the situation in fact had become. This review produced the following findings:

1. Many individuals were in post as managers who had received no managerial training at all. Others had undertaken a series of disparate short courses on such topics as 'time management', 'communications' and 'project management'.
2. There was an unacceptable level of loss among graduate recruits – most especially among the hard-to-replace specialist engineers. Approximately 35 per cent of graduate recruits left the company within four years of joining it.
3. A 'managerial audit' conducted by external consultants using psychometric tests and one-to-one interviews revealed that, even among very senior managers, there was an alarming deficiency in competencies related to marketing and entrepreneurship.
4. Smiths managerial stock was found to be characterized by narrow expertise and experience. Managers and others had progressed their careers by moving up 'functional chimneys'. The degree of inter-functional mobility was found to be very limited.
5. Although the company as a whole was large and varied, its managers did not enjoy the fruits of this. Inter-divisional career moves or transfers were rare. It was deemed that the company was not taking sufficient advantage of its size and complexity.

# Recommendations Arising from the Review

The management-development project team produced a lengthy report and made a series of recommendations for tackling these problems. Chief among the proposals for action were the following:

1. A central (i.e. corporate plc-level) management development function should be established and this should be headed-up by a group management-development director.
2. A prestige management college should be built or acquired.
3. A core training programme should be established and all trainee managers would be required to pass through its various stages. The syllabus for this programme would be devised centrally.
4. The managing directors and management boards of each of the constituent businesses (i.e. at SBU level) would be required to devise a management development policy tailored to the needs of their businesses. These plans, policies and progress against them would be included within the normal accounting review process, which takes place every six months.

5. Each of the five divisions would be required to establish a career review process. Succession plans and development plans would be tabled at quarterly meetings of the newly established divisional management-development panels. The degree of inter-business career transfer was expected to increase and it was hoped that more inter-divisional moves would be encouraged.

## What Happened Next

A series of 'programmes' were launched in order to put these recommendations into effect. These were being rolled out at a time when many other initiatives relating, for example, to manufacturing systems engineering were also being promulgated. For whatever reason, the messages from the top about the renewed importance to be given to training and development did not seem to be making a significant impact. Colin Brown, the new Group Management Development Director, did his best to make his presence felt around the group. He was usually given a polite hearing when he stood up to address a meeting but somehow the expected moves were not forthcoming. He probed members of various management boards in the different SBUs and he soon realized that his task was going to be far more difficult than he had anticipated. One managing director expressed what was apparently a received truth for many of the others:

Well, we can train and we do train, but at the end of the day the individual either has what it takes or he doesn't. No amount of training and development is going to overcome that basic fact. I myself didn't have any significant amount of management training. I was given a major assignment after 18 months with the company and it was a case of sink or swim. Fortunately I was able to swim.

In June 1991, Colin Brown was about to commission yet another team of consultants. He was not happy with the progress achieved during the past two years; nor were his senior colleagues. Brown was coming under increasing pressure. His position began to look, in some people's eyes, as untenable. The group managing director had captured the state of affairs succinctly when he had observed at a management board meeting that Smiths was now 'rather good at management training but pretty awful at management development'. Brown thought he had better do something about this.

He interviewed a whole succession of consulting firms, each of whom made presentations outlining their broad line of approach and *modus operandi*. Seemingly the full range of possibilities had been paraded before him: action learning, tracking management competencies, total quality approaches, training packages, performance-related pay systems and so on ... but still Brown hesitated. Having just gone through a full two years of strenuous effort in revamping the management development system he began to harbour suspicions that a more deep-seated analysis was required. But how to go about such an exercise was the problem he now toyed with. He consulted widely and the various suggestions he received from sources both inside and outside the company he listed as five main options. These were as follows:

1.  Win top management assent to a plan that entailed more stringent require-
    ments being placed on the divisional boards and their constituent SBUs to
    toe the corporate line on management development.
2.  Renegotiate his role: transform it into an advisory one. Cease entirely the
    attempt to claw back to the centre responsibility for management develop-
    ment. The group is now an entirely different entity to the relatively
    centralized company it once was and this fact should be recognized by
    devolving management development to the businesses. Diversity should be
    welcomed rather than being regarded as a 'problem'.
3.  Move towards an approach that places the emphasis on 'self-development'.
    Generate a central repository of distance-learning materials to support
    this.
4.  Broadly adopt plan 2 but red ring a cadre of managers who are either
    already at, or expected to attain, a certain senior level and treat this
    population as a 'group resource'. Brown should then redefine his own role
    as the keeper of this protected special group and the one who recruits new
    blood to this cadre.
5.  Treat with caution each of the above 'British solutions' and investigate
    forthwith the successful management development practices David Taylor,
    his Group Personnel Director, has discovered while working with a Japanese
    trading partner – a company comparable on many measures to Smiths
    and one that is now party to a joint venture with Smiths. Taylor suggests
    that Colin Brown reads the report he has compiled about this Japanese
    company and, if Colin is sufficiently interested in its findings, that he
    arrange a special visit to their joint venture company to explore the ideas
    further.

### Confidential: Report on the Management Development System at Watanabe Industries

Report compiled by Mr D. T. M. Taylor, Group Personnel Director,
Smiths plc

Watanabe Industries Ltd was established one hundred years ago. It used
to be part of a larger conglomerate (*zaibatsu*) which was broken up by
the Allies after the Second World War. Its core business today is electrical
engineering and it has diversified into electronic systems, new materials
and many of the activities pursued by Smiths. Its turnover in 1990 was
equivalent to £2.6bn. In Japan itself Watanabe employs 20,000 people of
whom 4,000 are female. Corporate headquarters and two of the main
production sites are located in the city of Yokohama which lies to the
south of Tokyo. But the company organization also extends well beyond
the Japanese islands. It has fifty overseas subsidiaries which operate in
every continent – with an emphasis on S.E. Asia, the United States and
Europe. Its overseas production accounts for some 20 per cent of the
total. The company in Japan is composed of eight divisions. These again
are somewhat reflective of the Smiths situation with a continued emphasis
on motor components and electric cables, though Watanabe has extra

divisions devoted to R & D, new materials (such as superconducting thin film) and optical local area networks.

David Taylor's report on Watanabe revealed the following pattern of features with regard to the making of managers in that company:

Its main source of management talent was through the graduate recruitment process. The company hires some 200 top graduates per annum — all drawn from just a handful of the country's best universities. Most of these recruits are engineers. The annual cohort of graduate recruits is husbanded as a distinct group for a number of years. Each cohort is put through a well-established induction and training programme. Even after a decade or so within the company most of a particular year's intake will use other members of that year as a key point of reference on progress. One of the many consequences of this pattern of resourcing is that the Watanabe company, like most other large Japanese companies, has at its disposal a managerial stock with a high level of educational attainment. For example, 95 per cent of Watanabe's present middle managers have degrees compared with 65 per cent of our own — and our figure is well above the British average of about 45 per cent.

The 'lifetime employment' system is still broadly intact. Most managerial positions are filled from within. External recruitment at middle or senior levels does occasionally happen but it is the exception. On the other hand, there are increasing signs that younger graduates are prepared to leave during the first few years but, again, this is still relatively unusual and it is not yet known whether this is the beginning of a trend. As part of this 'lifetime employment', the system is characterized by slow but steady progression for nearly all members of the annual cohort. The group moves forward more or less *en bloc* at least for the first 10 to 12 years. Hence there is little accelerated promotion based on merit.

Progression occurs through a structured hierarchy of *grades*. Each of these grades will have equivalent levels of supervisory and managerial *jobs* or *postings* but appointment to a grade does not necessarily involve appointment to one of these managerial posts. The emphasis, therefore, is upon what the Japanese call *Capability Development* and decidedly not upon special and distinct *management* development.

This structured progression is made even more systematic in that at each stage there is a standardized series of courses to attend, assignments to be completed, set books to be read and even tests to be passed. Term papers or essays for discussion with the boss also comprise part of the package.

Having emphasized the formal structuring of the Watanabe system of development it is necessary to also note, however, that in some other regards their approach is far more subtle and informal than ours. Key learning experiences reportedly derive from mentoring and coaching. Open plan is the norm and superordinates and subordinates seem to tackle problems together. Perhaps one of the most impressive aspects from our point of view was the way in which to take full advantage of these opportunities managers would frequently allocate tasks with *learning* being one of the prime reasons for giving it to one individual or group rather than another. This feature was reflective of a more general one and a vitally important one at that – i.e., managers at Watanabe (unlike most of our own it has to be said) really do take development of subordinates as one of the most important parts of their job. Not only is this aspect monitored in the appraisal and performance review system it is also deeply embedded in their consciousness as part of what it means to be 'doing management'. In this sense, capability development is part of the organizational culture. This is something I would dearly like to see us achieve – but how?

It is also more continuous. Even senior managers are expected (and more importantly appear to do!) correspondence courses which are related to business themes. They also attend seminars of professional bodies in their own time. I met some managers who would attend these early evening and then return to their work for another hour or so! Even less structured but still a seemingly vital part of the Watanabe system is the practice of learning from one's immediate boss. In part this is a direct coaching relationship, but in addition to that there is the practice of what Watanabe people term as 'watching the boss's back'. By this curious phrase they mean learning by constant and direct observation: What is the boss doing? How is he doing it?

Another key feature that impressed me was the fact that our colleagues in Japan appear to have sustained the same type of 'capability development' system for many years and at the same broad level. We, as you know, by contrast have chopped and changed and the training budget has been cut more times than I care to remember. We are undoubtedly suffering from that legacy: our General Managers suspect that soon our training commitment will wane again – and they are probably right. The Watanabe people have the other big advantage that all their managers know what the development system is and they broadly play by the rules. It may be a bit conformist for our tastes but at least they don't have the problems we have where a significant proportion of our line managers have only the flimsiest idea about what training provision is available. This is especially ironic given that some of our packages are of world class standard.

Perhaps the most enduring impression which resulted from my work with the Japanese was the way in which their training and development elements slotted together far more coherently than ours. Our 'system' is in effect a model drawn on paper – something we show on projector slides at conferences. But we would all have to admit that very few of our line managers are able to make the various bits and pieces slot together in a mutually coherent way in practice. You will recall that one of the main reasons why we continue to lose some of our best graduates within the first five years of appointment is that they fail to see any structured provision or progression once the two year graduate training period is completed. We are going to have to do something about that.

Another important point that struck me while in Yokohama relates to an issue that has worried me for some time about our own arrangements. When talking to many of the Japanese managers it became evident that they had some difficulty with the very concept of 'management development'. They were clearly more used to dealing with the problem of general 'capability development' irrespective of the kind of contribution, technical, design, commercial or managerial which people happened to be making at any one time. Capability development was a process to which all career employees were exposed. Hence, by the time a person was appointed to a specifically managerial position, most of the groundwork in training and development had already been accomplished. There was little need for the special kind of 'remedial' treatment to which we expose our new managers. In any case, many of the Japanese managers were moved on from their 'managerial' posting to some other type of role within a couple of years. Now clearly this all ties in therefore with the general pattern of career planning – and again we are surely going to have to address this soon as well.

It also has another upshot. Because the Japanese managerial postholders are 'developed' in the main *prior* to being allocated to a particular management job they would appear to spend rather less time on management training courses of a formal kind than do many of our own colleagues. Having said that, it also seems clear that the Watanabe managers are rather more attuned to other types of development opportunities than are Smiths managers. For example, they spend a lot of time in group working situations and they use this time to learn from others. Similarly, they seem to keep abreast of new developments in their field rather better by attending external seminars and similar events.

Perhaps the most impressive feature is the degree to which on-the-jobtraining (OJT) is apparently ingrained within Watanabe Industries Ltd. Line managers as a matter of routine take their people through a series of learning experiences. Moreover, they regard it as very much a part of their own responsibility to ensure that all members of their section or department are fully competent in the performance of a range of unit tasks and that the subordinate's future potential is further enhanced. Failure of a subordinate to perform up to required standard is seen as a poor reflection upon the responsible manager. In consequence of all of this, there is far less need for a constant stream of initiatives from a central training and development function. The prevalent British attitude of 'sending people on courses' as a way of discharging one's developmental responsibilities was largely absent.

## Meanwhile . . .

On this same day, the head of the capability development department at Watanabe, Mr Tanaka, called a meeting in his Yokohama office. He was concerned about a number of aspects relating to staff development. Heightened competition from various other South-East Asian economies was impelling a rethink of all aspects of the business. One particular worry was that the notorious 'groupism' of corporate Japan, a phenomenon reinforced by the long-drawn-out career development system, might be exacting a cost in terms of individual creativity. A perhaps not unrelated issue was the tendency, as yet still small scale but growing, for a number of younger graduates to leave the company within the first few years of engagement. In response, the company found itself increasingly participating in the external labour market. An element of performance-related reward had also been introduced within the past two years and this too was having repercussions beyond those that had been anticipated. Mr Tanaka had noticed also that fewer staff seemed prepared to work at weekends and late at night. The minuscule proportion of female staff at senior levels had also begun to be a point of contention. As Mr Tanaka pondered this catalogue of points, he began to wonder whether the long-standing system might now be requiring a fundamental reform.

## Case Study Tasks

You have been hired by Colin Brown as an external consultant to help him in formulating and implementing future developmental strategy for Smiths. In particular, you have been asked to begin by answering the questions posed below. Question 1, (a)–(d), can be tackled in a two-hour session; question 2 will require rather more extensive preparation.

1. What lessons of potential applicability to Smiths might Colin Brown draw from his colleague's report on management development in the Japanese competitor company? (*Note*: In moving towards an answer to this question, the following sub-questions might usefully be borne in mind – they should not necessarily be answered in the same sequence in which they are posed):

    (a) What are the *main* problems currently facing Smiths with regard to management development?

    (b) Which aspects of Japanese practice seem to be particularly advantageous to Watanabe's capacity for competitiveness?

    (c) How should Colin Brown conceptualize the meaning of the term 'management training and development'? What model or models might usefully be employed to capture the focus and scope of the concept?

    (d) What steps would you now advise Colin Brown to take? (In framing an answer to this part of the question, you should take into account aspects of process as well as content in the plan of action.)

2. Evaluate the Japanese system of managing managers and their development. What are its advantages and disadvantages? How sustainable is the system likely to be in the future?

## Essential Reading

Burgoyne, J. (1988) Management development for the individual and the organization, *Personnel Management*, Vol. 20, no. 6, June, pp. 40–4.

Storey, J., Okazaki-Ward, L., Gow, I., Edwards, P. K. and Sisson, K. (1991) Managerial careers and management development: a comparative analysis of Britain and Japan, *Human Resource Management Journal*, Vol. 1, no. 3, pp. 33–57.

## Additional Reading

Constable, C. J. and McCormick, R. (1987) *The Making of British Managers*, CBI/BIM, London.

Handy, C., Gordon, C., Gow, I. and Randlesome, C. (1988) *Making Managers*, Pitman, London.

Pedler, M. *et al.* (1990) *A Manager's Guide to Self-Development*, McGraw-Hill, Maidenhead.

Pedler, M., Burgoyne, J. and Boydell, T. (1991) *The Learning Company*, McGraw-Hill, Maidenhead.

Storey, J. (1991) Do the Japanese make better managers?, *Personnel Management*, Vol. 23, no. 8, August, pp. 24–9.

Storey, J., Okazaki-Ward, L., Edwards, P. K., Sisson, K. and Gow, I. (1993) *Managers and Management Development in Britain and Japan*, Blackwell, Oxford.

Trevor, M., Schendel, J. and Wilpert, B. (1986) *The Japanese Management Development System: Generalists and Specialists in Japanese Companies Abroad*, Pinter Publishers, London.

# Assessment for Development:
## Product Development — Ford Motor Co. Ltd

### Russell J. Drakeley, Ivan T. Robertson and Mike G. Gregg

## Organizational Setting

The Ford Motor Corporation is the World's second largest manufacturer of cars, vans and light trucks. Since 1967, Ford has been organized on a European basis, designing, building and selling a single range of vehicles for the Western European market. Ford Motor Co. Ltd, the British subsidiary, employs 45,000 people at 19 sites throughout the UK, co-ordinated centrally through its head office in Brentwood, Essex. Dependence on the motor vehicle as a means of private and public transport should indicate a healthy future for the motor industry but, despite the strength of demand for vehicles, the European market is greatly over-supplied. Too many individual companies compete with each other and the situation has been made more critical by the arrival of Japanese manufacturing plants on the European scene. The need to match Japanese quality and cost competitiveness, together with external pressure to reduce environmental pollution caused by the motor car, has forced the industry to invest heavily in research and development. Ford's British R & D activities are housed in a purpose-built Product Development Centre at Dunton in Essex, which was opened in 1964. The site employs over 2,200 salaried personnel, a large proportion of whom are graduate, or equivalently, qualified engineers. Such is the importance of product development to Ford that expenditure on R & D is currently running at £180 million per annum.

## Background to the Case

The Product Development Centre has a matrix management structure (Handy, 1985). Departments responsible for the design of components (fuel systems, suspensions, body and trim assemblies, etc.) represent the columns of the matrix. Each of these departments or 'component areas' is responsible for the development of its specific part of the vehicle but may be working on several vehicles at the same time. The responsibility for co-ordinating the development of components across a single vehicle line falls to the 'programme areas'. These departments join the columns of the matrix and ensure that, for example, the fuel injection system designed for a particular car in one component area will fit into the engine compartment designed for the same car in another area.

Given the enormous complexity and number of automotive components, and the wide range of vehicles produced, it is essential the matrix structure works well. Critical to the success of the matrix are the departmental managers in the component and programme areas (see Figure 24.1). They are very much the 'key players' in the system, having control over their own areas of the business while working together as a team to provide co-ordinated inputs to policy for product development as a whole. Their responsibilities include setting overall strategies, establishing budgets and negotiating for resources, liaising with the non-engineering parts of the company such as sales and finance, providing the overall technical direction for their own areas and, most importantly, managing the people in their respective departments.

Departments have a traditional 'pyramid' structure. At the base of the pyramid are the engineers and senior engineers who develop components and systems. The engineers report to supervisors who represent the first tier of line management. Supervisors in turn report to departmental managers. A typical department comprises four supervisors and up to forty engineers, i.e. the departmental pyramid is very 'flat' in organizational terms. This flat pyramid structure is important because of another feature of the organization: career progression is very largely restricted to movement through the engineering and supervisory grades into departmental management.

In fact this is the case in many R & D organizations and most specialist personnel have realistic opportunities for promotion only via a managerial

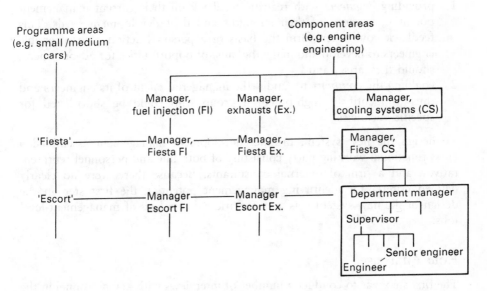

**Figure 24.1** Notional matrix structure of R & D

route (Bailyn, 1980). The so-called 'dual career ladder', which is intended to provide opportunities for R & D personnel to develop their careers along either technical or managerial routes, is not universally available and, apart from a small number of 'technical specialist' positions, this is the case in Ford. There are potential problems with this kind of unitary career system including the under-utilization of technical skills possessed by individuals (because they have been promoted to jobs that involve managerial rather than technical tasks) and the inability of people with high technical skills to cope with the demands of managerial jobs.

In product development, the virtual absence of a dual career ladder and the flatness of the departmental pyramid had two specific implications:

1. The opportunity for advancement beyond the engineering grades was severely limited. Most engineers were thus unlikely to be promoted to a departmental management position with its attendant rewards and status.
2. Promotion decisions tended to have been based on engineering expertise. This was partly because of a desire to reward engineering excellence (hence to motivate and retain the better engineers) and partly because there were no clearly laid-down criteria for assessing management potential.

The potential dysfunctional consequences of the above were widely recognized within product development and had been discussed for some time in the engineering and personnel communities. In the short term, the change to an extended dual career ladder was not considered (indeed, even where such a system is used there are doubts about its value – Allen and Katz, 1986). After much internal discussion, Ford decided to design and implement a new system of identifying management potential with a view towards

1. providing *engineers* with realistic feedback on their current management potential, in terms of their strengths and their development needs. This feedback could then form the basis of a personal action plan to enable engineers to develop and make the most of opportunities for advancement, should they arise; and
2. enabling the *company* to 'audit' the managerial talent of its engineers and thus to identify a high-potential group who could be short-listed for specific vacancies.

To design the new system, product development management assembled a cross-functional working party consisting of both line and personnel representatives, and a firm of external consultants. Because there were no clearly defined criteria for identifying management potential, the first step in the design of the new system was a systematic *role analysis* of management-level jobs.

## Role Analysis

The first step was to conduct a number of interviews with key personnel in the company, concentrating on the job of departmental manager. First, job-holders were interviewed to gather qualitative data on the content of their jobs, i.e. the *tasks* and *activities* performed by managers. Next, more senior managers were interviewed about the *skills* and *abilities* required to carry out these tasks successfully. The protocols from over sixty interviews were then reviewed by an expert panel of psychologists and line managers and used to construct a questionnaire that was distributed to engineers, supervisors and managers throughout the site.

The central section of the questionnaire consisted of a grid of tasks and skills the expert panel agreed were applicable across a wide range of departmental managers' jobs. Respondents were invited to rate the 'importance' of each skill for the successful execution of each task (effectively, a 'repertory grid' with tasks as the elements and skills as the constructs − see Kelly, 1955).

Using a consensus grid, derived from the individual managers' questionnaires, various statistical and interpretative techniques, including principle components analysis, were employed to reduce the original tasks and skills down to the following eight *performance dimensions*:

- Influencing skills (100).
- Technical innovation (85).
- Effective problem-solving (75).
- Systems/procedures orientation (75).
- Business/political awareness (55).
- Personal integrity (50).
- Incisive analysis (45).
- Results orientation (35).

The relative importance of each dimension for overall success as a manager was calculated, and this is indicated by the figure in brackets above (where the most important dimension, influencing skills, is arbitrarily scaled to 100). This index of overall importance was again derived from the consensus grid (although not used here, computer packages for analysing this kind of grid data are available − see Slater, 1977; Tschudi, 1988).

Thus, the job analysis enabled the company to define a set of criteria for identifying management potential across the entire engineering community within the Product Development Centre. These criteria were then translated into a programme for assessing management potential and giving feedback to engineers. Before outlining the programme, it is first necessary to describe some of the practical and conceptual issues that influenced the design of the system.

## Practical and Conceptual Issues

The first issue was the potential size of the population who would participate in the programme. With over 1,100 engineers on site, the programme had to be designed to process large numbers of participants quickly and efficiently. If spread over a long period of time the assessments on the first group of engineers would be out of date by the time the final batch went through.

Second, to ensure the credibility of the process, it was felt essential to use the departmental managers rather than members of the personnel department or the external consultants, both to assess the engineers and to provide feedback about their strengths and weaknesses. The amount of free time available to these managers was severely limited and, in any case, there were only 50−60 such managers employed on the site. The system therefore had to be flexible enough to ensure maximum management commitment to the output with minimal management involvement in the process.

The size of the problem suggested that some kind of pre-selection would be necessary. However, there were no arbitrary criteria (e.g. age, length of service, qualifications, etc.) politically acceptable to the company and the unions, and no method of identifying a high priority group of engineers (had there been, the new system would have been largely redundant).

Finally, it was thought desirable to involve everyone concerned with engineers' career development in the design of the programme. To ensure that the process was relevant and understood by all, the company convened a cross-departmental team of engineers, supervisors and members of the job analysis panel to construct the exercises and assessments that eventually came together in the finished programme.

## The Programme

The design team produced a programme with two phases: an 'exploration' phase and an 'assessment' phase (Figure 24.2). The purpose of the exploration phase was to encourage engineers to take ownership of their own personal development by either self-selection into or out of the programme at two distinct decision points. All of the engineers in product development were first sent an information pack and an invitation to nominate themselves for the programme. The information pack contained a detailed description of managers' jobs, an explicit statement of the performance dimensions associated with success as a manager, a colloquial account of a 'day in the life' of a typical job-holder and a description of the assessment phase of the programme (the 'model' for the design of the information pack was thus that of a vicarious realistic job preview − Meglino and DeNisi, 1987). The information pack was intended to enable the engineers to decide whether or not to nominate themselves for the programme on an informed basis.

Engineers wishing to participate in the programme, after receiving an information pack, were next invited to review their careers to date by completing a self-appraisal form. The engineer's experience and aspirations were then discussed at a review meeting with his or her manager. It was the manager's responsibility to give frank feedback about the company's perspective on the engineer's performance during this meeting. To assist in this process, the manager had a form similar to the engineer's self-appraisal, but completed by his or her supervisor. The purpose of the meeting was to *help* engineers decide whether or not they wished to continue onto the assessment phase of the programme; the manager had no right of veto but was able to advise the engineer as to his or her readiness for the assessments.

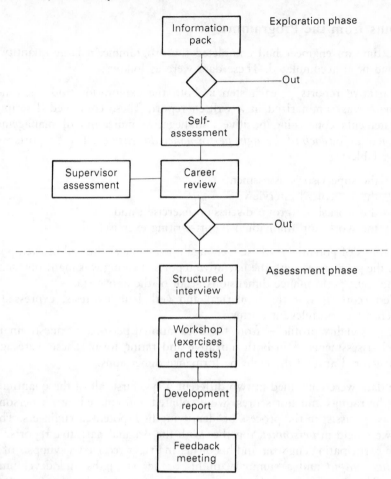

**Figure 24.2** Potential identification programme

The assessment phase comprised two stages: a structured, situational interview (see Latham *et al.*, 1980; Latham and Saari, 1984; Robertson, Gratton and Rout, 1990) conducted by a manager from another department, and a short assessment centre (Feltham, 1989; Woodruffe, 1990) or 'workshop'. Here, the engineers participated in group and individual exercises designed to simulate certain aspects of the work of a manager, while managers observed and assessed their performance on the relevant dimensions. The assessment centre was completed by the inclusion of tests of numerical and verbal reasoning ability (Saville and Holdsworth, 1985) to assess the engineers' analytical skills, a personality questionnaire (Saville and Holdsworth, 1984) and a self-assessment.

Engineers attended the workshop in groups of six. By timetabling flexibly, it was possible for three managers to process either 6, 12 or 18 engineers per day (depending on the size of the waiting-list) while preserving a 2:1 engineer-to-assessor ratio.

## Outputs from the Programme

By the time an engineer had completed the programme, a large quantity of data had been accumulated. These data were as follows:

1. Narrative reports — each step in both the exploration and assessment phase was summarized in a written report. These contained descriptive statements concerning positive and negative indicators of management potential for *each of the eight performance dimensions*. These reports were available for

   - the supervisor's assessment;
   - the structured interview;
   - the workshop (group discussion exercise); and
   - the workshop (individual report-writing exercise).

2. Ratings of potential — these were again available at the end of each phase in the process. As with the narrative reports, a rating was made on each of the eight performance dimensions at all of the above stages.
3. Test scores — for the numerical and verbal ability tests, expressed as percentiles on relevant norms.
4. A personality profile — from the occupational personality questionnaire.
5. Self-assessments — in both narrative and rating form. These were again structured around the eight performance dimensions.

These data were combined in two different ways. First, all of the quantitative data (the ratings and test scores) were collated and entered into a personnel database to assist in the process of identifying high-potential engineers. These data were held in *personnel*, together with the original narrative reports.

The participating engineer and his or her manager received a synopsis of the *narrative output* and a summary of his or her strengths and development needs. This 'personal development report' was written by the consultants involved in the programme, who where responsible for incorporating the results of the personality questionnaire into the narrative. It is important to note that this report did not contain ratings on the performance dimensions, or any quantitative data other than the percentile scores on the two ability tests. The report was thus solely intended to facilitate the process of feedback and development. While there was no guarantee of promotion, engineers received encouragement to help them make the most of opportunities as they might arise.

## The Problem

At the launch of the programme all eligible engineers received their information pack and an invitation to volunteer. From a total population of 1,100, 480 expressed a wish to take part immediately, while another 180 said they wanted to take part at a later date. The balance either declined to take part in the programme or did not reply to their invitation.

It is now nine months on, the first 80 volunteers have completed the programme and are in possession of their personal development reports. All of the managers involved in either the design of the programme or who had taken part as assessors were invited to attend a progress meeting. A measure of the success of the programme was that over 40 managers made time to attend. They were generally pleased with the way the programme was progressing, but expressed some concern over a number of issues. The following remarks illustrate their main areas of concern:

> one of my engineers filled in his self-appraisal over four months ago but he is still waiting for a place on the assessment centre. I'm worried that by the time he gets his report it will be too late for him to do anything about it before the next time he is interviewed for promotion ...

> the personal development report tells me *in words* what an engineer's strengths and weaknesses are; that's fine so far as it goes, but it doesn't tell me how he scores against other engineers – what's the 'bottom line'? – I need an overall mark ...

This 'bottom line' comment was in fact fairly common. Even though performance criteria scores were collated at each stage for all engineers it was never intended to feed these back to them in their personal development reports. The only scores included in the report were the percentile scores for the numerical and verbal reasoning tests. An unintended result of this was that both managers and engineers used the test scores as a surrogate 'bottom line': 'I've got a really good engineer in my area, and he's done well on the programme, but his scores on the tests are below average – I don't think he's below average, so what do the tests prove?'

Some of the comments were not so much about the process but about its implications:

> having seen the programme in action, I'm quite happy that it will help us find the high-potential guys – but what do we do with these people? We can't promote all of them, so how do we keep them motivated?

> I've got a brilliant component designer in my department, but he and I both know that he's not cut out for management – what's more the programme confirms that his strengths are mainly technical ones – what can we do for people like that? We need good engineers as well as good managers ...

> two of my engineers have received their reports and want to work on their development. We're pushed for time already – I can't afford to let them go off on training courses for weeks on end ...

Some managers expressed concern about the time commitment involved in conducting the interviews and acting as assessors on the workshop. Others disagreed:

> I've got a large department – over 80 engineers – if only half of them go through I'm going to have trouble conducting career review meetings

with them all. Do we need this stage? Very few people change their minds about going onto the next phase after the meeting . . .

I don't think the commitment's excessive. I spend one or two days per month on the programme at most and I'm convinced that my engineers value the outcome . . .

as an assessor I've seen engineers that I've never even met before and some of them are very impressive. Unless I get involved personally I'll probably never hear about these people . . .

The above and similar comments were made in a spirit of constructive criticism; managers were usually more concerned to debate ways of improving the process rather than to dwell over areas where the programme was working satisfactorily. An added 'edge' was given to the debate by one important development: the company was about to reorganize. This meant that a cross-section of engineers from other parts of the organization (some of whom had gone through similar, though not identical, programmes) would shortly be joining the population eligible for the programme. The net effect would be to *double* the number of engineers covered by the system.

## Case Study Tasks

Imagine you are a member of a management team that has been asked to look into the concerns raised at the meeting. You have been asked to prepare a brief presentation for the next progress meeting, which has been scheduled to take place in three months. Specifically, you have been asked to consider the following:

1. What are the major problems faced by the current system?
2. How can the overall throughput of engineers be improved? Should the process be streamlined and, if so, which stages (e.g. the workshop exercises)?
3. Should there be a 'bottom line' or an overall average mark? If so, how should it be calculated?
4. Should engineers get feedback on the performance criteria and their standing against the bottom line? How should this feedback be presented, and what dysfunctional consequences might result?
5. Should performance criteria scores and/or 'bottom line' scores be available to line managers or should they be held by personnel? To what extent should these scores be used to determine promotion?
6. How should the personality questionnaire be used?
7. Should there be a fast track for engineers with management potential? If so, how should it be managed? What alternatives would you consider?
8. How can the organization respond to the raised expectations of engineers who have received a personal development report?
9. How does the organization deal with technical specialists who are highly competent engineers but have little management potential?

10. How does the organization integrate new engineers into the programme? What criteria should be adopted to determine eligibility for the programme in the short, medium and long term?

## Essential Reading

Allen, T. J. and Katz, R. (1986) The dual ladder: motivational solution or managerial delusion, *R & D Management*, Vol. 16, pp. 185–97.

Feltham, R. T. (1989) Assessment centres, in P. Herriot (ed.) *Assessment and Development in Organizations*, Wiley, Chichester.

Handy, C. (1985) *Understanding Organizations*, Penguin Books, London.

## Additional Reading

Bailyn, L. (1980) *Living with Technology: Issues at Mid-career*, MIT Press, Cambridge, Mass.

Burgoyne, J. (1988) Management development for the individual *and* the organization, *Personnel Management*, June, p. 41.

Latham, G. P. and Saari, L. M. (1984) Do people do what they say? Further studies on the situational interview, *Journal of Applied Psychology*, Vol. 69, pp. 569–73.

Latham, G. P., Saari, L. M., Pursell, E. D. and Campion, M. A. (1980) The situational interview, *Journal of Applied Psychology*, Vol. 65, pp. 422–7.

Meglino, B. M. and DeNisi, A. S. (1987) Realistic job previews: some thoughts on their more effective use in managing the flow of human resources, *Human Resource Planning*, Vol. 10, pp. 156–67.

Robertson, I. T., Gratton, L. and Rout, U. (1990) The validity of situational interviews for administrative jobs, *Journal of Organizational Behaviour*, Vol. 11, pp. 69–76.

Saville, P. and Holdsworth, R. (1984) *Occupational Personality Questionnaire Manual*, Saville & Holdsworth Ltd, Esher, U.K.

Saville, P. and Holdsworth, R. (1985) *Management and Graduate Item Bank*, Saville & Holdsworth Ltd, Esher, U.K.

Slater, O. (ed.) (1977) *Dimensions of Intrapersonal Space*, Wiley, Chichester.

Tschudi, F. (1988) *Flexigrid Version 4.4*, Universitet I, Oslo.

Woodruffe, C. (1990) *Assessment Centres*, IPM, London.

# Subject Index

ACAS, 68
action plan, 65
affirmative action, 5, 96, 97, 102
age, 42, 85, 86
Air Navigation Services Ltd, (ANS), 88–89
air traffic control (ATC), 82–91
Applied Expertise Centre (AEC), 159–165
aptitude, *see* computer aptitude testing; psychological profile
'area working', 38, 40 *see also* team working
assessment, 4, 8, 45, 69, 83, 87, 90, 97, 144, 149–152, 170, 191, 194, 200, 204, 252, 259–264 *see also* performance appraisal; psychometric testing
Association of University Teachers (AUT), 200–202, 204
attitude, 6, 37, 58, 69, 97, 118, 126, 128, 132, 149, 150, 186, 229, 253
automotive industry, 30–41, 56–66, 246, 256–265
autonomy, 4, 5, 6, 7, 13, 60–64; 151, 182–183, 184, 199–200, 222 *see also* responsibility
Autospares, 238–245

bargaining, 2, 3, 5, 12, 15, 108–112, 137 *see also* negotiation
British Airways, 117–125
British Rail, 126–133
Business Review and Consultative Committee (BRCC), 70

business units, 57, 247 *see also* self-managing teamwork

Cableco, 67–72
Calendarco, 67–72
capability development, 251–254 *see also* development; management development
career development, 8, 258, 260–264 *see also* development
car manufacture, 4 *see also* automotive industry
case study, description of, 3; types, 4–8
childcare, 99, 102
Civil Aviation Authority (CAA), 83
climate, 139, 148, 186 *see also* environment
ComCo (North), 92–105
commitment, 2, 4, 6, 12, 13, 17, 92, 93, 117–125, 138, 194, 221, 228, 260
Committee of Vice-Chancellors and Principals (CVCP), 198, 200–202, 204
common cause, 95
communication, 4, 6, 11, 22, 24, 34, 36, 47, 70, 83, 87, 93, 131, 138–139, 141–142, 144–145, 148, 150, 151, 162, 179, 203, 228, 230, 248
Company Council, 34, 40
company policy, 79
competitiveness, 1, 2, 3, 5, 9–11, 14, 17, 39, 56, 67–68, 75–76, 79, 117, 127, 134, 159, 193, 228, 238, 239, 243, 253, 254, 256
computer aptitude testing, 69 *see also* recruitment

computer conferencing, 6, 144–156
computer-integrated manufacturing
  (CIM), 68, 69
computerization, 240–241, 242, 243
computer literacy, 69
computer-mediated communication, 144
conditions, of employment, 34, 67, 69,
  79, 93, 108–112, 137, 223
confidence-building, 118 *see also*
  development
conflict, 4, 6, 28, 36, 50
consensus management, 13, 166–168,
  177, 180, 181, 184, 185–186 *see also*
  management style
contract compliance, 96, 97
control, 5, 6, 7, 112, 190, 200
control strategies, 4, 40, 150, 180, 181,
  182
counselling, 93, 95, 97, 98
creativity, 84, 253
culture, 2, 3, 4–8, 9, 12, 13, 15, 17, 28,
  47, 49, 51, 58, 86, 102, 148, 150,
  154–156, 163, 177, 185, 187, 194,
  200, 222, 236, 240, 243, 244, 252
culture change, 5, 6, 9, 51, 117–125,
  126–133, 139–140, 151, 180, 186,
  187
customer service, 6, 45, 47, 57–58, 76,
  117–120,126–130, 132, 135–140,
  218, 224, 228, 241, 244

decision-making, 6, 7, 22, 27, 31, 90,
  112, 153, 154, 166–176, 177–178,
  179–186, 198, 199, 203, 222, 223,
  225, 243
delivery integrity, 46, 47, 50, 57
demand forecasting, 84–85
demarcation, 39, 68
demography, 12, 85
Department of Environment, 208
Department of Health and Social
  Security (DHSS), 16, 166
development, 4, 29, 53, 93–94, 118, 120,
  130, 136, 144, 146, 148, 150, 152,
  159–161, 180, 186, 187, 191, 197,
  198, 199, 201, 202, 208, 210–214,
  218, 224, 227–230, 234, 239,
  241–242, 247–254, 260, 262, 264 *see*
  *also* career development; management
  development; training
development grants, 68, 160, 162

diagnosis, 94, 131–132, 187 *see also*
  fault diagnosis; quality audit
Digital Equipment Corporation, 22–29
discrimination, 98, 137, 150
diversification, 12, 217, 246, 247, 250
division of labour, 5, 11, 35, 95, 105 *see*
  *also* functional grouping; equal
  opportunities

education, 9, 12, 85, 144–156, 190,
  197–206, 251 *see also* training
education, higher, 144–156, 197–206
electronic mail, 144
employee policies, 70
employee relations, 6, 35, 39, 94, 96,
  134–143 *see also* industrial relations
enterprise culture, 1, 3, 9, 15–17 *see also*
  culture
environment: changing, 28; climate, 89,
  92–93, 99, 164, 186, 195; dynamic;
  working, 77, 102 *see also* climate;
  culture
equalization, 169–174
equal opportunities, 5, 92–105, 168, 201
  *see also* gender issues
Equal Pay Act, 96
ethos, 94–96, 103, 104, 177 *see also*
  philosophy
evaluation, 4, 6, 53, 67, 131–132, 137,
  141, 144–153, 202, 254
experience, 98, 230, 243, 248

Falkner Wilks, 217–226
Fast Foods, 106–113
faults: detection, 33, 46; diagnosis, 46
  *see also* diagnosis
feedback, 64
flexible firm, 2, 3, 5, 6, 75–81, 142
flexible working, 40, 47, 90
flexibility, 2, 3, 4, 5, 9, 12, 13, 17, 27,
  31, 32, 37, 38, 39, 56, 67–71, 77, 93,
  94, 97, 99, 100, 102, 103, 126, 135,
  136, 151, 180, 183, 190, 202, 217,
  232, 260
food processing, 106–113
food retailing, 134–143
Ford Motor Co. Ltd, 256–265
Ford UK, 35–40
Fulham Football Club, 207–214
functional chimneys, 8, 248

functional groups, 4, 28, 35, 69

gender issues, 12, 76, 85, 86, 95–105, 151, 196, 205
greenfield site, 1, 4, 11, 67–72
Griffiths Report, 177–189
group working, 3, 253 *see also* team working
growth, 7, 8, 14, 217–226, 233, 238, 240

Harvey, SM (Engineers) Ltd, 227–237
Hiclas, 134–143
high-hazard operations, 5, 83
high-performance work-team, 4, 42–55
Home Cosy, 75–81
human resource management (HRM), 1, 2, 3, 5–8, 9, 11–14, 17, 30, 81, 105, 118–119, 123, 143
policies, 17, 68–71, 92–95, 104

improvement activities, 31
incentive, 241
individualism, 2, 5, 14, 17, 94–95, 102–103, 104, 117–120, 122, 199
industrial relations, 1, 2, 5, 9, 33, 106–113, 117, 134
information, sharing, 75 *see also* communication
information systems, 203, 223, 230, 239, 241
information technology, 2, 9, 11, 178, 180, 218, 242
innovation, 92, 94, 159, 160, 161–165, 183, 186, 218, 259
instruction, *see* training
integrated production, 37
internal labour market, 4 *see also* labour segmentation

Japanization, 17, 30–32 *see also* Japanese manufacturing methods
Japanese management style, 8, 11, 12–14, 184, 250–254
Japanese manufacturing methods, 4, 9, 30–41, 56, 256
Jarratt Report, 198
job characteristics, 5, 76–77, 191

job design, 2, 9
job description, 101, 232
job rotation, 31 *see also* multi skilling
job satisfaction, 136, 163
job security, 79, 93, 94, 95, 136, 163
job share, 99
Joint Industrial Council (JIC), 67, 70
just in time (JIT), 4, 12, 31, 37, 40, 56, 57, 62, 64, 68, 94, 100, 101

Kaizen teams, 33
knowledge, 6, 94, 98, 183, 197, 199–200, 202
knowledge-working, 9, 11, 15

labour segmentation, 67
labour turnover, 6, 78, 93, 137–138, 142, 248 *see also* volatility
leadership, 5, 34, 117–125
lead time, 46, 47, 50

management: development, 2, 3, 8, 120, 227–237, 246–255; practices, 13, 24, 30, 92–93, 94–95, 101, 141, 165, 217, 228; restructuring, 8, 42, 93, 120, 238–245; role, 229; strategies, 2, 3, 42, 119, 134–143, 205; structure, 2, 3, 4, 28, 107, 177, 180, 184, 185, 190, 198–199, 200, 220–222, 224, 230, 234, 251, 256; style, 117–120, 126, 134–136, 143, 166–168, 198; support, 58; teams, 21, 42, 108, 129–130, 221, 230; views, 79–80, 234 *see also* development; strategy
management, project, 221, 223, 224, 248
manufacturing, 2, 9, 11, 15, 150; engineering, 45, 249; methods, 30; strategy, 47–53; teams, 57; technology, 70 *see also* production
manpower planning, 2, 3, 5, 82–91, 184 *see also* planning
maternity leave, 99, 122
medical assessment, 83, 86, 90
Melthorpe International Airport, 89–90
mentoring, 251
mobility, 95, 96, 100, 248
'model working environment', 68
monitoring, 17, 77, 94, 97, 128, 130, 149–150, 178, 194, 198, 202, 220,

239, 241, 243, 252 *see also* quality
  audit
monitoring, computerised, 68
motivation, 17, 36, 70, 119, 149, 163,
  179, 242, 243, 263
motor-spares dealers, 238–245
multi–skilling, 4, 12, 27, 47 *see also* semi
  autonomous group working
multi–tasking, 227

National Health Service (NHS),
  166–176, 177–189, 190–196, 200,
  222
negotiation, 220, 240, 257 *see also*
  bargaining
new-company formation, 6, 159–165,
  227
Nissan UK, 32–35, 40
Norahs & Luap, Inc (N & L), 42–55

occupational psychology, 9
'on-the-job' training, 34, 45, 82, 86, 88,
  221, 251–253 *see also* training
opinion survey, 49
organization: behaviour, 2, 7, 17, 146,
  177; development, 2; functions, 75;
  hierarchy, 27, 132, 137, 201; skills,
  34; structure of, 2, 7, 8, 24, 27,
  154–156, 163, 198, 227–236,
  239–240
organizational change, 4–8, 21, 28, 113,
  153, 177–189, 190, 191, 196, 201,
  225, 236, 239, 242, 245, 247
organizational failure, 7, 8, 159–165
organizational setting of case studies:
  airline, 117–125; car manufacture,
  30–41, 256–265; civil aviation, 82–91;
  civil engineering, 227–237; computer
  assembly, 21–29; electrical
  engineering, 246–255; electronics
  company, 42–55; food production,
  106–113; food retailing, 134–143;
  government research laboratory,
  159–165; higher education, 144–156,
  197–206; manufacture of computing
  and telecommunication systems,
  92–105; manufacture of electric cables,
  67–72; motorspares dealers; 238–245;
  multi–plant, 106–113; National
  Health Service, 166–176, 177–189,

190–196; parts manufacture for car
  industry, 56–66; professional football,
  207–214; quantity surveying practice,
  217–226; railways, 126–133; retail
  distribution, 75–81;
ownership, 7, 46, 47, 51, 131, 207–214,
  260

pay, 38, 59, 60, 71, 79, 85, 93, 95, 97,
  100, 136, 137, 217
payment systems, 4, 5, 8, 67, 76, 200,
  241
pay structures, 15, 39, 45, 69–70, 87, 89,
  96, 108–112, 202, 203, 207, 224
performance, 7, 17, 49, 81, 94, 108, 155,
  160, 162, 177–178, 186, 197, 200,
  203, 238, 239, 242, 244
performance appraisal, 5, 7, 49, 53,
  93–94, 101, 149–150, 152, 178,
  180, 194, 197–206, 252; *see also*
  assessment
performance dimensions, 259, 262, 264
performance-related pay, 76, 95, 202,
  249, 253
personality assessment, 69, 261–262,
  264 *see also* recruitment
personnel management, 2, 4, 5, 9, 31,
  75–81, 128 , 223–224, 227–230, 233,
  236 *see also* industrial relations
philosophy, corporate, 5, 92–93, 94–95,
  96, 98, 101, 103, 104, 119, 136, 139,
  141, 177, 200, 217, 221 *see also* ethos
planning, 192 *see also* manpower
  planning
pressure, 90, 217, 249
privatisation, 2, 14, 117, 119, 127, 159,
  161
problem-solving, 1, 34, 37, 38, 44, 65,
  95, 128, 222, 259
product development, 256–265
production: 45, 46, 63; control, 59;
  growth, 26; processes, 43; schedules,
  69; flexible systems, 4, 21–29; targets,
  71
productivity, 27, 30, 36
product line, 43, 47, 51–53
product market, 75
professional firms, 217–226
Professional Footballers' Association,
  207–208
professionalism, 190–196

profitability, 12, 218, 223, 243, 246
progression, career, 257 *see also* promotion
project team, 68–69, 248 *see also* management teams
promotion, 5, 100, 101, 201, 221–222, 224, 225, 251, 257–258, 262, 263, 264 *see also* mobility; progression
psychological profile, 87
psychometric testing, 8, 87, 90, 261–262, 264; *see also* assessment
'Putting People First', 118–119, 122

quality: 2, 3, 4–8, 9, 11, 13, 17, 30, 32, 34, 38, 56–66, 126–133, 135–136, 149, 191–195, 198, 202, 217, 218, 256; audit, 43, 51, 58; control, 35, 191; culture, 58
quality circle, 36, 37, 40, 118
quality fair, 129–130
quantity surveying practice, 217–226

recession, 1, 12, 104, 151, 227, 228, 234, 236
recruitment: 4, 5, 32, 53, 69–70, 75–76, 77, 80, 82–91, 97, 98, 138, 163, 166, 167, 181, 217, 221, 223–224, 227, 229, 251; selective, 31; targets, 87
redundancy, 2, 5, 75, 117, 123, 124, 200, 222, 229, 247
reliability: operator, 82, 83; system, 83; technology, 83
research and development (R&D), 159–165, 256, 257–258
resource allocation, 6, 166–176, 177–178, 180–181, 190, 192, 198, 201, 224, 257
responsibility, 15, 16, 17, 35, 37, 48, 49, 50, 51, 58, 63, 69, 87, 118–120, 122, 126, 166–168, 170, 179, 180, 182, 183–184, 188, 193, 195, 198, 202, 204, 205, 212, 221–225, 227, 232–234, 239, 242, 243, 247, 250, 253, 256, 257, 260 *see also* autonomy
responsiveness, 11, 47, 217
retraining, *see* training
retirement, 229
reward systems, 4, 13, 53, 69, 70, 94, 241, 258
risk-taking, 118

role analysis, 258–259
role-play, 3, 4–8, 9, 53–54, 64, 104, 112, 187–189, 205
roles, 8, 53, 242–244
Royal Institute of Chartered Surveyors (RICS), 220
'rulebook' procedures, 82, 84

safety, 82–83, 87
salary, *see* pay structure
Saturday staff, 77–78
selection: criteria, 44, 98; procedures, 4, 5, 6, 33–34, 86, 97, 98, 100, 138, 142, 181; testing, 33, 87; *see also* recruitment
self-management, 200
self-managing teamwork, 4, 27, 50, 52 *see also* semi autonomous group working
service sector, 1–2, 3, 5, 12, 117–125, 126–133, 150, 159, 168, 188, 191, 197, 198
sexism, *see* gender issues
sexual harassment, 99, 103 *see also* gender issues
shifts, 39, 80
shopfloor, 35, 56, 63, 80, 227
skills: 4, 5, 11, 12, 17, 48, 69, 75, 77, 80, 85, 88, 100, 101, 191, 197, 218, 220, 221, 222, 223, 225, 229, 241, 243, 258–259, 261; development, 27, 119 *see also* training
skill modules, 69–70, 71, 242
Smiths (engineering company), 246–255
social benefits, 93, 147–148
Southglam (District Health Authority), 177–189
specialisation, 35
statistical methods, 58
statistical process-control (SPC), 52, 57, 60, 62 *see also* process-control
strategy, 2, 3, 7, 8, 10–12, 42, 49, 222–225, 238–239, 245, 247–255, 258
stress, 2, 9, 28, 118, 192
strikes: 2, 38; records, 33
supervisor: activities, 4, 38, 69, 77, 94, 95, 191, 251, 257, 260; attitudes, 80; function, 28, 93, 182, 191; systems, 68
supplier relations, 30, 31, 33, 37, 57
support, 6, 7, 82, 102, 103, 123, 178,

181, 191–196, 204, 208, 223, 227, 230, 239
system, integrated, 12, 83, 90, 94
systems design, 45, 144, 162, 258, 259


Taylorism, 186
teaching, 148, 170, 178, 199, 202, 203, 205 *see also* training
team building, 49, 140, 142
team: working, 4, 32, 35, 38, 39, 58, 69, 87, 129, 136, 180, 185, 192, 218, 221, 241, 248, 260
    multi-skilled team, 47
    pilot team, 47–51
    production teams, 32, 69 *see also* management teams
technology, 82–83
technology, new, 9, 14, 58, 68, 106, 144, 150, 153, 161, 162, 163–165 *see also* development
teleworking, 6, 144–156
temporary workers, 34, 75–81, 138
testing: product, 43, 46, 60–62, 100 *see also* assessment
time management, 248
time study, 76
tokenism, 102 *see also* equal opportunities
total quality control (TQC), 31, 37, 40, 56–66
total quality management (TQM), 4, 12, 94, 100, 128, 249
trade unions, *see* unions
training, 4–8, 11, 12, 21, 22, 29, 34, 37, 45, 48, 53, 57, 58, 63, 70, 76, 78, 79, 82–91, 93, 94, 95, 97, 98, 100, 118, 128, 129, 130, 132, 135, 140, 142, 180, 186, 190, 191, 197, 202, 220, 221, 239, 241–242, 247–254, 263 *see also* development; education; teaching
traits, *see* psychological profile unemployment, 16 *see also* redundancy

unions, 2, 4, 6, 12, 15–16, 31, 36–37, 40, 42, 56, 57–58, 67, 70, 93, 97, 106, 109–112, 123, 136–137, 140–141, 142, 166, 203–204, 260
    ACTSS, 106
    AEU, 34, 36, 38, 56, 106
    AUT, 200–202
    EETPU, 36
    GMB, 56
    MATSA, 70
    MSF, 106
    Management Association, 106
    TGWU, 36, 106, 136, 142
    USDAW, 106, 136, 142
United Kingdom Air Directorate (UKAD), 82–83, 85–88
University of Minterne, 144–156
unpaid leave, 78–79


value-added, 9, 11, 17, 47, 51
Valleyco, 56–66
vehicle evaluation system (VES), 33
Very Large Scale Integration (VLSI), 21–29
vigilance, *see* monitoring
volatility, 78


Watanabe Industries, 246–255
work flow, 46
working conditions, 107
workload, 190, 223
work organization, 4, 6, 21–29, 30–41, 42–55
work practices, 11, 33, 37, 39, 76, 85
work schedules, 45


yield: 46; increase in, 27


zero defects, 47